RANCH ON THE RUIDOSO

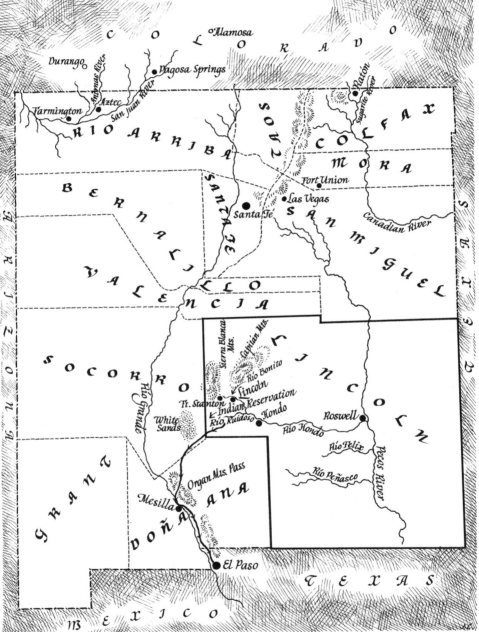

Territory of New Mexico
circa 1882

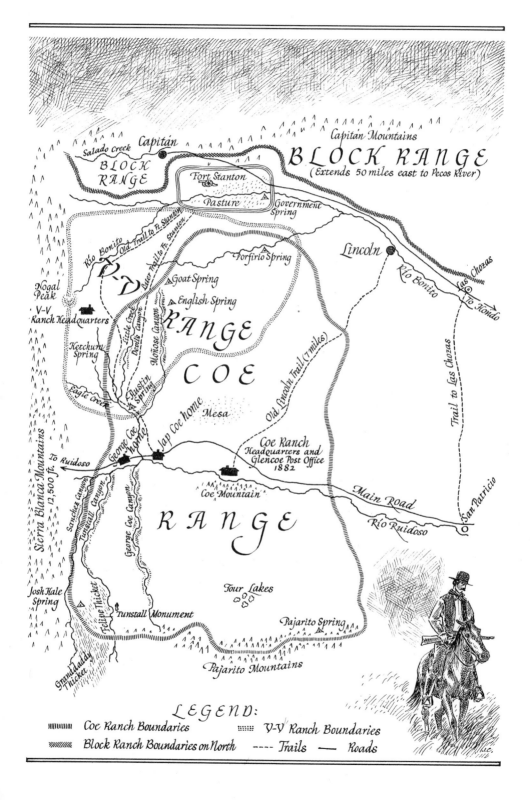

Capitán

Salado Creek

BLOCK RANGE

Capitán Mountains

BLOCK RANGE
(Extends 50 miles east to Pecos River)

Fort Stanton

Pasture

Government Spring

Río Bonito

Old Trail to Ft. Stanton

Outer Trail to Ft. Stanton

Porfirio Spring

Lincoln

Las Chozas

Río Bonito

To Hondo

V-V

Nogal Peak

Goat Spring

English Spring

RANGE

Little Creek

Devil's Canyon

Monose Canyon

V-V Ranch Headquarters

Ketchum Spring

COE

Austin Spring

Old Lincoln Trail (7 miles)

Trail to Las Chozas

Eagle Creek

Mesa

Sierra Blanca Mountains

12,500 ft.

To Ruidoso

George Coe home

Jap Coe home

Coe Ranch Headquarters and Glencoe Post Office 1882

San Patricio

Sanchez Canyon

Tunstall Canyon

George Coe Canyon

Coe Mountain

RANGE

Main Road

Río Ruidoso

San Patricio

Josh Hale Spring

Felipe Thicket

Tunstall Monument

Four Lakes

Pajarito Spring

Grand Daddy Thicket

Pajarito Mountains

LEGEND:

▥▥▥▥ Coe Ranch Boundaries   ▦▦▦ V-V Ranch Boundaries

▨▨▨ Block Ranch Boundaries on North   ---- Trails   — Roads

Peter Hurd's painting of the ranch on the Ruidoso

RANCH on the RUIDOSO

The Story of a Pioneer Family
in New Mexico, 1871-1968

BY WILBUR COE

With an Introduction by
PETER HURD

ALFRED A. KNOPF NEW YORK

1968

THIS IS A BORZOI BOOK
PUBLISHED BY ALFRED A . KNOPF, INC.

FIRST EDITION

COPYRIGHT © 1968 BY WILBUR COE

Library of Congress Catalog Card Number: 68–26490

MANUFACTURED IN THE UNITED STATES OF AMERICA

This book is dedicated to
the memory of my mother and father
Helena Tully Coe and Frank Coe

19840

INTRODUCTION

To MOST OF US living at the fast lope which prevails now it is difficult to conceive of the vast changes that have occurred during the lifetime of a person over sixty. These changes have far exceeded anything even dreamed of by the time of my friend Wilbur Coe's birth in 1894 or of mine ten years later. They have profoundly affected us all in nearly every phase of our lives from the physical to the philosophical and spiritual.

In this story of a family of pioneer ranchers the reader enters a world which would seem to be so remote from ours of today as to be beyond the memory of anyone now alive. But the author's possession of a rich and vivid memory, a memory which at times approaches total recall, disproves this. As a telephoto lens changes distance into foreground he brings us to a picture of the past, convincing and in clear focus.

What a transformation we have seen! In New Mexico until about the time we entered the First World War covered wagons were commonplace, and as automobiles increased the wagons became a nuisance if not a hazard on the narrow gravel roads. Most of these were used as freight carriers serving ranches and those communities not on a railroad. Others were the forerunners of today's trailers and campers; their occupants friends or families who were "just a-travelin'." People in no particular hurry. Trail herds also survived until the cattle trucks appeared in the 1920's. One of my duties as a boy on our farm was to listen for that indescribable sound of hundreds of cattle on the move: a continuous moaning, mooing, and bellowing to which was added, as the herd approached, the whistles and yells of the drovers. When this happened my job was to race away to close the main gates which gave entrance to our orchard and surrounding fields of lush alfalfa.

At West Point in the early 1920's cadets were instructed in mounted cavalry drill involving hand-to-hand combat with long, straight-bladed sabers. The other day my young grandson, delighted at hearing this, asked, "And were you a knight then—in armor and everything?" It now seems to me that perhaps those days did relate more to the age of chivalry than to our own.

In this book you will meet some colorful people, among them the best known is William Bonney, also called "Billy the Kid" or simply "The Kid." He died, aged twenty-one, killed by the sheriff of Lincoln County. Posterity has been kind to Bonney and with notable lack of evidence to merit this, the mantle of Robin Hood has descended on his narrow, bottle shoulders. For years a prominent highway sign stood near here on the road to Lincoln. Placed there by the State Tourist Bureau, it read: "Nine miles to Lincoln Town where in the turbulent days of the Lincoln County War there fought and bled such gallant men as Billy the Kid, Charley Bowdre, Tom O'Folliard, . . ." I quote from memory but vividly remember this overimpulsive use of the word "gallant." But perhaps they deserve it. People who knew Bonney said he had a sunny disposition. It has occurred to me that if only John Dillinger had been younger, sunnier, and had ridden a horse he might now be immortalized by the Indiana Tourist Bureau.

But to me the most colorful in all his cast of characters is Wilbur himself. Here is a man whom fate, it would seem, had marked early in life if not for failure then surely for a quiet, inactive existence. Not so. With a Scots-Irish heritage of cheerful dauntlessness combined with imagination, he has continued to ignore the disadvantage of a badly crippled leg. This did not even deter him in the past from roping wild cattle and riding raw broncs, activities that would discourage many a young man sound of wind and limb.

Introduction

Wilbur is a lusty and determined country fiddler. For years he and his wife, Louise (she at the piano or guitar), have played for dances at home or at the neighboring Bonnell Ranch. These affairs could not be described as stately cotillions: notably lacking is any air of stuffy formality and it is not unusual for exuberant guests who are musicians (or who have absorbed enough Tequila Cuervo to be convinced that they are) to seize whatever instrument is handy and join the players. Unperturbed by the cacophony, the original group plays on while the swaying dancers remain oblivious. Dinner parties at the Coes' are also lively and entertaining and, if well-briefed, a guest invited for the first time will arrive in a state of near-starvation, otherwise he will never do justice to the sumptuous fare. If a baile is scheduled he had best be well caught up on sleep, for the dawn may greet the entire company dancing a bouncy polca Mexicana.

In part at least it is from these social occasions that this book has evolved. Through the years friends of the Coes have delighted in Wilbur's reminiscences and as a consequence he would often hear someone say, "You know, you ought to write that." More persevering and methodical than some of us, he quietly decided to do so. Beginning fifteen years ago with a cardboard box as a file cabinet he began putting away snippets in his own longhand, old letters, photographs, clippings, etc. From this material, which quickly outgrew its original containers, comes this book.

Another author, Thomas Carlisle, also a Scot, wrote, "To interest readers, that is to say idle neighbors and fellow creatures in need of gossip, there is nothing like unveiling yourself." Perhaps so. But I should warn you, gentle reader, this book contains no gossip. Nor does it make any attempt at unveiling in the manner of certain tawdry biographies of today. Any skeletons that might exist remain snugly closeted—discretely ignored. On the other hand, it is no literary marshmallow: implicit through much of the book are the prevailing characteristics of the Coe clan—a toughness of spirit and body to equal "live oak bound with rawhide." An abundant sense of humor acts as a leaven in dealings with apple truckers and cattle buyers who are inevitably confronted with a guile equal to or excelling their own. Many a trader recognizing defeat too late leaves the scene with a wry smile of grudging admiration on his tight lips.

Throughout the years since their marriage Louise has played a tremendously important part in the continuing success and development of the Coe Ranch. They have been prudent ranchers always conserving, never plundering the earth that has nurtured them. Today their land holds visible evidence of the deep affection they have had through the years for it and for each other. They have set an example for the rest of us—an example, alas, too often disregarded—of the best methods of farm and range management. Earlier in this introduction I have referred to the lavish hospitality of the Coes, omitting to say that guests often enjoy meals entirely produced by the ranch—the only (and obvious) exceptions being sugar, salt, and coffee.

Sadly this kind of life is on the wane. Due to the problems in food production today, agriculture and stock raising are becoming less and less a way of life as it still is at ranches like the Coes'. The trend now is toward specialization; money-saving efficiency in which, as a result, farms and ranches will become in effect large impersonal food and fiber factories. When this change takes over completely something very special, something warm and wonderfully appealing in our life will have disappeared.

PETER HURD

San Patricio, New Mexico
March 26, 1968

FOREWORD

I PROPOSE TO TELL the story of how my family came to New Mexico, settled ultimately in Lincoln County, and developed our ranch. My story covers several decades, for I am in my seventy-fourth year. As I write this, I am blessed with a good memory. I can recall clearly details I heard my father and other immediate members of the family tell over and over again. The reader must realize that I make no attempt to write a complete history—neither of Lincoln County, famous for Billy the Kid and the Lincoln County War, or even of the Ruidoso Valley in which our ranch is located. Indeed, I am only concerned with happenings in which the Coes were intimately involved. My accounts of some events differ from existing ones, but what I write is based chiefly on family papers, to which other writers have not had access, and stories told repeatedly in the family circle before I was old enough to take direct part in any activities.

The reader must remember that during the early years of which I write, communication in the valley was crude, indeed in terms of today nonexistent. Consequently, much time was spent when friends and relatives got together in mulling over the old familiar stories in which the pioneers were leading characters. I might add that it was always my practice to keep diaries and notebooks in which I recorded accounts of any happenings that seemed to me at all notable.

I acknowledge with gratitude my debt to Amye Robinson of Hondo, New Mexico, and to my old friend Dr. John Frerichs of

El Paso for their considerable help in putting my text into final form. And to Peter Hurd for his introduction and his continuing interest in my writing.

WILBUR F. COE

Coe Ranch
Glencoe, New Mexico
July 12, 1968

CONTENTS

CONTENTS

ILLUSTRATIONS

(following page 76)

ILLUSTRATIONS

A view over the Coe Ranch in 1958.

Peter Hurd and Wilbur Coe posing as Billy the Kid and Frank
Coe.

The ranch house in 1960.

RANCH ON THE RUIDOSO

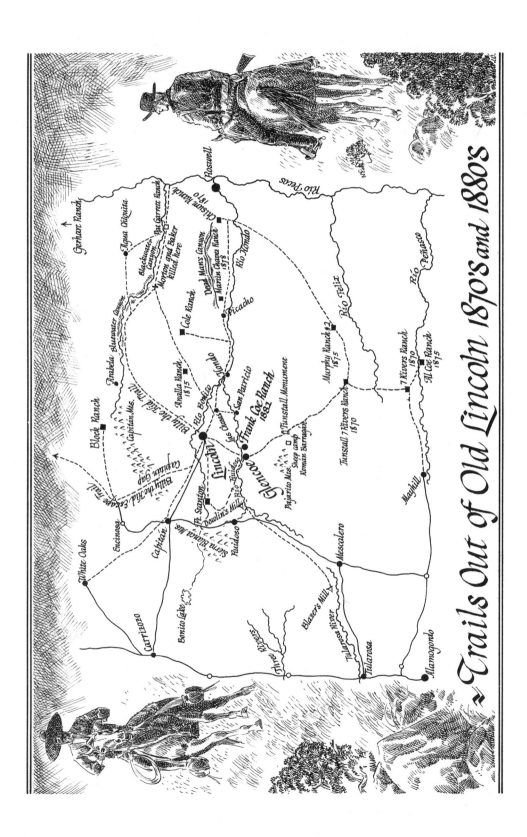

Trails Out of Old Lincoln 1870's and 1880's

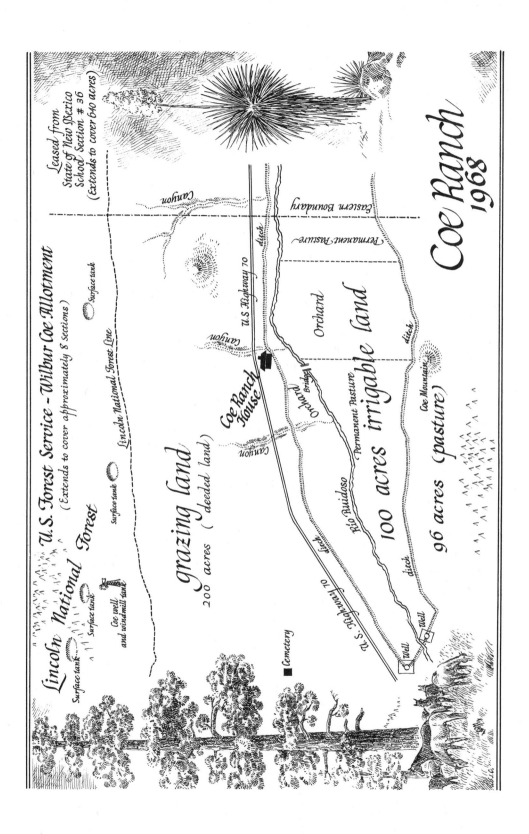

Coe Ranch
1968

Leased from
State of New Mexico
School Section # 36
(Extends to cover 640 acres)

Canyon

Eastern Boundary

Permanent Pasture

U.S. Forest Service – Wilbur Coe Allotment
(Extends to cover approximately 8 sections)

Surface tank

Lincoln National Forest Line

Orchard

U.S. Highway 70

Canyon

Coe Ranch House

Canyon

Orchard

Orchard Bridge

Permanent Pasture

Coe Mountain

Lincoln National Forest

Surface tank

grazing land
200 acres (deeded land)

100 acres irrigable land

96 acres (pasture)

Surface tank

Coe well
and windmill tank

Rio Ruidoso

ditch

ditch

ditch

ditch

Well

Well

Well

U.S. Highway 70

Cemetery

CHAPTER I

The Coes Migrate to NEW MEXICO

HEN MY FATHER Frank first saw Fort Union in New Mexico Territory, that dreary outpost had been guarding the California trail for a scant twenty years. The year was 1871 and Frank and his brother Al, both of whom had been champing at the bit for eleven long years to see the country their older brother, Lou, had settled in, thought the place a bit forbidding. Fort Union supplied the two young men with a place to rest up, but it offered none of the diversion and excitement of Independence, Missouri, over seven hundred miles behind them, where they had first joined the wagon train. When they were offered jobs to return to Independence for another load of freight, Frank refused, but Al accepted. He had been such a good cook the boss offered him a steady job and raised his pay to fifty dollars a month—too handsome a sum to be turned down.

Frank had been looking forward to this adventure since he was eight years old, when his older brother Lou joined a wagon train and headed for the new territory. Lou was then eighteen. In 1859 Lou had joined a wagon train going to Independence and took off down the famous Santa Fé Trail. Heading for new country was in the Coe blood, for the boys' father, Benjamin, had brought his family in the early fifties from West Virginia to a farm near Queen City, Missouri. At that time, the elder Coe's family consisted of his wife, Annie Kerr Coe, and five boys, Lou, Al, Frank, Jasper (nicknamed Jap), and Austin. The three girls, Mahalia, Mary Ellen, and Zebulah, were born later at Queen City. Benjamin was a good farmer, interested in growing fruit and, with the assistance of his boys, he planted one of

[5]

the first orchards in that part of Missouri. The life of a pioneer was rugged and hard, but Benjamin was never too busy or too tired to play his violin for a dance for his family's entertainment. Young Frank, with an ear for music, soon learned with his father's help to play the fiddle too.

When Lou's adventure launched the Coes west, Frank, who later became my father, could not have known that in that same year a certain William Bonney was born in New York City; nor could he have dreamed that in fewer than twenty years he would be involved with this man—known as Billy the Kid—in the bloodiest events in the history of Lincoln County, New Mexico.

When Lou went west the Mexican War had been over for eleven years, so he was an early settler in the area. Lou left the train in Colfax County, New Mexico. The valley of the Sugarite seemed to him a promising place to end his journey—plenty of good water to irrigate the fertile land that his young farmer's eye had noted. He staked a claim and threw up a rude hut and applied his strong back to the task at hand. His crops were successful and soon he had enough money to buy some cattle. Lou farmed his claim on the Sugarite for four years but, during the fifth, serious crop losses and some vexing litigations in progress over the Maxwell Land Grant that involved the settlers on the Sugarite (and perhaps the Coe wanderlust) caused him to join a wagon train headed for Lincoln County, in the south-central section of the territory. It was in 1866 that Lou left the Sugarite with his partner, Joe Storm, the only other unmarried man in the settlement. When they reached the tiny settlement of La Junta, now Hondo, which is at the junction of the Ruidoso and Bonito rivers about twenty miles from Fort Stanton, they settled down. Lou and Joe recognized the fertility of the soil and the abundance of the water and considered also, no doubt, that Fort Stanton, only twenty miles away, would provide a ready market for hay, grain, and beef.

Fort Stanton had been built as a part of the chain on

the California trail, an early outpost as protection of both travelers and settlers against Indian depredations. At that time there were approximately three hundred head of cavalry horses that had to be fed and Lou and Joe obtained a contract to deliver grain and hay to the fort. Prices were inflated in that frontier country and Lou and his partner seem to have prospered. With hay selling for sixty dollars a ton and grain for three dollars a hundredweight, Lou and Ed were able to increase their holdings by buying and trading with their Mexican neighbors. But despite all this prosperity there were drawbacks: pay-offs and kickbacks were common, the protection of the law was tenuous, and business life on the frontier hazardous. In any case, Lou, who had in his brief foray onto the frontier made more money than his father had accumulated in many years, decided to return to Missouri to marry his former sweetheart. Joe decided to stay on, so he took over Lou's holdings along the river. Lou's plan was to go back to New Mexico when the fruit trees he had planted began to bear. Like his father before him, Lou was as interested in fruit as in beef and had planted a considerable apple orchard on his land from seed his father had sent him from Missouri. The seedlings he replanted in neat rows twenty feet apart after the trees were a year old became the first apple orchard in the Hondo Valley.

Lou returned to Queen City in late 1866 and he brought with him glowing tales of the Sugarite country and of the new land he had homesteaded in Lincoln County. Good crops, wonderful climate, water aplenty, and the profits to be made filled his conversation.

My father was only sixteen when Lou returned, too young, even in those days, his family thought, to strike out for himself. But he and his brother Al, who was a few years older, must have listened to Lou's tales with growing determination to see the same country. Lou, my father remembered, soft-pedaled the tales of violence on the frontier, but it is doubtful that had he regaled his brothers with such stuff it would have deterred them. It was no surprise then that in April of 1871, Frank, now almost twenty, and Al rode off to Independence, as their brother had done twelve years before, to get a job with a wagon train hauling freight to New Mexico.

Somewhere along the trail as it wound its way up the Arkansas, the train must have overtaken the "end of iron" of the railroad-construction gangs. The rails had not at that time reached Fort Dodge and would not turn Buffalo City, the hide hunters' sod-and-tent settlement, into Dodge City until the next year. When the train passed through La Junta and Trinidad, Colorado, and reached the Raton Pass that debouched south into New Mexico territory, the boys were three full years ahead of the railroad, which did not reach the pass until 1874. By that time young Frank was a seasoned frontiersman, as we shall see.

The parting of the ways of Frank and Al was short-lived, for Al returned and launched a freight outfit hauling between Fort Union and Stanton. But the initial parting of the ways reflected to some extent the difference between these two brothers. Frank, though younger, was the more daring of the two; he was good with a gun and had a way with horses. Al was the steady and quiet one. Indeed, when he took the job as cook on the return trip he did so only with the wagonmaster's understanding that he would not be required to wear a gun and that he be allowed to quit any time the going got too rough for his peaceful nature. In fact in all his years on that wild frontier Al never wore a gun belt or packed a gun.

After Frank had said good-bye to his brother he looked around Fort Union for a job. The choices were limited and, besides, the offer to join a hide-hunting outfit appealed to his sense of adventure. The buffalo hunters, enjoying a windfall of profits slaughtering the southern herd, had moved out of Dodge City south across the Canadian River. It mattered little to these men that they were thus flouting the Medicine Lodge Treaty by invading the Indian country. Besides, the hide hunters were as often as not riffraff as renegades and the brutal life did little to improve them. The men in the outfit Frank joined up with in New Mexico were not any better and one season was enough for Frank. He later said that he found the slaughter of the great beasts just for their hides bad enough and the company of the men who slaughtered them even worse. Probably Frank got little chance at the hunting itself, for the young members of those rough crews usually had to do the skinning and drying, the meanest work in camp. When the first expedition was over, Frank declined to join up again, explaining to the boss that he was going to join his brother Al to take a freighting job. When Frank arrived at Al's place on the Sugarite, his brother was away on a haul. To pass the time until his brother's return, Frank went on a hunting trip in the Raton Range, taking with him a little pack mule called Kit and a small terrier who had attached herself to him and whom he had named Skip. The fort was a market for his fresh game. At a spot where pine, cedar, and heavy brush covered the mountainside, he built a shelter amid a hunter's paradise of mountain lions, lobos, coyotes, and other wild animals. Deer and turkey he shot from his doorway. Among the exciting hunting adventures Skip shared with him were those with a mother lion and her cubs and with an enormous black bear whose skin was taken to the fort and sold to the officers for a trophy.

Since there was no threat of heavy snow in the early winter of 1872, Frank remained in the mountains until December before loading his gear on Kit and returning to the fort. On his arrival there he learned that Jasper, the fourth of the Coe boys to migrate to New Mexico, had reached the Sugarite and was farming Lou's old claim there. Not knowing when Al would get back from Fort Stanton, he set out at once on the hundred-mile journey to the Sugarite. Frank not only was delighted to see Jap again after so long a time but to meet Jap's bride, Ada Saunders.

Jap and Frank worked the claim together, plowing, planting,

clearing more land, irrigating the fields, and building fences. Whenever a slack time came they mounted their horses and went hunting in the nearby mountains, or they hitched up the wagon and took Ada with them to visit a neighboring ranch. But it was at the dances that they enjoyed themselves most because cares, worries, and the rough jobs waiting for them at home were forgotten. And no one was more welcome at these shindigs than Frank Coe with his charm and ready wit. He was always willing to forget about girls and dancing for a chance to play the fiddle. Tunes he had learned from his father brought back memories of home to Ada, Jap, and him. When the occasional letters from Missouri arrived at the settlement, the Coes were all cheered. Their delight knew no bounds when they learned in the late winter of 1873 that Lou was planning to return to New Mexico in the spring and bring his family with him. Also coming was Jap's brother-in-law, Ab Saunders, and a cousin of theirs, George Coe.

Frank was especially delighted that George was coming. As boyhood chums they had hunted together. On the heels of this good news came Al's letter reporting that his trip to Fort Union in the late summer of 1874 would be his last. Tired of freighting, he planned to run cattle on a ranch he had bought in the Peñasco Valley of Lincoln County in another mountain range south of the Ruidoso Valley. There he found a cattleman's dream of open range, slow and dependable streams, virgin forest, and lush grama grass, a wild grass that grows from twelve to eighteen inches high and has a heading of grain. Pretty Molly Mayhill, whose parents had settled in the same area, had promised to marry him and he had already started to build a cabin on his land. Her decision, he stated, had been a brave one because it meant living where she would be the only white woman for miles around, surrounded by a wilderness in which wild animals and wilder Indians prowled.

After Al's last run to Fort Union he was planning to visit them on the Sugarite, and in closing his letter he asked his brothers to be on the lookout for some cattle for him to drive back and start his own herd.

As it happened, Al reached the Sugarite a short time before Lou and his two wagons arrived, and so five Coes were in New Mexico by the late summer of 1874—Lou, Al, Frank, Jap, and their cousin George.

By late fall Al left for his ranch on the Peñasco and his brothers settled down to serious farming again. Frank rented more land and entered into a partnership with Ab Saunders, so there was little time for hunting or community socials. At the dances George and Frank took turns playing the fiddle, and so long as the people stomped their feet the two Coes played for them.

But all was not peaceful in their pleasant valley. The trouble over the Maxwell Land Grant that had previously plagued Lou and others continued. Land claimed under the old grant caused disputes, lawsuits, interminable litigations, court trials, shootings, and feuds. Weary and disgusted by such conditions, the settlers along the Sugarite began to move out and file claims in other parts of the territory. Lou himself studied the possibilities of moving west to the San Juan Basin country, while Jap considered California where, he had heard, there were easier ways than farming to make money. To George it did not matter where he went so long as there was hunting in the area. Frank and Ab wanted to try another year on their claim, a decision they later regretted, for rustlers drove away most of their cattle during the winter.

Disgusted and with little hope of settling peacefully and permanently on the Sugarite, Frank and Ab decided to go to Lincoln County, whose climate and farming opportunities Lou had often talked about. In the late summer of 1875 they set out over the same trail Lou had traveled ten years before, and three weeks later they arrived at the confluence of the Bonito and Ruidoso rivers, the beginning of the Hondo, where they were able to rent the same land Lou and Joe Storm had farmed. And they too secured a contract to supply grain and hay for the cavalry at Fort Stanton. However, by the time these negotiations were concluded, it was too late to plant any crops, so they moved temporarily to the mesa land southwest of the fort and set up camp in the acres of tall, waving grama grass. Using the grain cradle Ab had brought from Missouri, they cut the natural wild hay and gathered it with a crude horse-drawn rake they had made. They loaded it loose on the wagon and tied it down with buffalo hides, which reminded Frank of the malodorous crew of the buffalo hunt.

On reaching the middle of the Río Bonito, they jumped from the wagon and began to throw water on the hay to help replace some of the loss of weight caused by the hot September sun that had been beating down on it since it had been cut. As the weighmaster at Fort Stanton had put them wise to the trick of wetting the hay, their consciences did not bother them. They assured him the water made it stick better and become more palatable to the horses. When the official handed them their weight slip, he winked good-naturedly and advised them to hurry their operations before a heavy frost put an end to them. Shortly afterwards a freeze did come and they moved back to the farm on the Ruidoso to begin plans and preparations for the spring planting.

Because of the limited extent of the land under cultivation, they enlarged their acreage, taking over nearby irrigable areas. Quick to see that the dams built by the Mexicans to divert water from the Ruidoso River assured better crops, they spent the winter cutting logs, building dams, and laying out ditches. This last operation was carried out with the able help of the Mexicans, who had a natural sense of the gradation of the earth and who knew how to build the ditches at the correct level, an art they learned by studying cow trails leading down the hills to the river. The dam and ditch work was completed by spring and the resulting corn crop was heavy and of fine quality. They had contracted to sell it for eighty dollars a ton on the cob, which made their farming operations financially worthwhile.

Both Frank and Ab wanted to continue farming where the profits were so good, but rampant lawlessness in the county caused them great worry. It was safer from Indian uprisings than at the time Lou had been there, but Lincoln County now had become a greater gathering place for rustlers, outlaws, and worse scum, all eager to share somehow in the lucrative business of cattle rustling, whose roots went deep in a situation that involved ordinary citizens, outlaws, influential cattlemen, lawmen, and politicians in high places.

It is not my purpose to detail the events of the Lincoln County War. This has been done many times and its complexities are often confusing. They found out that as citizens of Lincoln County they were forced to become participants or lose their property and perhaps their lives.

Frank Coe later referred to the Lincoln County War as a "cattlemen's war." He said it was prompted by greed. On one side was the Murphy-Dolan crowd which controlled vast herds of cattle and owned a large mercantile establishment in Lincoln. On the other was John Tunstall, a wealthy young Englishman, partner in the rival Lincoln mercantile firm of Alexander McSween, a lawyer. When they extended their interests to banking, the great cattle baron of the Southwest, John Chisum, became associated with them. Since the United States Government was paying a high price for the beef that the forts and the Indian reservations needed, these rivals competed for the contracts to supply the required cattle.

And how did this affect the ordinary citizens of Lincoln County? Through the experiences of Frank and George Coe much is to be learned. Frank and Ab Saunders were deeply troubled because they found the lawlessness incompatible with their desire to remain in Lincoln County and enjoy its superb climate and resources. They didn't want to be frightened away

by gunmen or become members of either of the factions even
though more and more men were joining either the Murphy-
Dolan or the Tunstall-McSween outfits. For the most part this
was done to protect their own interests and lives from the
rustlers hired by both sides to steal cattle. In the short time
they had been in Lincoln County, Ab and Frank had realized it
was doubtful that they could remain neutral much longer, so
they decided it was best to return to the Sugarite and talk the
situation over with Lou, Jap, and George. Before leaving the
Hondo Valley, Frank rented a farm on the upper Ruidoso
River, where, in another year, he hoped to run some cattle of
his own.

Frank and Ab realized before they reached the Sugarite late
in 1876 that they were willing to run whatever risks might be
involved in another venture in Lincoln County. Whether Lou
and Jap and their cousin George would want to try this was
another question. Lou and Jap had families to consider. When
they talked it over together at the Sugarite ranch, the arguments, pro and con, boiled down to the fact that there were
troubles to contend with and adversities to endure no matter
where they lived. Lou and Jap decided to remain on the Sugarite. Frank and Ab returned to Lincoln County, taking George
with them.

The year was 1876 and the stage in Lincoln County was
already being set for a showdown between the two big mercantile firms. Both were eager to fill the lucrative government
contracts. Outlaws, gunmen, and rustlers were in their employ
to see that there were enough cattle to fulfill the contracts.
John Chisum, who was associated with McSween-Tunstall, was
especially vulnerable. His "U" brand was clearly traced on
cowhides scores of miles away from his headquarters ranch at
South Springs near Roswell, mute testimony to the thieving
going on. The story is that as Chisum's cattle continued to
disappear in large numbers, Murphy became better supplied
with cattle and could thus inevitably make lower bids for the

beef contracts. Occasionally rustlers were jailed, but they usually escaped easily from the flimsy Lincoln County jail and its indifferent guards.

There was so much unchecked violence that no man's life was safe. People were shot down in cold blood and killings for revenge and retaliation were numerous. Thus when the Coes came onto the stage set with violence, greed, and injustice, they were unwilling actors in a drama not of their making and of which they wanted no part. Instead of the peace they had hoped for, they found increased reports of shootings as the bitterness between the factions deepened. Staying alive depended on the fast draw.

Ab went down to Analla (present-day Tinnie) in the Hondo Valley to look after a small farm they had rented, hoping he would be away from the feud. The valley of the Ruidoso was the territory of the Tunstall-McSween faction. George, Frank, and Ab had come to be associated more or less with some of them. Hatred of no one drove them into the conflict, but circumstances beyond their control caused them to drift along with others who took up arms to protect their lives and property.

The three worked hard that spring of 1876 to get in some crops. They avoided Lincoln as much as possible, for it was a gathering place for rustlers and outlaws. Occasionally they went to the cantina at San Patricio, five miles up the valley from the Hondo junction. Here the Tunstall-McSween cowboys gathered to talk, drink, and play cards.

Among the few scattered houses of the settlers in the Ruidoso Valley at which the Coes occasionally stopped on their way to and from San Patricio was the Brewer ranch, which occupied, halfway up the valley, one of the finest home sites along the river. At one time it had been run by Jack Gilliam, a former sheriff of Lincoln County who was killed in a gun battle. After his death the ranch was taken over briefly by the Harrold brothers, notorious outlaws from Texas. Frank had heard about their battles with the Mexicans over water rights and their other terrorist acts, especially the private war they had waged in Lincoln.

An old Mexican witness told how the Harrold "bandidos," aroused because one of their brothers had been shot, charged into the crowd on a fiesta day, firing their guns and killing and wounding several people. Afterwards, according to the story, they rode out of the country, leaving behind an unpaid bill of several hundred dollars at the Ellis store in Lincoln. This debt was assumed by Dick Brewer, who subsequently took over the land the outlaws had occupied. No more inviting place to stop over than the Brewer ranch could be found along the river. Under the cooling shade of huge cottonwood trees along the ditch, settlers passing up and down the valley rested and refreshed themselves.

Frank Coe later recalled many events that took place during his early years in Lincoln County. One that stood out in his memory was the day in midsummer of 1877 when he rode down to the Brewer place to find someone to help him and George with a big crop of oats; they were hurrying to get it in before a rain came. Frank thought it would also be a good opportunity to have Brewer replace a loose shoe on his pony. He asked Brewer if he would help them harvest their oats. Brewer replied that he had a small oat patch of his own that needed cutting but as soon as he took care of it he would pitch in if they still needed help. It was noon and, as Frank started to leave, Brewer invited him to have dinner with him. Frank, wanting to learn news of the lower valley, accepted. As they approached the house a young man rode up; he was well armed but had a pleasing appearance. Brewer asked him what his name was, where he came from, and what was he looking for. The stranger said his name was William Bonney and he was looking for a job. Brewer told him he did not need a hand at the time but that Frank Coe was looking for someone to cut some oats. He invited Bonney to join them for dinner. Brewer and Frank learned that the young man knew John Tunstall. Frank asked Bonney if he could swing a grain cradle and the young man quickly replied that he would like to give it a try.

After dinner, Frank and his new hired hand mounted their horses and started for the Coe place. A short distance up the valley, Bonney reined up his pony and pointed to some birds on the dead limb of an old pine tree in a small clearing. Frank never saw him draw but he did see three birds tumble down from their perches. As they rode along, Frank thought much about this friendly new hand. He was puzzled by the contrast between Bonney's smile and soft-spoken way and his superb marksmanship, perhaps indicative of gunfighting experience. Bonney was merry, always joking and full of tricks, and he particularly enjoyed hearing Frank or George play the fiddle, to which he would jig alone and cut amusing capers in the little room. The Coes' liking for him increased, although at times they were puzzled by his evasiveness and moodiness. He was a willing worker with surprising strength and endurance for his slight frame, and he asked no more from them than his chuck and a little silver to play monte bank at the cantina in San Patricio. He hunted with the Coes in Turkey Canyon and other wooded places. As time went on, Frank and George learned little more about Billy except some vague rumors about his past and his present association with known rustlers of the Tunstall-McSween outfit.

As the late summer rains had brought good grazing to the range, George and Frank were kept busy looking after stray cattle. Sometimes Billy went with them. On the days they did not need his help, he would become restless and would ride down to the cantina to play cards with the Chisum men. After they received fat bonuses for a raid on the Murphy cattle, they usually had plenty of spending money. One morning Frank told Billy that he and George were going to be busy for a few days rounding up strays. Billy asked if they needed his help. George said he thought they would find the cattle nearby and could handle them alone. They went out to saddle their horses, and when they reached the clearing where the horses were staked they found that Billy's horse had been stolen. Billy's face turned red with anger and he swore that he would get the thief who had played him such a low-down trick. They jumped on their ponies, Billy riding double with Frank, and took off at full gallop following the tracks, which were clearly visible until they reached the underbrush. Here the trail became dim and hard to follow. They decided it would be impossible for them to catch up with the thief and they returned to camp.

They told Billy he could use one of their horses, then they went to round up their cattle. Billy rode to San Patricio to join the gang at the cantina. It did not take long for him to get in a card game. He liked to play monte and hoped to win enough to buy another horse. The card game went on for several hours; whenever a player went broke, another took his place. By dark there was no one left in the saloon but Billy and Señor Zamora, who were still playing monte. Billy was losing but refused to pull out of the game. Finally he lost his last penny. All that remained for him to bet was his bridle and saddle on the borrowed horse. He put up his bridle and lost. He was sure his luck would change so he put up his saddle and blanket. When he lost them there was nothing left but the borrowed horse. He was desperate and wanted to take a last chance. When he lost the horse he felt sure that George and Frank would understand; he would repay them in some way. After an all-night session playing monte, Billy was tired and disgusted with himself. At daybreak he left on foot for the Coe camp about fifteen miles up the valley. On the way he stopped at Faustino Contrero's house to get something to eat. Faustino was glad to see him and Josefa, Faustino's wife, fixed him a pot of hot coffee, some beans and tortillas and goat meat. While he was eating, it began to rain.

When the roof began to leak, Faustino brought in a wide board to channel the water to the door to keep it from leaking on Billy's head. Finally Faustino dug a trench in the dirt floor to channel water from more leaks to the outside. After resting a while, Billy hurried on to the Coe camp. He knew he had to report to Frank and George that he had lost their horse in a card game. When Billy came in, Frank told him that he had good news for him, that his horse had come back with a short rope around his neck. It looked as if it had broken loose or perhaps the thief got scared and tried to make it appear that way.

Billy was glad to see his own animal and felt relieved because now he could offer it to George and Frank in the place of theirs. He was still determined, however, to win their horse back. The next morning, after borrowing some money from Frank, he rode back to San Patricio where he found the same crowd at the cantina, including Zamora. He suggested another game and placed on the table the five silver dollars he had borrowed. At first they began to grow; then they started to dwindle. Billy wagered the last of his stake and waited for the cards to show. His luck changed and his coins began to stack up; by mid-afternoon he had won back the horse and complete outfit.

At sundown Billy rode proudly into the Coe camp leading the horse behind him. At the door he yelled to the boys to come out and he told them he had won back the horse fair and square. Dismounting, he reached into his jeans and pulled out some silver, which he counted carefully into Frank's hand, paying him the money he had borrowed, plus interest.

Thereafter Frank and George were careful to stake their ponies as close to the cabin as possible, and before cold weather came they built a corral. With the arrival of winter, Billy became restless and spent more time at the cantina with the Chisum bunch. While the Coes were trying desperately to avoid involvement in the cattle war, Billy implicated himself inextricably in the affair. He became morose and did not even take his earlier pleasure in Frank's fiddle playing.

At supper one night in late December Billy announced that

he was going to hire out to Chisum until his promised job with Tunstall materialized in the spring. In a sense Frank and George were relieved because Billy's close ties with the outlaws had been worrying them. With so many of Chisum's cattle being rustled by the Murphy men, they knew he needed every good gunslinger he could get, and if that was what he wanted, Billy was his man. Yet the Coes tried to discourage Billy because they knew that law and order, not fighting, stealing, and killing, was the only solution to their problem. Billy was wading into deep waters that would eventually engulf him.

CHAPTER II

The 𝕮𝕺𝕰 𝕭𝕺𝕐𝕾
and the Lincoln County War

WHEN BILLY LEFT the Coe camp and hired out to John Chisum, he brought upon himself the stamp of approval of the Tunstall-McSween faction. The rustling and subsequent killings increased and as lawlessness gripped Lincoln County, George and Frank knew they must face up to the fact that they could no longer stay neutral. On both sides were base outlaws of whom they wanted no part. Because their economic and physical survival would be better protected by this faction, they thought the Tunstall-McSween side was the better one to be on. That their choice happened to be the same as Billy's was coincidental. They could only feel deep misgivings about the whole business.

Besides the competition to get cattle contracts, there was another thorn in the collective flesh of the Murphy-Dolan combine. Chisum had become associated with Alexander McSween in the banking business. McSween had been accused of mishandling, in fact stealing, a ten-thousand-dollar insurance award due the Fritz heirs, whose representative he had been. When later McSween refused to defend some Murphy rustlers, Murphy became vengeful and decided to use the fact of this missing money to make trouble for the Tunstall-McSween faction. The entire affair was obviously none of the doings of John Tunstall, McSween's partner. But Murphy decided to start trouble by making an aggressive move against Tunstall. Many found it hard to believe that a court order had been sworn out to attach Tunstall's thoroughbred saddle horses because of McSween's alleged theft. Sheriff Brady, whose allegiance and political affiliations reputedly belonged to Murphy, deputized

Billy Matthews to go to the Tunstall ranch and execute the order. He chose, according to the Coes, about twenty of the most desperate and unscrupulous outlaws in the county, including Billy Morton, Jesse Evans, Frank Baker, Bob Ollinger, and others, to help him, and set out for the Tunstall ranch.

At the time Billy was already in the employ of Tunstall. Billy told Frank at the cantina about reporting to Tunstall at his ranch on the Feliz and riding out with him to find his new foreman, Dick Brewer. On the way, Tunstall, an expert shot, suggested they try some target practice. Four hundred yards to their left were some bleached cow heads, looking more like small white rocks. They chose these for a target, and after Tunstall fired they found he had hit one between the horns. Billy missed his. Eager to show his new boss what he could do, he soon spotted some cowbirds trailing a bunch of cattle and downed four of them before they could get off the ground and a fifth one on the wing. He was proud of the praise his employer gave him. Frank and George were aware of the warm friendship that sprang up between the aristocratic Englishman and their friend Billy.

The Coes knew that Billy was in a dangerous position, for Tunstall had been marked as direct target of the Murphy-Dolan group. Knowing this, Billy was especially careful to keep near his employer in order to forestall, if he could, any attempt by the Murphy men to get him. He did his share of work around the ranch and told Frank that for the first time in his life he received full wages for doing a man's work. It seemed to give him more confidence in himself. He had known plenty of outlaws, rustlers, drifters, and down-and-outers in the saloons, but he had never claimed for a friend a law-abiding man of culture, education, and means. He was proud to be respected as Tunstall's friend. For Billy Bonney, not yet twenty-one, this was a new experience.

News of the court order reached Billy and Frank at the San Patricio cantina, where they met frequently; Billy left for the

Feliz at once, knowing that Tunstall's enemies would now get the chance they wanted—the opportunity to pull their guns on him. Shortly afterward, a messenger rode in desperate haste to the ranch to warn Tunstall that a posse would be up the next morning to seize his horses. Tunstall was sure that these men had no legal right to take the horses and early the following morning set out for Lincoln with them to see about the matter. Tunstall took with him Bob (the messenger), Brewer, John Middleton, and Billy.

What followed on this occasion was later told to Frank and George by Billy himself. On February 18, 1878, the group started to Lincoln. On the way Billy and Middleton spotted a flock of wild turkeys and took off to get one for Mrs. McSween. Tunstall, Brewer, and Bob rode on ahead. As Billy and his companion hunted in the brush, they failed to notice that they were being outdistanced by the others. Suddenly over a rise ahead of them a band of horsemen came riding fast, kicking up a cloud of dust. Tunstall's companions automatically wheeled and rode into heavy cover. Tunstall, unarmed and unafraid, remained on the trail. Not far behind, Billy saw what was happening and spurred his horse ahead to warn his boss to take to the brush. But Tunstall, who had told Billy that he was sure he could clear up the matter in the county seat, was willing to submit to arrest. There was no time to plead further with him, so Billy rode to join the others who had found temporary safety in bushes behind some rocky ledges on a hillside. Billy realized that it was suicide for them to try to shoot it out. They were outnumbered four to one.

From their position, Billy and his companions saw a score or more of men approach Tunstall and sashay their horses around him in a threatening way. They recognized the men in the posse, but they could only guess what was being said. Apparently Tunstall was trying to explain his intentions, but Ollinger, who was impatient to get on with the killing, drew his gun and fired. Morton and Baker followed suit, after which other mem-

bers of the posse added their bullets. Tunstall's body fell to
the ground. Morton shot his horse. Then Ollinger walked to
Tunstall's body, kicked it in the head, and put a final touch
to the ghastly spectacle by firing another shot into the victim.

Out of sight of the posse, but not out of danger, Billy and his
companions looked on helplessly, horrified witnesses to the
slaying. Billy told Frank later he felt the chills at seeing the
man who had befriended him shot down in cold blood. His first
impulse was to charge into the posse of murderers and kill as
many as he could before they finished him. But he wanted to
get them all. To do that he would have to wait. Engraved
indelibly in his mind with hate and vengeance were the names
and faces of every man in the posse.

This brutal killing of Tunstall touched off the Lincoln
County War, which had been brewing between the factions of
Murphy-Dolan and Tunstall-McSween.

Billy and the others knew that their next move had to be a
cautious one, for Ollinger and the rest were waiting nearby to
get them. They saw Ollinger turn Tunstall's body over roughly
to expose his face to the sun and thus hasten decomposition.
They heard derisive laughs from the posse as he put the saddle
blanket over the horse's face. Then the posse rode out of sight
and waited for Tunstall's friends to try to recover his body. But
the ruse didn't work.

The day wore on. Finally Billy suggested that Bob, Brewer,
and Middleton take a roundabout route to Lincoln to tell their
friends there what had happened. Billy proposed to ride to the
Coe camp to get someone to go after his friend's body. They
agreed and set out for their separate destinations. Billy probably never felt a more vindictive determination to kill.

He reached the Coe place after dark. On hearing hoofbeats
coming up the trail, Frank jumped from his bunk and grabbed
his gun from the belt hanging over the head of his bed. By the
time he reached the door, he heard Billy's voice. This incident

was so indelibly imprinted on his mind that many years later he could recall what was said, word for word.

"It's me, Frank. Open up quick. I've got terrible news. It means trouble for all of us."

Frank unbarred the door and Billy came in. Then he struck a match and lighted a candle. "My God, Billy, what in the world has happened? What's wrong?"

He barred the door again and returned to the center of the room where Billy stood dazed. "They've got Tunstall. The damned sneaking cowards have murdered him like a dog. His body is over in Sánchez [now known as Tunstall] Canyon."

Frank was shaken to the bottom of his boots. "Why in the name of God did they kill him? What did he do to make them shoot him down like that?"

Billy was too nervous to sit down so he paced back and forth in front of the fireplace; he related what had happened, ending his story with the solemn promise that he would never stop until he had killed every last man who had ridden in the posse.

Frank urged him to drink the coffee he had poured, but Billy did not seem to hear him. He explained that he wanted to get Tunstall's body out of the canyon. "I don't want to get you mixed up in this, Frank, but I want you to get someone to go to the canyon and take the body to the Newcomb place. The rest of us are goin' to have to stay under cover."

Frank said that he was sure Román Barragán would do the job. He had a sheep camp over near a seeping spring in a canyon not far from the scene of the killing. Billy agreed that Román would be all right. Then he headed for Lincoln to let Brewer know what he and Frank had planned. Frank knew that he dared not go for the body of Tunstall because any friend of Billy or Tunstall was a target of the Murphy-Dolan guns.

Next morning Frank rode across the hills to find the old

sheepherder. An hour later he came upon him gathering fire-wood near a brush corral. He told Román that Tunstall had been killed on the trail near the head of Sánchez Canyon. He said: "We want his body out of there pronto, Román. If you can get it to the Newcomb place, others will take care of it from there."

Román did not reply for a moment. Then, shaking his head thoughtfully, he answered: "No, gracias, Señor Covo. I do not want that I should get a bullet in me, too." At the thought of this he quickly crossed himself. Then he added that he did not wish to keep company with a dead man on such a long journey.

Frank assured him no one would harm an old man like him. Then he drew some silver from his pocket; Román accepted it and began preparing for the trip. Frank advised him to take along a covering with which to protect the body from brush. Román made fast the last knot on the pack and returned to his hut to get a greasy-looking blanket, which he tied on his burro, Gacho. He picked up the lead rope and started up the trail, and Frank headed for home.

Frank was sure the old man would find the body all right, but he could only surmise how Román would pray over it and struggle to get it on the burro. Frank knew the pack would be prone to slide on the hills, scooting up around the burro's ears on the down slopes and sliding back over his rump on the steep climbs. It would be an indescribable ordeal for Román to keep the filthy blanket around the body over the long, narrow, brushy trail. At times he would be tempted to give up but he had given his word and Frank knew he would do the job.

Frank was relieved later when he learned that Román had reached the Newcomb ranch with the body, which was hardly recognizable when it arrived because the trees and brush had ripped the blanket to shreds and the corpse, already full of bullet holes, was torn and lacerated beyond description. From Newcomb's the body was taken to Lincoln where, after an autopsy, a coroner's jury, of which Frank was a member, made its report. Since decomposition had already set in, it was necessary to bury the body as quickly as they could.

Two Negroes, "Mr." Bates and "Laughin' " Joe, were assigned the job of digging the grave. It was too risky to finish the grave by daylight as they were known to be friends of Tunstall, so the body was kept in a back room of the store until dark, at which time the digging was completed. A solemn, heavy-hearted, apprehensive little group gathered in the McSween parlor for the funeral services conducted by the Reverend Shields. As Frank, George, Billy, and Brewer lowered the body into the grave, a deeper gloom settled over Lincoln. The brooding look of the boy Tunstall had befriended was solemn, yet vengeful. Frank and George needed no one to tell them Billy's thoughts as he lingered at the graveside after the others had left.

Not long after Tunstall's death an incident beginning in a Lincoln hotel drew George deeper into the sheriff's net because the sheriff was reputedly a sympathizer of the Murphy-Dolan faction. A guest there, a native of Alabama, objected to what he thought was the insolent behavior of a drunken Negro cavalry trooper who insisted on sitting with him to eat. Since he couldn't persuade the intruder to go to another table and the Negro became more aggressive, he settled the argument by pulling out his gun and shooting him. He jumped on his horse and made his getaway over the trail to the upper Ruidoso, arriving at the Coe camp with his horse badly spent. He told his story to George, who, because he had good reason to believe that the man would be lynched without a trial if caught by the posse, let him have a fresh horse.

Soon after the fugitive had left, Sheriff Brady and an escort of Negro soldiers rode up to the Coe place. Brady was angry because George had helped the fugitive to make his escape. He ordered George to mount up to ride to the county jail.

Brady's rough handling of George showed plainly there was no love between the sheriff and the McSween men. His hands were lashed to the saddle horn and his feet were roped under the belly of the horse, the treatment usually given to dangerous criminals and not to a man willing to go peacefully to Lincoln and let the court decide his guilt.

With the lawman and his posse of eight or ten heavily armed troopers of the United States Cavalry, he started down the Ruidoso for the county seat. A drenching rain overtook them, soaking them through and causing George's ropes to tighten around his wrists and ankles. In the narrow places, sharp thorny brush tore through his clothing, and low-hanging limbs lashed at his face. Almost weeping at the agonizing pain in his wrists, George asked that his ropes be loosened. The commander refused. Not until they arrived at the Newcomb ranch, where they spent the night, did the sheriff loosen the wrist ropes. George was miserable in his wet clothes, his hands and feet numb, and his anger at a white heat. Next morning, he was so stiff and sore that he winced with pain when a couple of troopers hoisted him onto his horse.

At the courthouse he was placed under a five-hundred-dollar bond. He did not have that much cash, but he was permitted to go, under heavy guard, to the home of his good friend Ike Ellis, who went bond for him. Brady, glad to be rid of another prisoner whom he would have to feed, warned George as he left about what would happen if he did not show up when court convened in April. It happened, though, that the matter was regarded as of such small consequence that the case was never called up.

George returned home with his wrists raw from rope burns and his anger at the sheriff at a burning pitch. Frank's efforts to calm him did not help much. Shortly afterward Billy arrived, for as soon as he heard of George's run-in with the sheriff, he hurried to the Coe cabin. Frank agreed with George and Billy that the sheriff was going out of his way to make things tough for the McSween men. Still incensed over the death of Tunstall, Billy swore he was going to get Brady before George had the chance. He was so sure that he bet a pearl-handled six-shooter. At that moment George probably would not have tried to stop anyone who wanted to exterminate Brady; yet he and Frank argued that further killings would destroy any hope for peace that law-abiding people had in Lincoln County. Their efforts to convince Billy that Brady was only indirectly responsible for Tunstall's death were useless.

They had no doubt there had been some dirty politics behind the sheriff's election to office, but they did not think a man should be killed because he accepted favors and, in return, bestowed a few on those who had helped him. But to convince Billy of this was like trying to hold back the crashing waters of a flash flood along the Ruidoso River. In Billy's opinion Brady was personally responsible for the death of Tunstall because he had sent a deputy with a posse of killers to his ranch. That was the same as ordering Tunstall's death.

Knowing that it was useless to reason further, Frank picked up his fiddle and played a breakdown. When he switched to a schottische, Billy, in a quick change of mood, grabbed George and danced him around the table. In the middle of another tune, Frank put his fiddle on the table and looked at a calendar that hung on the wall under a gun rack. After some silent calculating, he suggested to George that they clear out of the area for a while and go to Las Vegas to get the threshing machine they had ordered from St. Louis. They had a fine piece of machinery on the way, which should interest people all over the three valleys. George was agreeable, but he was a little dubious about their good weather holding out. February could be a "changy" month.

They had eagerly awaited the arrival of their precious new purchase, which had cost them considerably. To get the needed money, they had taken out a mortgage on it from the bank in Lincoln. After they had made such a bold move, they had many misgivings, for in such unsettled times they wondered whether they would be able to find the time to assemble it and do the threshing.

On a bright, cold day they set out for Las Vegas, 170 miles by stage route. They got there easily, loaded the parts of the thresher on their two wagons, and began the return trip. On the first three days out there was some high cloudiness, not enough to cause concern, but on the fourth day there were definite signs of snow clouds building up down toward the Capitán Mountains. As the wind picked up, the cold intensified. By noon they had to walk beside their wagons and swing their arms to keep warm. There were no bright patches left in the sky as dark, menacing clouds moved in from the northwest. In the afternoon icy rain and snow lashed at them. Since it was open country there was no place to take shelter and so they had to keep going. All the while, wet snow clung to them and sifted into the loaded wagons, soaking everything.

Darkness came and bitter cold stung their bodies. Fortunately they reached a grove of scrubby pine and piñon, which provided some shelter from the wind and snow.

A bright sun the next morning warmed and cheered them as they made a pot of coffee and washed down some cold biscuits with it. As it rose higher the snow melted fast. By the time they reached the Hondo junction, there was little trace of snow remaining on the hillsides.

Hopes for earning money with the thresher faded when they learned that affairs in the county had grown worse; a couple of Murphy men who had been in the Tunstall posse, Morton and Baker, had been killed, allegedly by William Bonney. George and Frank weren't too surprised and conceded that the world was probably a better place without such outlaws but knew that their murders would bring more terrorizing and killing.

The next incident in the continuing hostilities was not long in coming, and the version given here is that of Frank Coe. The man who was shot was not shot by Billy; nor was he on Billy's list. His name was Andrew L. Roberts and he had settled on a little tract along the Ruidoso River. It was said that he was already carrying so much lead in him that he was called "Buckshot." He denied allegiance to either side in the conflict but was not above making deals with the Murphy men. Billy and Charlie Bowdre had sworn out a warrant stating that he had taken some shots at them from ambush in an arroyo near San Patricio. Dick Brewer was made a special deputy to bring him in, and a posse of thirteen including the Coes, Hendry Brown, Tom O'Folliard, Jim French, and John Middleton arrived at Blazer's Mill near Bent on the Tularosa River and stopped for a rest and some noonday chuck with the owner, Dr. J. H. Blazer, who had studied dentistry. Middleton was appointed to stand guard, for Buckshot reportedly was in the area.

Before long, Middleton saw a man on a bay mule cross the river and tie his mount to a corral post near the barn. Middleton shouted to him and asked what he wanted. The stocky little man paid no attention to his question or to a warning Middleton gave him; instead, he continued to walk toward the Blazer house, his rifle at the ready by his side. When he was a hundred yards away, Frank Coe, who had finished eating before the others, walked out of the house. When he saw Buckshot, he called to him, but Roberts paid no attention; he just kept on advancing. After they were within talking distance, Frank begged him to surrender and avoid bloodshed. Buckshot told him to go to hell and take the rest of his damned murdering friends with him. Then Frank explained he was outnumbered thirteen to one and didn't have a chance against all those guns. But Buckshot didn't give a damn and said so. To that he added that Frank could tell the rest of the posse he wasn't crazy enough to let them get their hands on him and turn him over to Bonney and Bowdre. They would riddle him with bullets before he would ever get a chance to stand trial.

Frank kept on trying to convince this stubborn fearless fugitive that he should give himself up, arguing that a dozen tough gunmen were holed up inside the house. It would be better, Frank reasoned, to surrender and be taken alive to Lincoln than it would to be shot down in a gun battle. Nothing he said changed Buckshot's mind, even though he knew the men were getting itchy to use their guns. Bowdre especially wanted to get on with the business. When he appeared around the corner of the house, he found Buckshot within gun range and pulled the trigger. Bringing up his rifle a little and shooting from the hip, Roberts knocked off Bowdre's gunbelt. When others of the posse came into view, he fired fast, hitting Middleton in the chest and knocking off George Coe's trigger finger at the middle joint.

Bowdre's bullet had gone through Roberts's chest, but he continued to advance toward the house. The men in the posse had all come out the back door and dared not try to re-enter now because of Buckshot's deadly aim, so they took cover outside. This enabled Buckshot to ease himself inside, from where he continued to pour lead at the posse. After he emptied his own guns, he picked up an old Sharps rifle and fired from the window as he lay on a mattress he had dragged over to it. One of the posse called to Dr. Blazer and asked him to try to bring the fugitive out, but he sensibly refused.

Behind a pile of scrap lumber near the sawmill, Frank, Brewer, and some other men debated about waiting it out. Roberts was badly wounded and would soon die or have to give himself up. But Brewer, in a hurry to get him, dead or alive, raised his head from behind a log during a lull in the firing to get a better look. As he did, Buckshot blew off the top of his head. After that no one cared to risk another look.

An hour later the courageous fellow who had gamely stood off thirteen men passed on to his dubious reward. Most of the posse left the mill then. Before leaving, George washed his injured hand in the clear, cold water of the Tularosa River and then, with Frank and some other men, started for Fort Stanton to see a doctor about his wound. But none was at the fort so he and Frank turned toward home. On the way they met a doctor from the fort who tore off the dirty bandanna and advised George, "Get to a doctor's office as soon as you can before gangrene sets in." As it was safer on the upper Ruidoso, George stuck close to their camp and never got the wound treated. In the meantime it healed rapidly and cleanly.

After Blazer's Mill, hostilities increased and new violence broke out. An event that rocked the entire area took place on April 1, 1878, as Lincoln dozed quietly in the early morning. Sheriff Brady, with his deputies, George Hindman and George Peppin, and court clerk Billy Matthews, was walking toward the courthouse from the east end of town. Suddenly a burst of gunfire came from behind an adobe wall east of the McSween store. Of the four men who had been walking along the street, one lay motionless, a second staggered in front of the Church of San Juan, a third disappeared completely, and the fourth fled to the safety of the Baca home across from the store.

The town was quiet again. Two of the six figures crouching behind the wall rose and walked boldly toward their victims. One of them, Billy Bonney, looked at the body of the sheriff and then reached for the dead man's rifle and six-shooter, but before he could get them a bullet creased his thigh. Another gave his pal a hip wound. They quickly rejoined their companions and rode out of town leaving the spectators aghast. Billy later told Frank he had wanted the guns for keepsakes.

For a direct witness's account of these events, let us look at it through the eyes of Sara Baca as she watched on that morning. Sara was the young daughter of one of Lincoln County's first and finest citizens, Saturnino Baca, who was born in Valencia County, New Mexico. As a young man he served in Company E of the First New Mexico Cavalry during the War Between the States, advancing to the rank of captain.

At the time of the Lincoln County War he owned land in Lincoln where El Torreón, an early fortification used by the settlers to defend themselves from Indian attacks, stands restored today. He also operated a mill on the Río Bonito. Saturnino had great pride in his family, and on the night a son was born he fired several shots to announce it, as was customary among the Mexicans. The Harrold brothers, the beforementioned badmen from Texas, were riding into Lincoln to start a ruckus about that time and, on hearing Saturnino's shots, thought their plans had been discovered. A Mexican riding with them later told Saturnino that he was the first to put the spurs to the horse and ride away in the opposite direction from the Harrold brothers, who raced for the protection of the tall timber of the Arabela country. Frank heard this story more than once because Saturnino always enjoyed telling about his small son's unwitting part in averting bloodshed. When he had the infant baptized by the local priest, Padre José Aguillo, he gave him the name of Juan Salvador—John, the Savior.

In 1879 Saturnino was appointed the first probate judge in Lincoln County and followed his distinguished work there by serving for three years as sheriff of the county. In a battle between the sheepmen and the cattle ranchers he lost an arm. He had a long and colorful career, much of which was spent in the service of his country. His death, just a few months short of his seventy-fifth wedding anniversary, ended an eminent career that included, in addition to these other offices, some time in the Territorial legislature as a representative from Socorro County. Here he introduced the bill that created the sprawling cattle empire of Lincoln County.

Saturnino's daughter Sara spent her entire life in Lincoln. On reaching a marriageable age, she caught the eye of the handsome, dashing Francisco Salazar. Like Sara's father, Francisco possessed much of the Old World Spanish dignity and courtesy. According to Frank, no one could tip his hat to a lady more graciously or acknowledge an introduction with greater courtliness.

At the age of ninety Sara dictated to her daughter an ac-

count of the happenings about to be related. With this she sent
the following letter:

Lincoln, New Mexico
Agosto 25, 1955

Mr. and Mrs. Wilbur Coe
Glencoe, New Mexico

Mis muy apreciables amigos,

   *Aquí les mando lo que acuerdo de la guerra del Billie the
Kid. Yo estaba muy chiquita pero me acuerdo lo que decían
en mi casa, y don Sipio Salazar también me platicaba. Si
tengo algún equívoco, me dispensad. Ya ahora estoy muy
vieja y muy mala salud.*

Su respetable amiga y S.S.S.
Sara B. Salazar

Sara remembered that she was playing in the Baca yard
close to the adobe wall of the house. Some squatting Mexicans
were talking in the warm sunshine in front of the McSween
store. As Sara looked up to watch a spiraling whirlwind of dust,
she saw four heavily armed men almost in its path. One of
them she knew was the sheriff. They were on their way toward
the courthouse where, she had heard her papa say, they were
going to hold a session that day.

Suddenly there was the crackling of gunfire. Frightened,
Sara saw that of the four men who had been walking along, one
lay motionless a few steps away, another was staggering along
in front of the little Church of San Juan, and one had disappeared as if the earth had swallowed him. The only one still on
his feet fled past her into the Baca home. Two men who had
crouched behind an abode wall east of the McSween store
vaulted it and went over to one of the bodies. As one of them
reached for the rifle and six-shooter of the sheriff, a shot rang
out from the Baca house. The men dashed back behind the
wall, one of them holding his hip.

Then the door of the Baca home opened and Sara's mother rushed out to pull her child to safety. Some who were watching from the shelter of their homes called to her to hurry back inside. "Let them kill me," she cried. "I won't let a dog eat the blood of a human being." Stooping, she picked up a rock and hurled it at a mongrel that was sniffing the air and drawing closer to the body of the wounded man. She hit him and his mournful howl sent up a requiem for Sheriff Brady. Then the mother hurried back into the house, leading her daughter by the hand.

Sara clearly remembered the silence that settled over the town that night. Behind their locked doors, those who lived near the church talked of the dying groans of the deputy as he called for someone to bring him water. No one dared go outside to help him. When night came the villagers barred their doors with extra caution and put flour sacks over the windows. Neighbors of the Bacas slipped in and talked to them in hushed voices. Sara was the center of the curious group. Had she actually seen Billy Bonney jump from behind the wall and try to get the sheriff's guns? Would no one give the dying deputy a drink even though he begged for one? Sleep refused to come to the little girl as she huddled on her mattress. She could still hear the shots fired from behind the wall and see the sheriff grab for his stomach as he fell forward into the dust.

News of the deaths of Sheriff Brady and his deputy Hindman, who had staggered past the church, swept like a grass fire and soon reached the Coes. Even though they had no liking for the sheriff, they deplored Billy's actions, which set back the cause of peace. Alexander McSween bitterly denounced Billy's part in the slayings, but he, as well as others, knew that nothing would silence Billy's venomous hatred and demand for revenge except a bullet.

Every move Frank and George made had to be a cautious one. But they too were angry at the atrocities their enemies had committed. Their feelings reached a new high after some of the Murphy outlaws swooped down on their Analla farm where Frank and Ab were clearing brush from a ditch, burned down the house, and drove off most of their livestock. Frank's most cherished possession—his fiddle—burned with the house. George was on the upper Ruidoso farm at the time.

Lincoln was an especially dangerous place for them. As much as they could they avoided it, but a business matter came up not long after the sheriff's death that required them to go there. They had already stored their thresher for safety at the Ellis place, for with so much turmoil they had little hope that they would be able to use it when the grain was ripe. A note on the machine was now due at the bank, so they had to go to the county seat to borrow money, if they could, from their friend, Uncle Ike Ellis. Ab and Frank had arranged with George to meet him at the Ellis place in Lincoln.

On the appointed day Frank started out early ahead of Ab in order to stop at Billy's hideout in a rocky gorge of Bluewater Canyon where a McSween man had told him he and his gang were hiding. Since Billy was in close touch with what was going on, Frank wanted to talk to him before going on to Lincoln. Frank had good reason to remember his conversation with Billy because his friend warned him to be careful not to get any holes shot in his new sombrero. Billy was as angry as Frank about the Analla raid. He would see that the Murphy men paid for that, too. Frank had other occasions to observe Billy's loyalty to his friends. Frank did not tarry long with Billy and the dozen saddle-weary companions, among them Charlie Bowdre, Doc Skurlock, and Tom O'Folliard. All were laughing over the chase on which they had just led Sheriff Peppin and his posse from Roswell. When Billy offered to go with Frank to Lincoln, Frank cautioned him to take no chances because he had the most valuable hide in the territory.

Luckily Frank met no one as he proceeded to Lincoln. Just on the outskirts he passed a couple of drunks who silently lifted their hats in a grandiose manner and rode on. It was late afternoon and Mrs. Ellis was getting supper for her husband and a couple of McSween friends who had just come in, so Frank joined them. They did not sit around the table long after dinner. Wearied and worried over the general situation, they went to bed, leaving a man to stand guard until midnight, when another would relieve him. Frank was too disturbed to go to sleep. Except for his boots, he lay fully dressed on the bunk, tossing about, wondering why George and Ab had not arrived. If they did not reach the Ellis place by morning, he would know that something had gone wrong.

But his fears in that respect proved groundless. About noon the following day George and Ab rode up, accompanied by Hendry Brown and Frank McNab. The Coes attended to their business at the bank and then all five took the road east out of Lincoln. At Las Chozas, George and Hendry took the trail to San Patricio while Frank, Ab, and McNab continued down the Bonito.

What followed soon afterward was to become for Frank the most memorable incident of the Lincoln County War. When he, McNab, and Ab reached the Fritz Spring, ten miles out of Lincoln, they pulled up to get a drink and water their horses. But unknown to Frank and his companions, Sheriff Peppin and his posse, still hoping to collect the large bounty on Billy's head and following the cold trail after him, had arrived at the spring ahead of them. They had just finished their camp supper when they saw Frank, Ab, and McNab approaching and dispersed to ambush them. It is easy to imagine that they were eager to get three of the McSween men at once. This would please the Murphy men.

Just as Frank was getting ready to dismount the shooting began. When McNab dropped to the ground, the posse yelled with delight. He was an old Chisum man who had been with Billy when Brady and his men were ambushed. Desperately Frank raked the side of his horse in the vain hope that he might get out of range of the guns. By this time Ab had gone down.

Frank's only hope was to outride them, but he knew there was little chance that he could put much distance between himself and his attackers.

Frank was riding at full speed and looked back and saw the posse coming over a ridge from which they had him in clear range. By the time they opened fire, Frank's horse had reached a deep arroyo, which he could not cross. All Frank could do was make a sharp right turn and ride parallel to the arroyo. This left the horse exposed broadside, and when one of the posse fired an "impossible" shot from twelve hundred feet, Frank's pony went down with a bullet behind his right ear. Thrown off and with only his reflexes working, Frank rolled into the arroyo, his six-shooter still in his hand.

The fall had not hurt him and he had bettered his position by tumbling into the protection of the arroyo. After a few seconds he began to fire back at the posse, being careful not to expose himself too much or to waste bullets. During a temporary calm he pulled himself up and saw that the posse was keeping well out of his range, hoping he would soon run out of ammunition. Lead whined all around him as he crouched low and clung to the bank.

When the firing died down, he was curious to know what was going on, so he risked another quick look and saw that they were having a parley. He wished desperately for his rifle which was in the saddle scabbard under his pony. He stuck his head up again. Whan-n-n-g-g!! A bullet ripped through the crown of his hat and knocked it off, and he thought of Billy's warning. But the look was worth the cost, for he saw that the men were fanning out in all directions. All he could do was to wait to see what they were up to. In the meantime he fired all of his fast-dwindling supply of bullets. From all sides he now was being shot at; but soon there was a silence. As risky as it was to give himself up to the killers, he knew this was his only chance.

Taking out his bandanna, he tied it to the pistol and stuck it in the air. There was a coarse laugh, and a voice he recognized as Wallace Ollinger's yelled, "Got enough, Coe? Are you surrenderin'?"

Then the sheriff shouted, "If you mean what that flag says, toss out your guns, Coe."

"You know damned well if I had any ammunition left, I wouldn't be puttin' this flag up." After a few seconds he added, "All right, here's my gun."

With that he tossed it toward the posse. Raising himself to an upright position, he climbed from the arroyo and walked toward the men. It was the longest walk of his life, for at any second he expected to get a bullet in him. But there was no click of revolvers as he advanced. As soon as he reached them, they surrounded him.

"It took you a damned long time to find out when you'd had enough," Ollinger greeted him, running his hands over the prisoner looking for another gun. "Git some rope, boys, and tie up the bastard."

The sheriff admonished his men to tie him up good and tight. As he stuck Frank's gun in his own belt, he said, "Yo're under arrest, Coe."

"Have you a warrant, sheriff? You know you can't do this to me without one. But I'm not worryin' about myself. What about those other men you shot? They are my friends and I want to see if I can help them. You can't let them lay there like dogs."

The sheriff said he did not need a warrant and told Frank it was too bad that they did not get him along with his pals. He ended by saying, "I don't guess yore friends back yonder need yore help. McNab's got what he had comin' to him. He's dead-er'n a door nail. The other one's hurt too much to care what happens, so you don't need to worry about him."

There was nothing he could do for McNab, but Frank wanted to burst his ropes to get to Ab. "He's my friend, and

I've got to see him. Why did you have to shoot down a man like him who hasn't done harm to anyone?"

If the sheriff heard this, he showed no sign. As he gave the ropes a final jerk, he told him Ab had been taken to the Fritz place. From there the "dead wagon" from Fort Stanton would pick him up and take him to the doctor.

Relieved to know that much at least, Frank objected no longer. He knew he had been lucky. Except where a bullet had nipped his heel as he rode away from the spring, he was the only one of the three who had escaped death or serious injury. His sorrow over Ab knew no bounds. They had been close friends and partners since the days on the Sugarite. Ab's only crime had been that he was a friend of Frank and George Coe.

One of the men brought McNab's horse for Frank to ride and they proceeded to Lincoln, avoiding the Ellis place on the main road because a number of McSween men were holed up there. The brush was safer. At the outskirts of the town they made camp and Frank spent a miserable night roped at the wrists and ankles, prodded by the butt of a rifle if he dared move around to ease his cramped position.

In the meantime there was mourning at the Ellis home. The grapevine had spread the word that all three men had been killed at Fritz Spring. George was deeply grieved and violently angry when the news reached him at the Coe ranch. He rode at once for Lincoln to join the men at the Ellis house, who were in a mood for quick vengeance. Lookouts were doubled, and with the exception of two men who slipped in after dark, no one dared to move.

After a night upset by hoofbeats on the road, morning came and with it an unnatural quiet. Before noon a few more of the McSween men joined those at the Ellises', and later one wormed his way through the brush along the river behind the house and brought word that Frank Coe had not been killed but taken prisoner. An unbearable weight was lifted from George's heart and there was joy among the others.

Added lookouts were placed to guard against a surprise attack. From a post on top of the house, George and Hendry commanded a view of the mountainside at the back on the other side of the Bonito River. From this spell together as guards came a story George never tired of telling. They had not been at their stand long when Hendry thought he saw something move near some mesquite clumps. He took up an old seaman's telescope and peered through it. Then he handed it to George, who looked and agreed that there was a man far up on the hillside. Evidently he felt he was too secure at such a distance to get hit; sitting on a bleached cow's skull, he boldly kept tab on the movements at the Ellis place.

George raised the glass again and told Hendry he thought that the spy was ready to be picked off. Hendry said it was impossible. With their naked eye they couldn't be sure a man was there. When George picked up his rifle, his friend warned him against starting a fight. Once again George took the spy-glass and studied the enemy scout's position in relation to a large boulder and some tall brush. Then he took careful aim and fired. Watching through the glass, Hendry could not believe his eyes when the man rolled from his perch. At a distance of a quarter mile George had hit the target.

Hendry's prediction was right, for this amazing shot was the opener for the battle that followed. All at once guns on both sides began barking. At the outskirts of the town Frank Coe heard them and hoped the McSween boys were giving a good account of themselves. Wallace Ollinger, who had been left to guard him, was uneasy, probably because he did not care for the job of looking after the prisoner. He knew Billy would storm the gates of hell to rescue Frank Coe.

"What do you make o' that shootin', Coe?"

Frank guessed it was in answer to the ambush at the spring. Frank could see that the continuing gunfire in the town didn't cheer Ollinger, especially when the sounds of it came closer to them. They listened for a while, and then Ollinger suggested they try to sneak on down to the Murphy store, where he could lock up the prisoner. Frank was of the opinion that any spot would be better than where they were. He thought they would have a better chance of making it if they would cross the river and stick to the brush along the opposite bank. After thinking it over a minute, Ollinger untied Frank's ankles and they started for the Bonito. By the careless manner his captor held his rifle, Frank concluded he must have little interest in whether he ever reached the store with him. When they were opposite the Murphy place, they crossed the river and circled widely to the rear of the establishment and entered by the back door. Frank saw some men gathered in the front part watching the street and listening to the gunfire going on at the other end of town. They paid no attention to Ollinger and his prisoner.

At Ollinger's inquiry about a safe place to put Coe, a clerk told him there was an empty room at the top of the stairs. But he cautioned him there was no key and that he would have to stand guard. It was obvious to Frank that this did not please his jailer, who ordered him to go up the stairs ahead of him. Into a room containing only a wooden bench and a stool with a broken leg Ollinger herded his prisoner. After taking a quick look out of the window, he returned to the hall and sat down across from Frank's door, tilted back in his chair and rolled a cigarette. Curious to get a look at things, Frank peered out on the street. There was no one in sight, but the sharp crackle of gunfire came to him. As this went on, he noticed Ollinger was getting restless. Finally Ollinger went to the top of the stairs and yelled for Buck Somebody. There was no answer. Then to Frank, he said, "Why in the hell don't someone let me know what's goin' on?" He sat on the chair and glared at his prisoner. "Coe, if I turn you loose, kin you take care of yourself?"

Frank suspected Ollinger was getting shaky because he had

no legal right to hold him. "Just try me, Wallace. No one's goin' to care about me gettin' away. You know it's Billy they're after."

Wallace then got up and said he was leaving. With that, he went down the hall to the stairway, purposely leaving Frank's own rifle propped against the wall. Frank waited until he heard Ollinger's feet on the last stair; then he stepped into the hall, picked up his rifle, checked it, and advanced cautiously to the stairway. As he was about to start down, several Murphy men started up. As surprised to see Frank with his rifle leveled as he was to see them, they automatically put up their hands. At his command they turned and went back down with Frank at their heels. At the foot of the steps they stood holding their hands in the air while Frank left by the back door and dropped quickly out of sight. They made no effort to pursue him.

Frank rushed for a rain barrel at the corner of the store and ducked behind it. When no one came out to try to stop him, he dashed for some lilac bushes next door to wait until he could make a run for it. From the house next to this, Jimmie Dolan (of the Murphy-Dolan outfit) rushed out to try to get Frank who was heading for the street that he had to cross to reach the Bonito River. Dolan tripped over a root and hit the gound with a thud. There he lay on his stomach, and Frank heard him cursing and yelling in the same breath for someone to get him a doctor and to stop Frank Coe. Frank later found out he had either broken or seriously injured his leg and was howling with rage and pain as he was carried into the house.

Fortunately for Frank, Dolan had diverted attention from him, so after crossing the street, he made his way to the river and approached the McSween house from the rear. As the tempo of the firing had increased, it was too dangerous to join the men there; instead, he kept close to the riverbank and arrived safely at the Ellis place. He never forgot his welcome there. George wrung his cousin's hand and inquired about Ab. Frank could tell them no more than the events at the spring, but later in the evening one of the men slipped down from the McSween ranch and told them the Fort Stanton ambulance had picked up Ab and also the man whom George had shot from a distance; he had received only a leg injury.

By morning, the siege at the Ellis and McSween places was still in progress. According to what Frank later learned, Sheriff Peppin grew weary of his hunt for Billy and decided to order soldiers from Fort Stanton to capture him at the Ellis home, where he suspected he was hiding. With Billy he would bottle up the entire gang. Shortly afterward he rode up with a troop of U. S. Cavalry. On the order to surrender, the men came out, but to the keen disappointment of the sheriff, Billy was not among them. Neither was Hendry Brown, for he had made a quick exit to the cover of the river brush. He was a prime fugitive who had been with Billy when Brady was killed. George jumped on a bunk, pulled up the covers, and when an officer and soldiers came into the room, he was moaning in pain because of his "shot-off" finger! They didn't bother him.

Those who surrendered were taken to the fort, and as soon as Hendry saw them leave, he returned to the house. At dark he and George rode quickly for the safety of the Ruidoso. At San Patricio they met Billy and hashed over the Fritz Spring ambush with him. By morning Frank returned home because the military, which had arrested them, had no charge against him.

Later Bowdre and Billy arrived at the Coe ranch and rode with George and Frank to the fort to see Ab. To play safe, Billy and Bowdre waited for them at a sutler's store near the stockade. When the Coes returned to join them, they brought back word that Ab was suffering from severe wounds in his stomach and back. The four rode away together and at the parting of the trail Frank and George sadly went back to their farm.

Tempestuous spring gave way to extreme summer heat in that memorable year of 1878. The long, dry winter was followed by heavy deluges that started arroyos running, and the rivers of the three valleys flooded the fields. Little work was done on the farms or elsewhere. The Coes, along with others, brooded over disappearing cattle and wanton killings. Bodies tensed at the slightest sound as the last act of the Lincoln County War shaped up. Lincoln, to which Billy and several of his men had moved after a minor incident at the Chisum ranch, was the focal point.

It was known to the Coes and other McSween followers that the Murphy side had gathered together a band of fifty or sixty men, all ready and able with their guns. Not to be outdone, McSween, with thirty or forty Mexicans from the upper Ruidoso, rode down the street in a show of their own strength and also as a support to Billy and his cohorts, who had arrived and were holed up at the McSween store. With them were the Coes, who well remembered barricading themselves behind the doors with sacks of grain and barrels of flour. East of the McSween place a number of his followers under Martín Chávez prepared for the battle behind the thick walls of the Montaña and Patrón homes. In the west part of the village the Murphy forces held the Murphy hotel and store. Guns were in readiness, and only the slightest upset was needed to trigger an explosion.

This came after one of the Murphy snipers on guard shot at Martín Chávez as he stepped outside his house. It was all the provocation necessary, and with it began the "three-day battle" that climaxed the Lincoln County War. From that moment on guns blazed along the main street of Lincoln. Soon McSween's attackers started a fire in a wing of his twelve-room adobe house. Thanks to the direction of the wind the fire spread slowly, but two days later the breeze changed and the rest of the house started to burn. On the third day those inside knew that they would have to make a run for it. After securing a third truce (two had already been granted so that Mrs. McSween could appeal personally to Colonel Dudley of Fort Stanton, who was camped nearby with his troops, to put an end to the senseless killings), Mrs. McSween and two other ladies were permitted to leave the house safely.

Then the men prepared to make their uncertain dash to escape. At a signal from Billy, who had come to the house, they all rushed from the front door, their six-guns spewing lead—all except Alexander McSween, that is. McSween, who had always gone unarmed, walked alone from the house into a burst of gunfire that riddled his body with bullets. Billy and most of the remaining men sped safely through the barrage and reached the shelter of the enfolding hills nearby. In a short time they were joined by Frank and Bowdre, who had stayed in the store. George and Hendry had already made a safe exit to San Patricio.

Such was the end of the bitter feud. In the final count, it has been reported that six men lost their lives in the three-day battle, but no accurate count could possibly have been made. And although the bitter feelings of that time have subsided today, one can without difficulty still find people who feel strongly about it. Ironically, Murphy never lived to gather any profit, for before the final battle he died in Santa Fé, a bankrupt man. But the lawlessness he had helped support did not end. In spite of all the killings, the most wanted gunman in the West was still at large. And with him were the Coes, who now found themselves branded as outlaws. They had little choice but to go with Billy and his friends, a part of the outlaw gang yet not belonging to it. To Frank and George, Billy's career had been and still was a lawless one. Never for a moment did they consider continuing their present roles as hunted criminals. Somehow, somewhere, they must return to the existence of law-abiding men.

The outlook was discouraging because their lives were still in danger. They went to Fort Sumner and made their headquarters at the Gerhart ranch. Frank and George were especially welcome, for the owner had known Lou Coe. He certainly could not have regarded Billy and the others as assets, but he did want to help Frank and George if he could.

This chance meeting caused the two fugitives to consider seriously Lou's previous offer to come to the Sugarite and work for him. He had acquired a ranch in the San Juan Valley and was soon to drive some cattle to his new place. He wanted their help for the long journey. Both agreed that this was the best thing to do, so in a day or two they started out. Billy rode with them for a short distance. Frank remembered Billy's somber look as he slumped in the saddle and listened while the Coes urged him to change his mind and go with them. Doubtless the most happiness Billy had ever known was that which he had shared with them in their lonely cabin. They reminded him of Governor Wallace's promise of amnesty for participants in the Lincoln County War, and urged him to accept this and start all over again. But Billy told them that he would never surrender because he would not have a chance if he did. In addition, he had a job to finish—that of getting the rest of the men in the Tunstall posse. He forced a smile as he told them in parting that they would all celebrate at Las Chozas when they returned again to Lincoln County.

By the time Frank and George reached Lou's ranch their depression had lifted and they began to feel more enthusiastic about a new life as peaceful citizens. To their surprise and joy they found the Al Coe family there. Because the rustlers had thinned out so many of his cattle, Al had decided to leave the upper Peñasco. With the help of Cal Brown he had driven the remainder of his herd to Lou's and was now planning to go to the San Juan country until his cattle would again be safe in Lincoln County.

In October 1878 Frank and George accompanied Jap, Lou, Al, and their families to their new place near the Animas River in New Mexico's San Juan Basin. There Frank, who was tired of his rough and purposeless existence, was to meet the girl who would inspire and help him achieve a new life.

CHAPTER III

Frank Coe Wins
the Belle of the San Juan Valley

IVING IN THE SAN JUAN VALLEY near Farmington, New Mexico, at this time was the John Tully family. Mr. and Mrs. Tully had come from Chicago in 1878 to live with their son Fred, who had settled there for his health. With them were their three children, Helena Anne, fifteen, Jim, fourteen, and Edith, eight. Their oldest son, Kivas, was already an established architect in St. Louis. John himself was an architect who, after marrying a beautiful and talented young girl from Toronto, Canada, had opened an office in Chicago and had been burned out by the Chicago fire. After several more years of practice, the family moved to Farmington at Fred's insistence, although Mr. Tully was not very happy there. He thoroughly disliked roughing it and was never able to adjust to the hardships of frontier life. Soon after arriving at Fred's place, he went over the line to Colorado and opened an architect's office in Durango, where he died less than two years later.

Later, Helena Anne wrote an account of their coming to New Mexico. She told that her mother remained at Fred's ranch with the three children and saw that she and Edith practiced their music, for they had brought with them their most precious possessions from Chicago, a piano, a sewing machine, and a beautiful green carpet. Her mother wrote to her father regularly and told him of Jim's indifferent progress in his studies and of the girls' musical accomplishments. An able musician herself, Anne Tully tutored them. Fred had promised to send Edith, when the time came, to St. Louis to complete her musical education. It seemed that her mother's chief worry at the time was about Helena Anne herself. Already she was attracting beaux and her mother was afraid she might marry some uncouth rustic. But Helena Anne considered none of them seriously.

At social gatherings she was popular. She loved to be whirled in the fast Mexican polka or the graceful waltz in one of her elegant Chicago dresses which she hoarded carefully. It was to such a frontier party, a housewarming a few miles away, in late July of 1880, that Helena Anne went in the wagon with her family. Idly she noted that patches of grain stubble skirting the road matched the color of the moon. Fred and Jim, on the front seat, talked about a threshing machine brought into the valley by a couple of farmers, newcomers to the area. Helena Anne was more interested in who was going to be at the dance. Maybe some handsome young frontiersman would notice her. At seventeen she was already beginning to feel old!

They arrived near dark at a cabin in a clearing surrounded by cedar and pine. The mother inspected her daughters carefully by the light of a lantern swinging outside while Jim and Fred unhitched the team. Inside the house an odor of coffee, pitch, and new pine logs met them as they greeted friends and neighbors. From the far end of the room came the discordant sounds of two fiddlers and a guitar player tuning up. Soon the music began and Fred, as was his custom, danced the first number with Helena Anne, "to show her off to the cowboys." At the end he returned her to her mother and joined the men outside.

A scrape of the bow announced a little later the beginning of another number, a Mexican polka. The first to reach her was an awkward cowboy who could not get the hang of the fast steps of the dance. As it was a "gentleman's choice," he was soon tapped on the shoulder by a trim-bearded man neatly dressed in a gray suit. He had arrived late and had been standing near the door with another late arrival when he noticed Helena

Anne and her partner as they made the first turn around the room. On the second time around, he left his companion and tapped Helena Anne's partner on the shoulder. As they started dancing he said, "I'm Frank Coe, sort of a stranger around here." His friendly polite manner made her forget she had not been properly introduced to him.

At the end of the dance Fred came up and shook hands with Frank, saying something about there being no need to introduce the late arrival who, with his cousin, was threshing grain in their neighborhood. He cautioned her laughingly: "There may be some things you don't know about this fellow, but you needn't worry. Everyone in the Animas Valley will vouch for him."

Fred then introduced Frank to the rest of the family. Frank danced as many numbers as possible with Helena Anne during the rest of the evening, while George replaced a fiddler whose bow arm drooped lower and lower from taking too much from the bottle in his violin case. Helena Anne was very disquieting to a man of twenty-six who had never given serious thought to a girl.

Mrs. Tully found Frank to be a charming and gentlemanly person, even though he did wear a menacing-looking gun. She was not surprised when he asked permission to call on Helena Anne, and consented as if he had been the most eligible suitor in the territory. Later in the year when he proposed marriage to her daughter, she gave them her blessing.

In the precious moments Frank and Helena Anne spent together during their engagement their talk was often serious. There were some things she must understand about the danger in which he was still involved. She must know, among other things, that the Murphy men might still come to the San Juan Valley to get him. Could she endure life, dreading every knock on the door, waiting terrified for him to return after each absence from the house, listening with a fluttering heart at the sound of hoofbeats riding up in the night, and living in constant fear of the gun he wore during every waking moment and placed by his bedside at night?

Sitting close to Helena Anne by the fire in late autumn, Frank looked at her and wondered why he had ever found it so much fun to go with Billy Bonney to the dances at Las Chozas. Whenever his thoughts returned to Billy he felt sad. And then he would think of something else about Lincoln County he had not told her. One day he pulled out of his pocket a worn, soiled envelope from which he took a clipping from the editorial page of the Mesilla Valley *Independent.* The editorial is still in the family's possession, and says in part:

Coe . . . has been hunted down by . . . the Dolan-Evans faction with the tenacity of sleuth-hounds; his house burned down, his crops destroyed, farming implements destroyed, and he himself driven out of Lincoln County. . . . It can be seen from this the injustice that has been done and the suffering that has been endured by many of the peaceable, law-abiding citizens of Lincoln County. Frank Coe has never been mixed up in any way with the troubles, but on the contrary refused to take sides with either party. The unfortunate circumstance of his happening to be present when Roberts was killed was sufficient for the "Dolan" party to place his name in the list of those marked for the bullet. The cry raised against the "Coe boys" was scarcely less than that against McSween. . . . Taking all things into consideration we don't know but Coe ought to be thankful for the final result. After being robbed of the fruits of long years of toil; harassed and driven from home, and thrown into prison and loaded down with chains, he has upon first legal examination of the charges against him, been triumphantly acquitted.

At the finish of the reading Helena Anne's face was troubled. Try as she might, she could not grasp all the complexities of the war. Then she scolded him for returning to Lincoln County to get the thresher.

Frank often told of this trip to Lincoln. He had started from Farmington to go to the Ruidoso and return with the thresher. When he arrived in Santa Fé, Marshal Sherman threw him into jail on the old charges that he had taken part in the Blazer's Mill battle. From Santa Fé he was taken to Las Cruces because court was in session there. Locked up in a vermin-infested cell, he fretted over the delay this meant to his threshing operations. After several days of misery, the lawmen got around to studying the charges against the prisoner and found that there was not enough evidence to convict him and so he was released. The men in charge knew full well that Governor Wallace would not uphold them in any unfounded legal prosecution. As soon as he was released, he caught the stage from Las Cruces to Santa Fé, paid the livery stable owner out of his small supply of cash for taking care of his team and wagon, and went on to Lincoln.

The grapevine was quick to pick up the news that Frank was in town. Across the rocks and arroyos to a hideout in the Capitán Mountains a rider took the word to Billy Bonney. He and Tom O'Folliard started for Lincoln at once to find their old amigo. They had not seen him since he had left the Gerhart ranch. As there were orders to bring in Billy and his friends, dead or alive, the two were extra cautious. Knowing that the most likely place to find Frank was at the McSween store, they stopped their horses there in the deep shadows of a tree.

What Billy didn't know was that Mrs. McSween was honoring his friend with a party that night. For that purpose she had fixed up a wing of the store for a dance and musicale because she knew how much Frank loved music. Among the guests were three officers from Fort Stanton, who were stationed in Lincoln for the purpose of bringing in William Bonney and all other outlaws. To furnish music for the occasion she had arranged for Zebrioen Bates, a talented musician and former member of the Negro cavalry at the fort, and Solomón Montaña, good on both the fiddle and guitar.

Leaving Tom to stand guard, Billy advanced toward the place from which the sound of music was coming. If he was surprised at what he saw when he opened the door and stepped inside, he gave no sign of it. He only pushed back his hat and smiled broadly at Frank, whom he had spotted immediately on his left. On his right, seated near the wall, were the officers from the fort. Frank gestured toward them to warn Billy. He indicated that he had seen them by bringing up his rifle so that it could be fired from his waist like a pistol, its barrel pointed directly at the Fort Stanton guests.

At Billy's unexpected entrance the music came to an abrupt and discordant halt, conversation broke off, and a chilling silence enveloped the room. Billy's hurried glance and quick smile in his direction told Frank his friend knew he was there. In that instant only did Billy take his eyes from the three men at his right. With Frank at his rear he felt safe. However, no one made a move to take him as Billy exchanged words with the officers seated near the wall. They looked extremely uncomfortable, especially when Billy advanced a few steps toward them. They didn't question the fact that Billy was in a better bargaining position than they, but they let him know they were there to keep the peace and take in any outlaws. In reply to this Billy made it clear he had not come there looking for trouble or to stir up a ruckus in which some innocent people might get killed. He was there to see a friend, nothing more, nothing less. In a quiet voice he told them that if they wanted to take him in, now was their chance. In answer to this they assured him they were not after him alone; they were ordered to bring in all outlaws.

When the guests heard this exchange of words, they breathed easier. They saw that Billy had not come there to make any trouble. Tensions were all eased when Billy cried out for Bates to strike up his favorite tune because he'd rather dance than eat. To the three-four time of "Sobre las Olas" he began to sashay back and forth directly in front of the officers, keeping a few feet distance between them and him. He moved gracefully from left to right working closer to them with his finger on the trigger of his rifle and his eyes boring into theirs.

As his sweeps became more exaggerated and he advanced closer to them, their nervousness increased. They squirmed on their seats when he brushed their knees with his rifle, hastily giving their chairs another backward shove which brought them against the wall. Finally they got up, stood behind their chairs, and flattened themselves against the side of the building.

Just when Frank began to fear he was pushing his luck too far, Billy started backing away from the officers until he reached the door through which he had entered. As he stood framed in the darkness outside, he called to Frank to meet him at Chozas the following night. Frank indicated he would and Billy backed out. In seconds the hoofbeats of two horses were heard leaving Lincoln. The musicians picked up their instruments with shaky hands and began a lively dance tune. Soon couples were on the floor stepping to it, and Mrs. McSween hurried with a plate of cookies to serve the onlookers standing against the wall.

The following night Frank rode out to the adobe hovel that served as the cantina at Las Chozas and spent a great part of the evening talking with Billy. Tom remained on guard outside until late. It was past midnight when Frank rode back up the valley to the Ellis home and Billy headed for his camp in the foothills of the Capitáns.

Again Frank had seen it proved, as he had on other occasions, that Billy had a lot of friends. But arguments to get him to lay down his guns were useless. It was Billy's good fortune, Frank thought as he drove his wagon back to Farmington, to have many more friends who wished him well than enemies who wanted to see him dead.

In January of 1881 Frank and Helena Anne made their wedding plans. The family agreed that because of her father's failing health it would be better to have the wedding in Durango. The date was set for February 7. Her wedding gown was chosen from the dresses she had brought from Chicago and was heavy gray-and-green silk brocade ornamented with wide bands of velvet on both the blouse and the overskirt, which was gathered in the back to make a bustle. Frank had never seen her wear it so she kept it a closely guarded secret.

Another secret was well guarded too. Since Frank's arrival in the valley his reputation as a musician had grown, but the only fiddles he played were borrowed. When it became known that he and Helena Anne were to be married, their friends took up a collection to buy him a fiddle for a wedding present. Nothing could have pleased Frank more. Now he could join the musical Tully family on an equal footing; and because music was to draw Helena Anne and him closer together and deepen their love, it became an enduring part of their life together.

February 6 was close upon them before they knew it. It was very cold and the trip to Durango was made under freezing, blustering conditions. Traveling by carriage and on horseback, the wedding party set out from Fred's place in a light snowfall that grew worse as the trip progressed. The ceremony was to take place at the Howards, close friends of the family, and by the time they reached the house a foot of snow was on the ground.

At noon the following day Frank and Helena Anne were married. The bride came into the parlor on Fred's arm, accompanied by Joe Shram, who was the best man. As soon as the ceremony was over and Frank had kissed his pretty bride, he hurried to the front hall to get his gunbelt which he had promised not to wear during the ceremony. The wedding party then went to the Durango Hotel where the owner, a friend of John Tully, was giving a supper and dance in their honor.

When the dancing began, Frank reluctantly allowed his friends to dance with his lovely bride. This did give him a chance, however, to play his new violin, for the guests insisted he perform for them. Helena Anne danced dutifully with the others, but she was impatient to get back to her husband and let him guide her over the floor. If anything clouded her happiness, it was the bulge under his coat where his gun rested. The sight of it on such a happy occasion brought back her fears for his safety.

At midnight the dance broke up, and the events that followed were remembered vividly by both Frank and Helena Anne. They took place after the long-drawn-out good-byes and well-wishing and the last guest had been helped down the front steps. Ed, the owner of the hotel, bade them good night and they ascended the stairs to their room.

They had no more than reached the inside and lighted the lamp when they heard a soft knock at the door. When Frank opened it, he found Ed with a worried look on his face. He stepped inside and in a hushed voice explained that there were four tough-looking desperados downstairs who claimed to be friends of Frank. They wanted to see them so they could wish him and his bride happiness. Then they were going to escort them safely out of town. Frank reached for the gunbelt he had just hung on the bedpost. He had a pretty good idea who they were and what they would do to him if they got their hands on him. Helena was pale as she crossed to the door where Frank stood and placed herself in the loop of his arm. Unable to say anything, she tried to gather strength from her husband's calm manner as he asked Ed whether the men were wearing any hardware. When he said he had made them stack their rifles outside, Frank knew they had not come there for any Sunday-school picnic. He knew his life depended on some quick thinking and acting. He explained to Helena Anne he wouldn't have a chance if he went down there, outnumbered as he was. "Helnee-Anne [for he always called her that], they wouldn't dare harm you. It's me they're after. Now you must do as I say." After he instructed Ed to slip down the hall to get Fred, he went on to explain to her that she and Ed were to go down to the lobby to stall the men while he and Fred went out the back way and returned home. The men would not risk doing any shooting and rousing the hotel guests. Tomorrow Joe Shram would being her back home in the hack. By the time he had finished these instructions, Fred came down the hall carrying his boots. Ed followed them down the back stairs and bolted the door after them.

Weak and terrified though she was, Helena Anne realized the extent to which her husband's safety depended upon her. She grabbed her Paisley shawl and started down the dimly lit stairs. Ed followed behind her. At the bottom of the steps she almost turned and ran back up. Through the door to the lobby she saw four of the hardest-looking men she had ever beheld. Trail-worn, unshaven, dirty, and cold, they hovered around the stove. At the sound of her steps, they had unholstered their guns and held them leveled at the doorway. Looks of surprise and disbelief came to their faces when they saw, not the man they were hunting, but a pretty, proud-looking girl. They lowered their guns, too astonished to know what to say for a moment.

Then one of them doffed his dust-streaked hat and said, "Me and the boys, ma'am, have rode a long ways to wish Frank Coe good luck. Now you'll oblige us by tellin' where he is at."

Another with a scar across his cheek added, "He's right, lady. We shore have come a fur ways jes to see he gits out of Durango all safe and sound."

By this time Helena Anne was more angered than she was afraid. She knew that she had to keep them talking, for the longer she delayed them the farther Frank and Fred would be able to ride from the town. "Don't you think that the hour is late for you to be making such a suggestion?"

"No, ma'am, we don't. And all yore Sunday-school teacher airs ain't goin' to change our minds. How about it, men, shall we go up and flush him out?" He gestured to the stairs with his gun. "And be sure yore hawlegs are in workin' order. We want Coe to feel well pertected."

"You're a brave lot of men, four of you coming here in the middle of the night to get one man. I am sure if Frank Coe wants to get out of this town safely he'll have to put his trust in a Higher Power—and not in cowards like you."

"Now yo're spunky, ain't you. But we're on to your trick. Tell us where Frank Coe is at. We've come to get him. If we don't git him now, we'll trail him back to San Juan County and finish the job."

"Tom's right," said another.

"Well, let me tell you that Frank Coe doesn't scare easily either. If you men persist in trying to get my husband, you do it at your own peril. He is considered pretty fast on the draw himself."

"So yo're his new bride? I guessed as much by the way you wuz gittin' all riled. He's shore goin' to hate to leave a purty girl like you and go with us." He winked at his companions.

Helena Anne was now red with anger. "Furthermore, Frank Coe has a lot of friends—and they are all good shots, too, so why don't you leave here and quit trying to start trouble?"

The men were getting impatient. "Look here, you'd better hold that tongue of yores and step out of the way so we kin git yore husband," one ordered.

During this conversation Ed had remained in the hall ready to rouse the guests if trouble developed. Over Helena Anne's shoulder the men had seen him. The indications were that they did not want to start trouble and arouse others. To smooth things over, one suggested they call off their "party" and get Coe later.

Helena Anne could see that they had lost their nerve. With relief she watched them walk toward the door, holstering their guns as they did. After the last one had mounted his horse and ridden off into the night, she sank into a chair and wept tears of joy for her husband and brother, who were by this time out of their reach.

The next morning Ed sent for Joe Shram, who shortly afterward drove up to the hotel in a buckboard. With the buffalo robe over them they rode off through new snow to rejoin Frank at the Coe home near Farmington.

CHAPTER IV

Frank and Helena Anne Coe
Migrate to Lincoln County

THE HARDSHIPS OF THE FRONTIER were not new to Helena Anne, so she adjusted readily to her new role of homemaker. She was not yet nineteen. At first she feared some of the Murphy outlaws might make another attempt to get her husband, but as time passed and none appeared she grew less apprehensive. There was little to mar their happiness until after the birth of their first child, named Sydney, in November of 1881. The baby progressed well but Helena Anne's strength did not return. Days wore into weeks with no improvement. From her persistent fever she grew weaker. Waited upon by her mother, her husband, and a neighbor lady, she spent most of her time in bed, getting out for a short while each day to rock her daughter. Even that became too much for her and so Frank neglected his work to remain with her. Her brother, Fred, who had studied medicine in Chicago, made frequent trips to see Helena Anne but her case baffled him. It was he who first suggested that she see a doctor in Durango. Frank and her mother urged this also.

Finally she agreed, and Frank padded the back end of the hack with old quilts and pillows to make her as comfortable as possible for the rough trip. They went to a doctor recommended to them by the Howards. The doctor said little to her, but he bluntly told her husband that she would be an invalid for the rest of her life, which probably would not be a long one.

Frank was stunned. In the days that followed, Helena Anne could only guess at what lay behind his forced smile and sad expression. She took her medicine dutifully and tried to pretend that she felt stronger, but those who watched her knew better. Her husband encouraged her but she could only hope and pray.

Frank remembered how thin and flushed with fever she looked one day soon after New Year's 1882. There were tears in her eyes as she stubbornly vowed that somehow she was going to get off that bed and look after her house and baby as a wife should. He went to the bed and kissed her. When he made some noise pulling up a chair, she motioned him not to awaken little Sydney, who was sleeping at her side. Taking a letter from his pocket, he read her the news he had just received from Al, who had returned to the Peñasco Valley. Its contents showed his enthusiasm for Lincoln County, especially the climate, which he thought might help Helena Anne. Moneymaking opportunities there were better since wholesale rustling had been stopped. He urged Frank to come back and file a claim. His family could stay with him and Mollie until a cabin was put up. In the James Canyon was some fine cattle country that had just been opened up to settlers. All Frank had to do was to file a claim and prove up.

Helena Anne listened as he read the letter. To his surprise she began to ask questions about the county from which he had been driven over three years ago. For the first time since their marriage she wanted to talk about Lincoln County's mountains, mesas, and streams.

"I'll do anything to get up from this tiresome bed," she promised her husband. "I want to get well so I can look after you and the baby. But how can I travel to Lincoln County when I can't even sit up for over five minutes at a time?"

Frank answered her by saying that he would make a bed for her in the back of the hack as he had when they had gone to see the doctor at Durango. She could lie there while he sat in the front, held Sydney, and drove the team. He explained that the Terrell and Slain families were leaving soon for Lincoln County and he could get one of the Terrell boys to drive his wagon. Preparations would have to begin at once so that they could be ready when their neighbors left. Helena Anne gave her consent and Frank began to make arrangements with George and his brothers to dispose of his holdings on the ranch.

They had learned during this time that Billy Bonney's guns were no longer a threat. Frank never liked to think about how in July 1881 Sheriff Pat Garrett had shot Billy in a darkened room of Pete Maxwell's house in Fort Sumner. He was sorry it had to happen that way. To Helena Anne the subject of Billy the Kid was a blessedly closed book.

In bright, warm February 1882 the small caravan started out. From her pallet in the rear of the hack Helena Anne jolted uncomfortably while her husband sat in front and managed the team and Sydney. When she was not too tired, she talked to him about their future plans and watched uneasily the territory they rode through. She had never forgotten her horror of the Indian stories she had heard around the campfire when the Tullys came by wagon train on the last leg of their journey from Alamosa, Colorado, to Fred's "Valley of Dreams" in northern New Mexico. She did not know that these tales had been told for the benefit of the tenderfeet from Chicago. She had then asked her father to let her sleep under the wagon with him and Jim, but when he told her a wild animal might bite her, she wedged herself between Edith and her mother inside the wagon. Most of the time as she and Frank rode along she said little, but she did wonder about what was before them. She worried, too, about a visit Frank must pay to New Mexico's governor, Lew Wallace, when they reached Santa Fé, to ask for the pardon that had been promised the participants in the Lincoln County War.

To Frank's dismay, for a couple of days Helena Anne seemed to show signs of ever-greater weakness. Then on the third day there was a change; she ate almost hungrily of a squirrel he had taken pains to cook for her. At a midafternoon stop the next day she asked to be helped from the back of the carriage so she could sit in the sunshine and eat with the others. While the women were preparing the meal, she sat and held Sydney and played with her. When the wagons started to roll again, Helena Anne begged her husband to let her ride in the front with him and the baby. Confident that she would soon tire, he nevertheless helped her to the front seat. She spent the remainder of the day there, and from that time on she sat beside him and held Sydney.

By the time the wagons reached Santa Fé, Helena Anne was able to visit some of the big mercantile stores and sit in the charming Old World plaza to watch the town's colorful citizens. At their camp outside the city Frank dressed himself carefully before calling on the governor. He waited nervously in an outer office of the Governor's Palace, which had housed the Spanish rulers long before the *Mayflower* touched the shore of Massachusetts. Finally he was admitted to the inner sanctum of the Territorial Governor of New Mexico. Etched in his memory was the scene when the governor rose from behind his immense carved desk and extended his hand across it and inquired the purpose of the visit. As briefly and simply as he could, Frank told him that he wanted to take advantage of the amnesty declared for the men involved in the Lincoln County War. The governor called a clerk to get some papers from a file. He studied them for a few moments, pulled one from the stack, and said warmly, "I am happy that you are taking advantage of the pardon offered you, Mr. Coe. I only wish that others involved in the controversy could have seen it the same way." Frank surmised that the governor was referring to the death of William Bonney, in whose interest he had made a special trip to Lincoln to persuade him to lay down his guns.

Frank answered, "Governor Wallace, no one more than I wants to see the old wounds healed. The sooner I can fix it up with you, the happier I'll be. All I want is to live at peace in Lincoln County."

Rising to indicate that the interview was over, the governor again extended his hand and wished him happiness. As he rode toward their camp, Frank for the first time in many months had a feeling of inner peace.

Helena Anne, eager to reach her new home, thought the journey would never end. She was awed at her first view of the grandeur of Sierra Blanca Peak. On their route lay White Oaks, later to become a boom town famed all over the West; from there, a short but mountainous way to Fort Stanton. On the mesa near the fort the men staked their horses in the tall, lush grass and made camp. The following day Al arrived as had been prearranged by letter.

During their stay at the fort Frank would want to trade the hack for a light mountain wagon and so in a few days they drove into Lincoln. At a blacksmith shop he met a saloonkeeper who needed a hack and they made a deal, Frank throwing in five dollars to boot. Afterward Frank and Helena Anne went to call on Mrs. McSween. Frank was proud to present his wife and the baby to old friends he met on the street, but Helena Anne was not so calm as she appeared because she was afraid her husband might run into some members of the Murphy outfit. She was glad when the visit was over and they could return to the fort.

After the horses had rested enough, Frank made plans to leave and loaded the wagon with supplies for the months ahead. With Al driving one wagon and he the other, and the Terrell and Slain wagons following behind them, they headed east out of Lincoln and followed the Bonito Valley to its junction with the Ruidoso Valley. By nightfall of the second day they pulled up under the cottonwoods of the Miller ranch, where Frank Coe first met Billy the Kid. After an overnight stop the Terrell and Slain families moved on up the Ruidoso Valley, but at the insistence of the Millers, Frank, Helena Anne, and Al remained another day to visit with them. Frank brought out his fiddle for an evening of music. The twelve-year-old daughter of the Millers fell in love with little Sydney and helped take care of her during their stay. Regretfully the families said good-bye.

The Coe wagons started up the canyon toward the Peñasco Valley through a desolate country with deep ravines, abrupt mountain slopes, and thick brush. The sight of such lonely vastness made Helena Anne's spirits sink, and she held her baby closer to her and edged nearer her husband. She scanned the heavy timber anxiously, fearful that a ferocious beast might attack them. No cabin of any kind bordered the trail. It might be a paradise for cattle, but it was a nightmare for her.

By noon two days later, the wagons pulled up at a small clearing with a cabin in its center, and Molly Mayhill Coe, Al's wife, who had been staying with a neighbor, ran out to greet them. They moved on ten miles farther to Al's home, where they stayed while Al helped Frank put up his own cabin another ten miles deeper into the wilderness, a place of incredible beauty and wildness.

Frank filed his claim and bought a herd of cattle to run, leaving Helena Anne alone much of the time while he looked after them. As soon as he left in the morning, she put the heavy bar across the door and did not dare lift it until his return, even though she needed sometimes to go for water and wood. She trembled at every sound and peeked through a porthole to look for the Indians she was sure were going to creep up and scalp her and the baby. Frank begged her to learn how to shoot and left his rifle on a rack near the door. But never did Helena Anne fire a gun; she claimed she could do as much with a broom. In lighter and happier moments she and Sydney watched the deer who came through the clearing with their fawns cavorting around them. All the game they needed for the table could be killed from their doorway.

Cold, brisk winds blew early in the canyon country. Helena Anne became depressed, knowing they would be hemmed in later on by snows. She felt buried alive among the trees, brush, rocks, wild beasts, and Indians. Thoughts of the future weighed heavily on her mind and heart. Where would Sydney and the other children they wanted go to school or attend church? The latter she especially missed. Frank, knowing the James Canyon country would remain a wilderness for many years to come, had no answer to these questions. All he could say was, "Time will take care of everything, Helnee-Anne. You mustn't worry over the bridges we don't have to cross right now."

Frank's cattle fattened well on the heavy grass the early summer rains provided. With some of the profit from them he planned to add another room to their cabin. He decided to go to Lincoln before an early snow blocked the trail, so he could get some materials he needed for this project. Because Sydney was fretful and a sick baby on such a trip would make it a difficult one, Helena Anne stayed with Molly and Al, and Frank went alone.

In Lincoln he loaded the wagon with the things they needed, remembering to select some yard goods so his wife would have some sewing to occupy her time. On the return trip he stopped at the Miller place overnight and, among other news, learned that their ranch was for sale. They wished to go to a place where their daughter could get an education and therefore they were returning to Missouri. Miller planned to take up freighting operations again.

Helena Anne was relieved to see her husband return. After spending the night at Al's place, they started for their own cabin. With so little news of the outside world reaching them, she listened eagerly to every morsel Frank could remember. It was not until they were nearing home that he told her the Miller ranch was for sale.

Helena Anne was busy with her restless baby and did not answer him at once. After Sydney quieted down she remarked wistfully that it was a nice place. She had never forgotten her visit there on the way to the James Canyon . . . was it only six months ago? It seemed much longer to her.

"How much does Mr. Miller want for the ranch?"

"More than we could ever get together, I guess. Four hundred dollars is what he told me."

"Do you suppose he'll find a buyer soon? I guess it is a lot of money."

Frank didn't "reckon" he would. Money was very scarce. A lot of people never saw that much in their entire lives.

They were almost to their dooryard by now, so the matter was dropped. But later, after Helena Anne had cooked their supper and washed the dishes, she inquired of her husband again about what the Millers had asked for their place. Frank was tired and planned to get up early the next morning to go after some strays. He was surprised when his wife wanted to know how much profit he thought he could make on his cattle when he sold them. He had not given it much thought.

But Helena Anne had. She began to prod him with questions and emphasized the good points of the Ruidoso Valley. "Think, Frank, how that valley will be building up in a few years. It wouldn't be too long before we could have a school maybe— and a church. And there's good land for grazing cattle, too. But here in this canyon there will never be anything for you to do but to run cattle. At the Miller place you can also raise grain and have an orchard and garden."

On the back of an envelope he took from his pocket Frank began to do some calculations. "I believe we can make it. If I can find a buyer for my cattle and get Al to help me round them up, I might scrape together enough money."

The next morning Frank rode out to find a buyer for his cattle. He figured that if the Millers sold the ranch before they got there, they would look for another place to buy in the same area. At home Helena Anne began to pack, caring little that they had not lived in the James Canyon long enough to prove up on their claim. She wanted to leave the place. Of that much she was sure. After looking around, Frank found a buyer for his cattle and later delivered them to a ranch on the Feliz River.

Proudly he counted out the money on the kitchen table—almost four hundred dollars!

Hurrying lest early snow shut them in, they loaded their possessions on the wagons and prepared to leave. Helena Anne, who had never before picked up the reins of a horse, climbed on the seat of the wagon and drove the team. She was determined to get out of the James Canyon if she had to pull the wagon herself! To keep Sydney from bouncing off the seat, she sometimes had to put her on the floor of the wagon bed. On the steep hills it was with great difficulty that she held the horses with both hands, worked the brake with one foot, and kept Sydney from rolling around with the other. Her arms ached, her legs pained her all the way to her waist, and her hands were stiff from holding the reins.

When the Millers saw them coming, they ran out to greet them. Frank had no trouble crossing the narrow bridge over the irrigation ditch near the Miller house. But Helena Anne in her excitement dropped a line and then began pulling on the other one. This caused the team to turn sharply to the right and the front wheel missed the bridge and dropped into the ditch. With her foot still pushing on the brake, she screamed for help. Frank and Miller ran quickly and helped her and Sydney out of the back. Frank took over, and with Miller's help, they were able to get the wagon out of the ditch without any damage.

After supper the Coes got around to talking business. Frank barely could meet the terms set by Miller. To do so, he had to throw in a team and wagon. But when the deal was completed, he was the owner of almost 300 acres of irrigable land along the Ruidoso River.

The Millers delayed their departure for two weeks so the families could visit. When the last good-byes were said and the tailgate of the Miller wagon had disappeared down the valley, Frank and Helena Anne knew that their life had taken an important turn.

CHAPTER V

Settling on Coe Ranch
and Bringing Up a Family

HE MILLER RANCH now became known as the Coe Ranch, held in 1882 under squatter's rights. In addition to the irrigable land, Coe Ranch had access to thousands of acres of open grazing. Frank saw that the free use of this vast range with an abundance of water would give him a chance to build up a large herd of horses and cattle.

The house was one of the first built in the Ruidoso Valley. Its low walls of sun-baked adobe brick, eighteen inches thick, had withstood the onslaught of sun, wind, rain, snow, rifle bullets, and Indian arrows. It consisted of a single room twenty by forty feet with a dirt floor, no windows, and a single door. Portholes served for ventilation and light, and were also used to shoot through if necessary. The flat roof was supported by vigas with boards across them covered with a thick layer of adobe mud. This kept the house warm in winter and cool in summer.

Frank and Helena Anne moved in with their few belongings. Their most prized possession was a Tully heirloom, a mahogany clock given to them as a wedding present. This was placed on a shelf above the beehive fireplace in one corner of the room. They also brought with them a walnut dining table, a bed, cook stove and two chairs with rawhide bottoms.

There was no money for improvements. Frank put in crops of corn, wheat, and barley, which brought him good prices. He sold most of his crops to the government at Fort Stanton. With the money he received he was able to buy from his Mexican neighbors a few cows and a bull. This was the beginning of the large herd of cattle that Frank gradually developed. There was a vegetable garden that furnished enough food for the table in the summer and plenty to can for winter. Frank also planted alfalfa and set out a small apple orchard. In the rich soil and with plenty of water the trees made rapid growth, and justified his belief that this would be a good fruitgrowing country.

Helena Anne was left alone much of the time, and with no neighbors she was often lonely and afraid. When she found that she was going to have another baby she worried over getting someone to help her. About this time there was a welcome development that was to make life for her and her family much happier.

Because of the approaching announcement of the homestead law, which permitted only 160 acres to each claimant, Frank had written to his cousin George and asked him to come back to Lincoln County and file on a homestead to help hold the river land. George had married Phoebe Brown and settled in Colorado just over the line from New Mexico. They did not like it there and were glad to come to the Ruidoso Valley, where they moved in with Frank and Helena Anne.

Frank had recently gone to Dowlin's Mill on the upper Ruidoso and bought the best lumber available. With this he built a smooth floor in the house. He and Helena Anne wanted to give a dance to celebrate the arrival of George and Phoebe, so the neighbors up and down the river were invited to come and dance on the new board floor. Frank and George tuned up their fiddles and thoroughly enjoyed playing together again. This was the first of the dances which became regular Saturday night affairs at Coe Ranch for many years.

As soon as possible George and Frank went up the river to select a site for George's house. They found it about a mile and a half up stream. George selected this location because nearby a spring of water gushed from the hillside.

The Jap Coe family came from California in 1884 and settled midway between Frank and George, to help hold the valuable river land. The Coe wives were now in a position to help each other when the babies came. During the rush to complete George and Phoebe's home (for an expected child), a second daughter, Annie, was born to Frank and Helena Anne in 1884, a short time before the birth of Phoebe's daughter, whom they named Grace.

Houses grow around here according to the needs of the family, and there aren't many that did not start with one room and increase, one at a time, until the family needs were finally well met. Helena Anne began to urge her husband to add a room for the growing family and, with the help of his two faithful Mexican workers, Timio and Fabián, Frank made the necessary adobe bricks—whose proper curing requires months —and began the construction. From then on it was a race between construction of home and growing family. The second room was connected to the original house by two large doors that could be thrown open to provide a wide passageway for entertainment and dancing. No sooner did they plan their third room than another child was on the way. At completion, the house had a "T" shape, with three rooms forming the cross-piece and four the trunk. The first post office in this immediate area was established at our home and was called Glencoe. Frank was postmaster.

Winnie, the third child for Frank and Helena Anne, was born in 1886. Not quite three years later another girl, Agnes, was born. It was about this time that the Coe families, all of them growing fast, had to do some serious thinking about their children's education. Sydney was almost eight and had received no schooling except what her mother had taught her. As yet no public-school laws had been enacted in the territory, so any provision for school had to be undertaken through private initiative. Only land and children were plentiful.

The Frank, George, and Jap Coe families agreed that each would furnish one third of the materials and labor required to build a schoolhouse. In addition, each family would board the teacher a month and pay her twenty-five dollars. A three-month term was all they thought they could afford.

To get the construction moving quickly, Jap donated the adobes he had made the previous summer for his house. He also offered the use of his front room for a school until the new building was completed.

The next problem was to get a teacher. This task fell to Helena Anne, and a difficult one it was in a community where no qualified persons were available. Finally, through her brother Kivas in St. Louis, she advertised in a newspaper there and found a Miss Poole, whom she employed. She took over her duties in Jap's front room while the Coe men worked on the schoolhouse.

Built of adobe bricks and covered with a roof strongly supported by stout vigas, the Coe schoolhouse still stands today. It has served the community for almost seventy years in varying capacities after it became too small to house the growing school population. Opposite the entrance is a fireplace that was fed by wood carried in by the children. There were homemade benches for them and a pine desk for the teacher. A handily placed bundle of switches was also a part of the equipment in the days when the rod was used to take care of the wayward child.

The school was an object of pride to all the Coes, but to Helena Anne it was the realization of a dream, one that began as she lay ill on the hard pallet in the rear of the hack, jolting on her way to Lincoln County.

Frank's four girls grew, as he often said, like weeds on the banks of an irrigation ditch. Three years after the birth of Agnes, when Helena Anne knew her fifth child was on the way, she hoped and prayed that it would be a boy. Strong arms and bold hearts were needed on the frontier. To the joy of everyone, on October 4, 1893, I was born. Immediately I became the center of an adoring family even though I could not have been much to look at. I was named Wilbur Franklin, partly after my father, who began at once to make great plans for me at the ranch. My mother, who was deeply devoted to all her children, gave me all the care and attention possible. Josefa, the faithful servant who had been nursemaid for the older children, hovered over me in delight, I have been told, pouring forth endearments in her soft, mellow Spanish.

To understand better the illnesses of children, Mother continually studied her mail-order medical guide *The Home Book of Health and Medicine,* for the services of a doctor were hard to get on the frontier. Her extensive knowledge was eventually drawn on over a wide area. When sickness struck, Mother was the first person called. Taking off with her guidebook and an interpreter, if necessary, she hurried to give whatever aid she could, and by prescribing simple home remedies and urging stricter sanitation, she saved many lives in a settlement that had its unhappy share of diarrhea, dysentery, consumption, and other diseases that were often fatal to infants.

At home her children received routine doses of castor oil, which she consistently administered for all internal ailments—and woe to any of us who backed away from the spoon. For external troubles her stand-by remedy was coal oil, generously applied to scratches, bruises, bites, blisters, burns, and rusty-nail injuries. Although a strict dry, Mother would recommend whisky for medicinal purposes; to make sure it was used only for that, she kept it locked in a cabinet. As regularly as the first green apples appeared, "cholera morbus" doubled us up with pains in our stomachs, so she had ready Jamaica ginger mixed with castor oil.

But there were many diseases against which Mother's home remedies were powerless. This became tragically evident after an epidemic of spinal meningitis struck the entire area of the three valleys. Since there was no known treatment for it the victims died like flies; Indians, Mexicans, and Anglo settlers alike. Once the disease struck, it was usually fatal. The Coe mothers, like all parents in the settlements, were deeply concerned.

At the time I was six months old. Before anyone else in the family noticed something wrong with me, Mother became aware of it. She studied her medical book constantly, waiting with terrified heart lest any symptoms of the dread disease appear. When spots began to appear on my body and I started having convulsions, the heartbreaking truth became known.

All she had to rely on was the medical book, for the nearest doctor was ten miles away at Fort Stanton. He could not make calls except in extreme cases. With the disease so prevalent, my case was only routine. Following the directions in her medical book, Mother put me into a tub of hot water, a treatment similar to that of Sister Kenny years later. This procedure went on day after day. Unquestionably, this way of caring for me, added to her dogged determination to save my life, brought results even though at one time my heart stopped beating. Mother, however, was one who preferred to render unto Caesar the things that were his and to God the things that belonged to Him, thus maintaining her deep belief in the efficacy of prayer, which probably saved my life.

As soon as possible the doctor from Fort Stanton came to the ranch. He could only marvel, as he looked at my feverish emaciated body, that there was the breath of life in me. At the time he prescribed nothing more than the treatments Mother was already giving me. At a later date he suggested that an electric current passed through my body might stimulate the lifeless muscles of my legs. To get me to endure the tickling sensation, my sisters joined hands with me in a circle while someone turned the crank which spun a coil inside three magnetos. The faster it turned, the more power it generated and my sisters and I screamed and tugged, trying to let go of each other's hands. I cannot say by what miracle it ever came about, but my body from the waist up was spared the ravages of the

Portrait of Frank B. Coe in 1878.

Frank Coe with his gun in 1922.

Portrait of
Helena Anne Tully Coe in 1880.

Helena Tully Coe in 1922.

Jim Tully and three vaqueros saddled for a roundup of beef steers on Fort Stanton mesa.

Old Man Goss, the cook, in front of Coe ranch house around 1900.

A twenty-dollar mare and her five-hundred-dollar family.

Edith Coe in her mother's gray-and-green silk brocade and velvet wedding dress from 1881.

The Coe Ranch in 1910 looking toward the Pajarito Mountains.

The first cold storage on Coe Ranch in 1915.

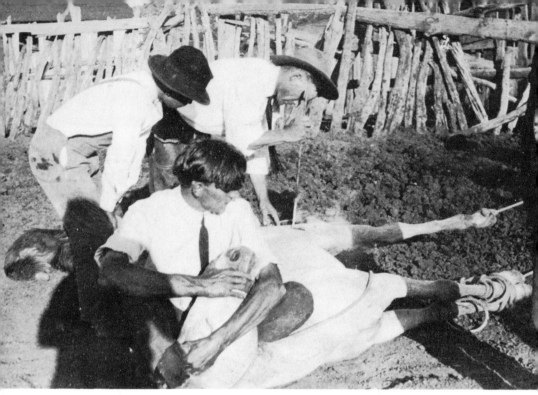

Frank Bunting, Frank Bonnell, and Wilbur Coe branding a colt.

Working cattle on the Coe Ranch in 1912.
Wilbur Coe is the rider on the right.

Helena Anne Coe playing the piano brought from Chicago in 1878.

Phoebe and George Coe and Frank and Helena Coe on a Sunday in 1925.

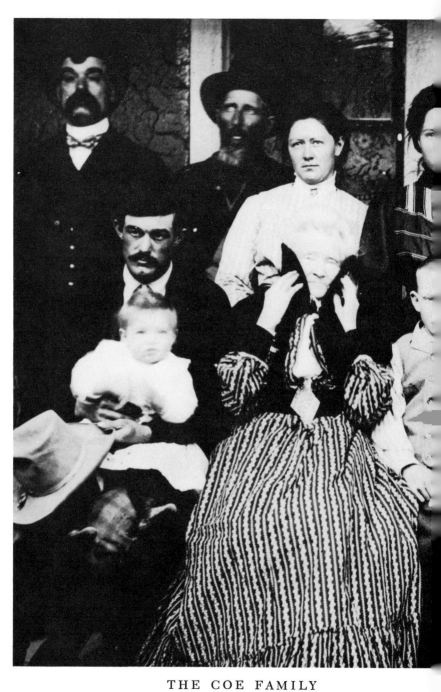

THE COE FAMILY

*Left to right: baby, Bert Bonnell, Granmaw, Wilbur,
Mother, Helena Anne, Edith, Sydney.*

Back row: Rev. Scogins, Frank, Annie, Winnie,
unidentified man, Jim Tully, Agnes.

Wilbur Coe before a cattle drive in 1912.

Wilbur Coe sculpturing driftwood from the Ruidoso.

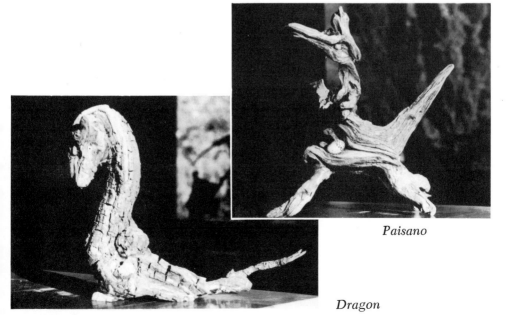

Paisano

Dragon

The living room of Coe Ranch.

The apple orchard in bloom, 1964.

A view over Coe Ranch in 1958, looking south.

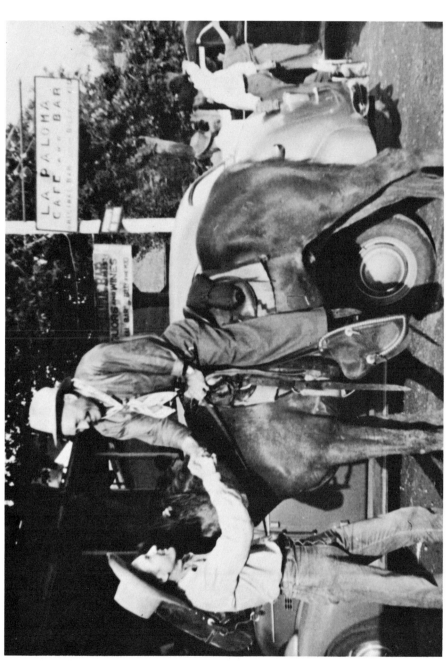

Peter Hurd and Wilbur Coe posing as Billy the Kid and Frank Coe as they met in 1879.

The ranch house in 1960.

disease. And I retained partial use of my stricken lower limbs.

It was Mother who conceived the idea that the hot mineral baths at Pagosa Springs, Colorado, might be beneficial to me, so after another baby, Edith, was born in 1895, she decided to take me there. The springs are just over the New Mexico line not far from where the Tully family lived. This enabled her to visit with her family at the same time. As it was too much for her to make the trip with me alone, she took sweet-natured Winnie, who was only eight, to help look after me. Baby Edith was left with Aunt Phoebe. Dad took us in the carriage for the long, dusty four-day trip to San Antonio, New Mexico, to catch the train. When we reached Durango, Uncle Fred met us.

At the time of our visit Pagosa Springs was famed more for its mines than for its health-giving waters. Because there was more money in ore than in mineral water, promoters had done little to develop the facilities there. Coming from the underground extremely hot, the spring water had been piped into a trough to cool and from there it flowed to the bathhouse, which was little more than a shack containing some private baths and a steam room. No living accommodations worthy of the name had yet been constructed, so Uncle Fred fixed up some sleeping quarters for us in an abandoned schoolhouse. He rigged up a tent adjoining the schoolhouse to use as a kitchen.

In order to take all the advantage possible of her visit, Granmaw and Aunt Edith went to the springs with us and we made a family party of it. Granmaw Tully was suffering from inflammatory rheumatism, but she was too modest to go to the public pool where the rest of us splashed together so she soaked her aching joints in a private bath, wearing an old house dress over her underclothes and her long cotton stockings. With Winnie and Aunt Edith, Mother's younger sister, to look after me, I was taken to the public baths, where special care was taken to see that my muscles were exercised as much as possible. On ropes stretched across the water I began then to develop strength in my arms, which later became prodigious.

But it always took considerable effort to swing my legs and walk.

At the time we went to Pagosa Springs I was too young to retain any memory of the place, but I somehow kept some remembrance of my Aunt Edith, who was at that time in her late teens. Perhaps this was because of her beautiful black horse, Midnight, on whose glossy back I rode with her two miles through the pine forest to a place upstream where we could find a safe spot to cross the Animas River to reach the springs. Or perhaps it was because of the tragedy that occurred years later. Anyway, I must have been as near heaven as a little boy can get, riding on the sidesaddle in front of her. Talented and beautiful and the pride of Granmaw and Uncle Fred, Aunt Edith was planning to attend a music conservatory in St. Louis. Granmaw was especially proud of her accomplishments because she had tutored her through the years.

When our stay at the springs was over, we boarded the train for San Antonio, where Dad met us to take us to the ranch.

On the ride from San Antonio, Dad told Mother of his plan to convert the carriage shed on one end of the house into a store. She was delighted and could hardly wait until the store was finished so that she could send off an order for some hats to sell. Of course, she expected people to buy them, but while waiting for customers she and the girls could wear them if they would be very careful not to damage them. As a girl, Mother had planned to become a milliner and for many years after she came to the Ruidoso Valley she sent orders for her hats to a Chicago wholesale establishment where for a short time she had been apprenticed.

As soon as my sisters were old enough, Dad taught them to ride and round up the stock. Annie early showed signs of becoming an excellent rider. To my mother's dismay, the girls preferred riding to doing ladylike tasks around the house. Although they cared little for books, Mother saw that they spent some time with them and with their musical studies, which at first was guitar and the rudiments of music theory.

Memories of Granmaw's piano were dear to my mother. She often yearned to run her fingers over its keyboard again. The realization of a school had been a dream come true, to own a piano was still just a wishful hope. Cash was always in short supply despite the fact that Dad was a good trader. His hay and grain found a ready market at Fort Stanton. I recall he once bought a little brown mare about two years old for twenty dollars. She ran on the open range for the ten years we kept her, bringing in a colt every spring, and these brought a profit of more than five hundred dollars.

One year Dad sold some crops to Fort Stanton at a higher price than he had expected and so he had some extra cash on hand. He asked Mother what she would like for the house. As she looked around at some of the boxes and crates that served as furniture she saw the obvious need for some new pieces. Yet the thought of depriving herself and her family of a piano any longer was an unpleasant one. She chose the piano and immediately wrote to her brother Kivas to select one and have it sent to El Paso, Texas, by railway freight.

After weeks of anxious waiting, the piano arrived in El Paso. Dad and Timio drove a four-horse team hitched to a heavy wagon the 170 miles to get it. On a long haul, he usually took along something to sell to pay expenses and for supplies or equipment needed for the ranch. On this trip he hauled a load of shelled corn, which he had contracted at a good price delivered in Tularosa. The only road to El Paso at that time was up the Ruidoso Valley, through Dark Canyon and the Mescalero Apache Indian Reservation to Tularosa. After delivering the corn they traveled west along the edge of the White Sands over the San Agustín Pass to Mesilla. From there they followed the winding road through the sand dunes along the Río Grande to El Paso.

When the box containing the piano was safely loaded on the wagon, they started home. The trip was uneventful until they reached Mesilla. There Dad met a man who wanted to sell some hives of honeybees. He offered them at a bargain. When Dad saw that they were filled not only with bees but with good honey, he bought them. He knew they would not only provide honey for the family but would be valuable for the pollenization of the apple blossoms. The hives were placed on top of the big, flat piano box and securely tied down with ropes. These were the first honeybees brought into the Ruidoso Valley and through the years were an important asset to Coe Ranch. Dad and Timio had no trouble on the return trip until they reached within a mile of the ranch. There had been torrential rains for several days and pulling up the last hill the wagon wheels bogged down to the hub in the heavy mud. The horses pulled and tugged as best they could but were unable to move the wagon. It was getting dark, so Dad and Timio unhitched the tired teams, mounted two of the horses, leading the other two, and rode bareback the last mile home.

Mother was glad they had arrived home safely but was disappointed that the Steinway grand piano would have to stay on the wagon overnight. Early the next morning Dad took fresh teams and brought the wagon and its precious load safely home.

After the beehives were carefully placed on a knoll near the orchard, the piano was unloaded and set up in the parlor. Mother immediately began to play and sing. This was the first piano in the valley and it brought pleasure to her family and to the entire community for almost fifty years. The piano is still in excellent condition and belongs to my sister Edith.

At the turn of the century Mother's last child, Zebulah Helena, was born. Yet with her brood of six girls and one boy, she found time to give the oldest of us piano lessons. We all loved music. It was not only a means of passing lonely hours where ways of recreation were few, but also a part of living itself.

Mother's expanding ranch house kept her busy. Most things she could cope with but there was one problem she couldn't solve. Green lumber was used over the vigas, or heavy logs, which supported the boards across the ceiling. On top of these, three inches of mud plaster had been smoothed on and on that several inches of dirt were thrown. The result was a continual sifting of dust through the cracks of the lumber as it shrank. During the rainy season trickles of muddy water came down. Most people just moved from under the dust or water, depending on the season.

Mother wanted to put an end to the nuisance. One time when Dad was going to Lincoln on business, she told him to bring back some heavy muslin. She and Josefa tacked it under the vigas, thus making a second ceiling below the first to catch the dust. Neighbors looked at it with admiration when they came to see us.

But Mother's satisfaction was short-lived. Soon bulges, which grew larger as time passed, appeared. The weight of the dust was straining the tacks holding the muslin. Something had to be done. With Josefa to help her, she set a coffee box on top of a table. By standing on it she was able to reach the ceiling. After Josefa handed her Dad's hunting knife, she made a slit in the biggest bulge. As the lump deflated, a washtub caught the dust. With deft stitches she sewed up the hole. This procedure continued until she had emptied the largest pockets of dust. Later when the muslin became streaked with mudstains and the slits too numerous, she replaced the material. This went on for years until Dad finally coated the ceiling with plaster.

About this time a dismal tragedy brought lasting and indescribable grief to the family. I was still quite young at the time. Dad had just returned from Fort Stanton in the afternoon with the mail. Part of his job was to carry the local mail to the fort to be put on the stage headed east; on his return trip he brought back the mail for the settlement. As he turned the sack upside down to empty it, he saw a yellow Western Union envelope that was used to mail telegrams that could not be delivered otherwise. It had on it the San Antonio, New Mexico, postmark, our nearest railway station.

I was playing at the woodshed with an old gristmill when Annie and Winnie came running to tell me the news. I could tell by their faces that something terrible had happened. Annie told me that Aunt Edith and Uncle Fred were dead. I remember wondering whether beautiful Midnight had been killed also. It was some time before the circumstances surrounding their deaths were made known to us. The telegram was a week old when we received it.

We found out later that Aunt Edith, home from St. Louis during her vacation, had set out with Uncle Fred in a light wagon to go to Aztec, a small village about twenty miles away, to transact some business. Their route lay across a ford of the Animas River, which at the time was very high. Even though they were both good swimmers, Fred must have surveyed the rushing water carefully before urging his team into it. But he evidently miscalculated the swiftness of the current and forced the horses into the deeper part. Too late he discovered his mistake. With a tremendous rush the swirling water overturned their wagon and engulfed them both.

When the team came back to the house dragging the doubletrees with river debris still clinging to them, Granmaw Tully was terror-stricken. Running to the nearest neighbor, she told of the team's return and of the disappearance of Fred and Edith. Soon the news spread through the whole area and men started out to find them. At first the search parties hoped they would find them alive, but with the passing hours the grim truth had to be accepted. Two days later Uncle Fred's body was discovered wedged in the crotch of a tree. It was two weeks before Aunt Edith's was found at the headgate of an irrigation ditch. From the evidence put together it was concluded that, in overturning, the wagonbed had been torn loose from the running gear and gashed Fred on the head, either

killing him outright or knocking him unconscious. Edith doubtless was pinned beneath the bed and was drowned.

After Mother had partially recovered from the shock, she
sent her brother Jim, who had come to Coe Ranch sometime
previously to work as a cowboy, to Farmington to get Grandmother and bring her back to live with us. Part of Granmaw
had died with the two children. Stunned by grief, she let Jim
dispose of all her property except a few household possessions
which could be loaded on the wagon. With tear-dimmed eyes
she looked for the last time at the beautiful rosewood piano she
had brought from Chicago. There was not room enough for it
in the wagon, and Jim, impatient to be off, had sold it to a
neighbor rather than make other arrangements to send it to the
ranch.

At the end of her tiresome journey from the San Juan Valley,
Granmaw walked stiffly from the wagon into the outstretched
arms that awaited her at Coe Ranch. When I gave her the
biggest hug I could, she kissed me on the cheek and said I was
as strong as an old bear, which pleased me very much.

The day after Granmaw's coming, the family gathered in the
parlor with joy and anticipation to welcome her into our musical circle. Although I was too young to join it yet, I waited
impatiently for the performance to begin. After Dad had tuned
up his fiddle, he turned to Granmaw and said, "It's been a long
time since you played for us, Granmaw, and we are pleased to
have you join the Coe orchestra. We'd like for you to take your
place now at the piano and start us off with my favorite
march."

Within her sorrowing heart Granmaw was carrying a grief
that she took to the grave; yet she was determined not to allow
it to cast a shadow over the lives of her children and grand-
children. Smiling bravely, she walked over to the piano and
twirled the stool until it was the proper height. As she sat down
she said, "When I had to leave my own piano behind, it was a
great consolation to know I would find another at Coe Ranch.

Thank you for inviting me to become a member of your orchestra."

From then on Granmaw was a participant as well as a strong promoter of music in our valley. She was strong in her belief that it was a binding force that helped hold people together. No matter how much the men wrangled over water rights or fences during the week, come Saturday night the people would all get together for a dance. On Monday they could take up their arguments anew.

From the beginning Granmaw was a strong force in our lives, and to our music she added a fresh impetus. She gave special attention to Sydney and encouraged her to play by note rather than by ear; in the hours spent with Annie she urged a more technical and scientific approach although Annie played the violin and mandolin by note as well as by ear. Agnes never learned to play an instrument but had a very important role in organizing and criticizing the orchestra. She was less tolerant of discords than Granmaw. She insisted that her favorite tunes be played over and over again until we were worn out from her special numbers. She always looked to Granmaw for the final word, for she was awed by Granmaw's rendition of Paderewski's "Minuet" and other classical compositions.

While still not old enough to take much of a part in the musical performances, I had my own problems, some of which were knotty ones. Mother had seen to it that my life was made as nearly normal as possible, so I took part in all the games and sports my sisters and I could devise. But I always had to strive hard to do the things other children did easily. Despite Mother's fears that I would be hurt riding, I was put on a horse as soon as I could hold on to the saddle horn. From that moment it must have been my unswerving ambition to become a cowboy. But not until I was tall enough to reach the saddle horn and had sufficient strength in my arms to lift myself over the horse and into the saddle was I able to make much progress.

To take part in games, I had to learn to handle my partially paralyzed legs well enough to keep up with the other children, and in everything except a foot race I could hold my own. In haying time we climbed up to our cupola playhouse in the hay shed, accessible only after the fresh, fragrant alfalfa had been piled as high as the hayfork and pulley horse could stack it. By grabbing hold of the rope on the pulley track, we were able to shin the rest of the way up to the cupola, which was floored around the sides and open at the center. We took with us our dishes, dolls, kittens, and anything else suitable for a playhouse.

The tougher the game was, the harder I tried to keep up with the others. If Annie, in playing "follow the leader," took us around the edge of the hayloft, where to keep from falling we held precariously to the cracks in the walls and at the same time kept our feet on the narrow side of a two-by-four, I would sweat it out. Or if we found the swallows nesting in the comb of the roof and wanted to dislodge them by tearing down their nests, I was the first to reach them because this involved swinging by the arms on the rafters and here, with my strong arm and chest muscles, I had the advantage. To get down, we just dropped to the hay below.

Getting to the Coe schoolhouse a mile away presented a problem that I tackled with all the ingenuity I possessed. My first year I trained a team of dogs to pull a little red wagon over the trail through a little canyon. But the uphill stretch was too much for them so I had to walk or ride my "stick-horse," pushing as best I could with my legs. It was a speedy method. Uncle Austin once told my dad he had seen me "skedaddle off across the mesa faster'n a jack rabbit," a comparison that pleased me even though I knew it would have to be a crippled rabbit he was talking about.

In bad weather I rode my pony Kate. But she had to be tied up and fed, so I preferred the dogs, Towser and Tag, hitched to the wagon. I even tried a team of goats. They were so hard to handle I ended by picking out a husky calico-colored wether and putting shafts to my wagon. But I still had to walk up hill.

So I sought out old Miguel Sedillo, our goat herder, who had a couple of burros he used for packing camp gear. We always called him "Hoso" because, like a bear, he liked to eat raw meat. ("Hoso" was our own pronunciation of the Spanish "oso," meaning bear.) As he didn't need his burros at the time, he let me try out my scheme. This necessitated making a larger wagon, which brought on more difficulties than I had anticipated.

One of Hoso's burros was slow, lazy and stubborn while the other, though faster, was twice as obstinate. As I never liked to be late anywhere and since I could not predict the burros' moods, I left early to allow for them. On the uphill climb, their added pull made my trips pleasurable until a contrary streak hit them just as the cart and I were slanted at a sharp angle. This happened once when the very stubborn one balked and sat down, so I gave him a sharp crack with my stick. He jumped as if he had been stung by a bumblebee, breaking the single tree and turning the wagon over on top of me. Then they both pulled loose from the wagon tongue and started for home, leaving me to get there as best I could.

But I did not give up. Not much later as I was leaving the ranch in a hurry to get to school, one of the burros took a stubborn spell just as Hoso happened to be coming along. He watched me for a while, grinning through his yellow teeth which were pointed like a bear's, and then said, "Pícale la cruz," which meant to take the sharp point of my stick and punch the burro in a tender spot where the color of the hair on top of the shoulders forms a cross. It worked like magic. But it was so sudden it turned over the wagon and I landed on my head.

I decided then that if two burros could give as much trouble as those had caused me, one would make only half as much. After hours of work in the shop I fastened a pair of shafts to the cart and drove a single burro. This was a fairly dependable system, and to share my success some of the other kids sat across the rear end and dragged their feet in the dust. My last year in the Glencoe school, I went back to riding my little pony Kate. She was small enough for me to get on and off easily. She always waited until I climbed on, and when I pulled up the reins she was ready to go. She could pace and single foot in addition to the standard gaits. I always carried my lunch and a bag full of oats for Katie tied to the saddle horn.

By the time I was old enough to go to school, the Coe children and a few others belonging to nearby settlers nearly filled the room. In Uncle George's family there were Grace, Will, Roy, who was my best pal, and Mina. Uncle Japs' numbered nine: Lily, Ross, Ed, Charlie, Harvey, Ben, Sadie, Bertha, and Jessie. And from our own family there were Sydney, Annie, Winnie, Agnes, Edith, Helena, and I, making a grand total of nineteen Coes!

Learning was never taken too seriously by any of us. But in our family hookey was not frequent because of Mother's stern ideas about the importance of education. Miss Ward, the teacher when I started to school, was also an example of correct demeanor to my sisters. She was so painfully modest that it was embarrassing for her to get on a horse for fear she would show her ankle or maybe the calf of her leg. Once primly mounted on her sidesaddle, she would blushingly pull down the long skirt of her riding habit so that only the tips of her shoes showed. To make sure none of us kids saw her mount, she would leave very early for school, and by the time the children arrived, she'd be changed into her regular clothes. I doubt she approved of my sisters in their divided skirts riding astride a cowboy saddle. Obviously her desire to be a lady was greater than her wish to be a good horsewoman, for her riding did not improve.

During vacation Mother kept Miss Ward with us so we could go on with our studies. However, at the end of the second session she left us, greatly to Mother's sorrow, for she knew it would be hard to find another such ladylike person to take her place. But losing such a fine teacher was only one of Mother's educational problems. The Coe school was becoming overcrowded as new settlers came into the valley. Overage and indifferent to learning as some of them were, they did what they could to make life miserable for the teacher. In time Mother knew she would have to find other means to get us the kind of education she wanted for us.

She had tried to do this on a previous occasion with disastrous results. When Winnie and Annie were in the fourth grade, she took them to Roswell to put them in school. There the specter of Billy the Kid arose, as it did on many occasions, and put an end to her plans. Well-meaning friends of the family with whom the two girls were boarding advised them not to harbor any of Frank Coe's children under their roof. It was unthinkable that anyone related to a McSween sympathizer be sheltered there. Chagrined and angry, Mother brought them back to the ranch and enrolled them in the Coe school again.

When that session ended, Mother began her routine "house cleaning," which entailed setting up living quarters down by the river not far from the house. To this spot we took our bedclothes, cooking utensils, and food staples. We made an arbor where we cooked and slept during the renovations. Mother and Josefa, with whatever help they could get from Timio and Fabián, scrubbed, painted, put new straw in the bedticks, washed and ironed curtains, and did other things necessary to get the house ready for another year.

When the wind blew the cupola off the hay shed, Dad had it moved down by the river. Mother used it for a summerhouse. Tents were set up nearby to sleep in. When weather permitted, the cooking was done outside. We children peeled tubfuls of peaches and pears, which were cooked in the big iron pots and put into large glass jars to be stored away for winter use. We were always sorry to return to our regular quarters.

CHAPTER VI

My Trips with Dad
and Attending the "Baptist College"

ONE TIME when several bushels of peaches were in the summerhouse waiting to be peeled, I was delighted that Dad asked me to go with him on a trip to the Spindle Saw Mill in the Capitán Mountains for a load of lumber. In preparation for the drive we put on the brake block a new lining, made from the leather of an old boot. We stored necessary supplies in the chuck box and tied it on the running gears of the wagon, along with log chains, bedrolls, ax, pick, and a shovel. We took the short cut, which began over the mesa in front of the house and required going down the banks of arroyos, picking our way among trees, and loosening large boulders enough to push them out of our way. If Dad could not maneuver the teams around the smaller trees, he had to cut them down.

At the end of the first day we stopped at Capitán Gap. While Dad hobbled the horses, I gathered firewood. As I was doing this, I spied some wild turkeys coming toward the spring, so I alerted Dad, who grabbed his rifle and shot down a couple. We cleaned and fried the young one and hung the other in the cool night air. After supper we took a final look at the horses and then climbed into our bedrolls. Silence was all about us. Suddenly a coyote that had probably smelled the turkey gave a blood-curdling yelp, the most terrifying sound I had ever heard. Inching closer to Dad, I huddled against his back and whispered something about the coyotes being after the turkey. To satisfy me, he fired his rifle a few times in the direction of the howling. After that all was quiet and I soon fell asleep.

We rolled out of our blankets in the brisk morning air and cooked breakfast. After hitching the teams we started on our way, taking the other turkey as a present for Andy Richardson, the manager of the Block Ranch Store. He welcomed us warmly and called a cowboy to take care of our teams. Then we went inside.

It still lacked an hour until dinnertime and Andy, after filling my pockets with gumdrops and licorice, took Dad into a back room, leaving me to amuse myself. Fascinated, I began to wander around, chewing on some licorice. I walked the length of the long room, which was lined on either side by shelves of merchandise, filling my mouth with more licorice. I wanted to save my gumdrops to take home for a candy-spitting contest with my sisters. (The object of this game was to put a gumdrop in your mouth, spit quickly, and then let someone guess what flavor it was.) Evidently a big-wheeled freighter had recently come in from Las Vegas, for a lot of merchandise was heaped on the floor inside the front door—sacks of flour, bundled slickers, coils of rope, a dozen ax handles wired together, a stack of leather gloves tied in a bunch, and other mercantile supplies. To the side was a fifty-gallon barrel of whisky, which I somehow connected with the prolonged stay of Andy and Dad in the back room.

I wandered in this direction and came to the section where there were some ready-made clothes—chiefly socks, work pants, and men's long drawers in two parts. Behind a showcase filled with smaller items such as combs, shoelaces, and buttons were the yard goods; boots and shoes hung on nails driven into an upright two-by-four. Their leathery smell combined with the odor of hemp rope and coal oil from lanterns. A sign on a stack of Navajo blankets read "six cents a pound." Sitting on them to wait until dinnertime, I looked around at all the commodities on nails, pegs, shelves, or propped against the wall—saws, harnesses, kerosene, lamps, coffee grinders, rubber boots, kegs of horseshoe nails, buggy whips, and wooden buckets of candy. The smell of vinegar came from the grocery supplies. Curious to know what was on the labels of patent-medicine bottles next to the canned goods, I went over to read them. Some were for livestock, such as White Horse Liniment, "guaranteed to cure all the external ailments of man or beast." Across the room was medicine of a different kind—guns and ammunition.

Then spying some spurs suspended from a horse collar on the wall, I took one and ran the rowel over my stern to see how it felt on the side of a horse. At that moment the front door opened and a bunch of Block cowboys came in, pulling at their gunbelts and taking off their gloves. I was quick to spy Ross Coe, who was the best-looking one in the bunch. He was Uncle Jap's son. When he saw me he smiled and came over to shake hands, telling the others that I was his cowboy cousin from over on the Ruidoso. I told him I had come with Dad to get some lumber and that he and Andy had gone into the back room. Ross winked at the others and said something about "Uncle Frank probably was bitten by a snake coming through the gap." They all laughed at that. Then Ross put his arm around my shoulder and drew me to the back of the store where there were some rickety slat-bottomed chairs, most of which were wired at the rungs. I could not have been any happier, for Ross was my idol and as handsome and daring a cowboy as there was in the territory. I wanted nothing more in life than to be like him—which was a big order for a small fry like me.

As we reached the rear of the store, Dad and Andy came out of the back room, refreshed and smiling. At this moment Doc, one of the Negro boys who worked in the kitchen, banged a hammer against a plowshare hanging outside on a post and yelled, "Yawl come'n git it." We went through a door to the dining room at the back and ate hungrily of steak, gravy, biscuits, and a big helping of prunes, a traditional dish at Block Ranch. I looked at the weather-beaten faces of the cowboys, the rope burns and scars on their hands, the lips swollen and cracked by wind and sun, and wished I would hurry up and become like them.

In a short time chairs scraped on the floor as the men finished eating and returned to their loafing place in the back of the store. There they sat picking their teeth, smoking, chewing tobacco, and talking for a while before going back to work. They listened with interest to news Dad gave them of the Ruidoso Valley. Then the conversation turned to a nester named Hunt who had recently moved into the area with his family. I thought he must be an awful scoundrel from the way they talked about him.

Imagine my surprise the next morning when Dad told me we were going over to the Hunt place to look at a water system supplied from a spring high up in the mountains by means of a wooden flume. We followed a lonely trail until we came to their isolated cabin situated comfortably in an oasis of green. Clear mountain water sparkled as it traveled down the flume to supply the needs of the Hunts. Four or five of the nester's children saw us coming up the wagon road and ran for cover like scared rabbits. Then from their hiding places they peeked at us and whispered to one another.

Hunt came out, cradling his rifle in his arm and looking surly and unfriendly. Abruptly he inquired about our business. Dad explained who he was and why he had come; only then did the nester show some friendliness. He walked ahead, leading the way to the barn, where he helped us unhitch and throw some hay to the horses. Then he took us to the house and introduced us to his wife telling her (to this lonesome lady's pleasure) that we were going to stay overnight.

By this time the children had emerged shyly from the bushes and had come up to me, asking if I would like to get a drink. We went to the trough and I eagerly lowered my face into the flume where the water was running rapidly. Then I learned why the Hunt kids were so eager for me to get a drink. When I put my mouth into the water, I filled my nose as well and brought my face up, coughing, sputtering, and strangling, much to the delight of the other youngsters.

We spent the remainder of the afternoon looking over the water system, for Dad was always interested in anything that transported water from one place to another. Hunt explained that the two-mile flume worked well except when a bear or deer knocked off a section of its props. It aslo sometimes became clogged with leaves or pine needles and cones. Hunt seemed proud of his oldest son, who had helped figure out the system. Later I came to admire the ingenious mind of this boy, Orville, who came in about dark from a hunting trip. At the time he was planning to join up with one of the big ranch outfits.

When we said good-bye to the Hunts the next morning, I was still wondering why the cowboys at the Block Store had called them such awful names. Over a rough, winding road we reached the heart of the Capitán timber country about noon. Dad loaded all the lumber he thought our teams could pull, and climbing on top of it we headed for the gap where we had spent the night on our way over. From there we kept to the main road through the Bonito Valley, not daring to risk the short cut with such a heavy load. At Las Chozas we turned off and took the San Patricio trail over which Dad and Billy the Kid had ridden many times. It was rough enough and the descent of one hill was so steep that even with the brakes locked, the wheels skidded so much that we had to cut down a big piñon tree to use as a drag behind the wagon. At dark the second day we arrived home. Mother had kept some supper for us on the back of the stove. I was almost too tired to eat, and as I started to my room, I heard Dad say, "Helnee-Anne, if we just had water like that up at the Hunt place, you could have water running right into your kitchen."

Edith, who had been disappointed because she did not get to go to the lumber mill, had been promised a trip to the V-V

Ranch. More than a year had passed since Mr. Cree had stocked his V-V range with a large herd of Black Angus cattle imported from his native Scotland.

Dad was eager to see them and find out how they were doing and what advantages they had, if any, over the white-faced Hereford. One day Dad, Edith, and I set out on horse-back headed for the V-V Ranch. On the way we stopped at the Brown place on Little Creek to visit with them and get the local news. They were friends we met at the camp meeting every summer. It was getting late and they insisted that we stay with them for the night. Edith and I were pleased when Dad consented. The Browns had children our age and we knew we would have a great time together.

Near noon the next day we reached the V-V Ranch. As we came near the headquarters we could see the house and build-ings in a green valley surrounded by pine, juniper, piñon, and cedar on two sides and by a rough high country combed with steep hills and canyons to the south. Like those of the Block Ranch, the Cree holdings were vast. More than a thousand longhorn cattle, along with some three or four hundred Black Angus, roamed over thousands of acres of open range. As we rode up to the house, I looked at a fresh-killed beef hanging up in a juniper tree in the yard and anticipated some good steaks for dinner.

Mrs. Cree, who spoke with a real Scotch burr, came out to welcome us. A cowboy took our horses and we went inside. We talked for a while and then she showed us around the house, which was built of native stone. When we had finished looking at the ground floor, she took us into the kitchen, from which we descended by means of a trap door to the clean, cool stone-lined cellar. She lit a lantern and by its yellow light we could see shelves along the walls filled with canned fruit and vegeta-bles. Above a potato bin was a shelf of homemade yellow soap, and in stone crocks on the floor were eggs stored in coarse stock salt ready for the slack season. As Mrs. Cree swung her lantern from one display of food to another I kept wondering where a sickening smell was coming from. Everything was immaculately clean. Edith must have caught a whiff of it too, for she nudged me and held her nose.

We soon found out. As we proceeded farther to a back part of the cellar Mrs. Cree held her lantern high and pointed proudly to twenty or twenty-five dressed chickens hanging on wires stretched across the ceiling. She explained they were being "cured" according to the Scottish custom. This made them much more palatable. They had a golden color and the odor was stronger now, making me feel as if I wanted to vomit. I was glad we did not stay long. I made up my mind then that if I ever traveled to Scotland I would never eat chicken because I would still see them hanging by their skinny legs and smelling to high heaven.

When the dinner gong sounded a short time later I sat down as hungry as the others. Mr. Cree and some cowboys who had been on a coyote hunt joined us. Mrs. Cree's hired girl, Ida Barrett, helped her bring the food to the table. From my chair next to Dad I began looking up and down the table for the steak. But instead of huge portions of beef in rich brown gravy, there was a mound of fried chicken on a blue-willow platter. I began to have a funny feeling in my stomach all over again as visions of yellow malodorous chickens floated before my eyes. As Mrs. Cree started the plate of it around, she said, "I know you folks can have fresh beef any time so I cooked some chicken for you as a special treat."

Dad lifted his eyebrows when he saw me dig around for the smallest piece of chicken on the plate. When the mashed potatoes came around, I put a big pile of them on, almost covering up the meat. By taking a nibble of chicken and following it with a big forkful of potatoes or a huge bite of biscuit, I managed to get rid of most of it. Later when the platter went around again, Dad gave me another quizzical look when I didn't take any. Three helpings of potatoes and as many of biscuits made my stomach feel as if it was ready to burst, but when Ida put a succulent cherry cobbler on the table I scooped a large portion onto my plate. Where I would have room for it, I did not know.

After we left the table, I sank heavily and drowsily into a rocker in the sitting room and began to thumb through a gun catalogue. Mrs. Cree and Edith went into the bedroom to look at some "pretties." She was particularly struck by Edith's winsome ways and brought out her beads, earrings, and dresses to show her. Her new lavender-and-yellow foulard she had bought especially to wear at the next camp meeting. Edith admired everything, but what really took her eye was a pair of hand-made riding boots Mrs. Cree pulled from under the bed, still in a box. Edith was delighted when she asked her to try them on. Then Edith was asked to walk up and down the room in them. Convinced that they fit her well, allowing some room for her feet to grow, Mrs. Cree told Edith she could keep them. Then she explained they were too small for her own feet, and having noticed Edith's small ones, size three, she wanted her to have them. She could never thank Mrs. Cree enough for "the prettiest boots in New Mexico."

When we left the next day Edith had them on and through the years they remained her most cherished possession to be worn only on Sundays, Fourth of July celebrations, and other special occasions. Today they are in the Lincoln Museum.

While Miss Ward was with us we had to keep on with our studies even during the summer vacation, but after she left we spent more time studying music. Practice on the piano, guitar, violin, and mandolin went on at all times under the guidance of Granmaw and Mother. I was now becoming more actively interested in participating in the family musical performances, and toward that end Winnie had given me some preliminary lessons on a guitar Granmaw had purchased from a mail-order house. I was always Winnie's pet, but that did not keep her from threatening me with horrible punishments if ever I got any scratches on her guitar.

That is why I was glad Dad decided to take her with him to Nogal Lake to help round up his herd of goats. Raising goats was a profitable side line of Coe Ranch, their fine mohair bringing in top market prices. Winnie wanted to go with him yet she hated to leave her guitar in my custody. I had to cross my heart a dozen times and promise her I would not let any harm come to it when I went out to the woodshed to practice. I never wanted anyone to hear me make so many sour notes, especially Granmaw, so I usually went there or to the buggy shed.

However, Winnie soon forgot about her guitar as she rode away with Dad early in the morning. When they arrived at Nogal Lake in the afternoon they found Hoso camping at a brush hut near the flock. Dad and Winnie began at once to fan out through the brush and drive the goats out into the open mesa. This took two or three hours, and by the time the last strays had been rounded up it was too late to start back home. They had not brought bedrolls so they had to look for some place to spend the night.

A Gallegos family that Dad knew lived in the vicinity, so they rode in that direction. As they approached the house, Torivio came outside and told "Meester Covo" and his "niña linda" he was glad to see them. Dad explained his predicament and was given a cordial invitation to spend the night with them. "Ésta es su casa" Torivio kept saying as he helped them put up their horses and feed them some hay. When they went into the house, his wife, who was turning tortillas on the stove, told them the comida was ready. Not long after they ate they were shown one of the two beds in the one room that housed the adults and their numerous children. After they removed their boots they dropped gratefully on the uncomfortable mattress and were soon asleep.

How long Winnie slept she did not know, but suddenly she

awoke, sat straight up, and began scratching in a dozen places at once. About the same time Dad, who rarely swore, came to a sitting position and said, "Damn." It still lacked some time until daylight so all they could do was sit in' the bed, miserable and desperate, and fight the bedbugs. They could not offend their host by telling him their trouble. He was snoring peacefully in the other bed with the pests probably crawling all over him. Never were two people so happy to see daylight. Getting out of bed, Dad explained to Torivio that they wanted to make an early start back to the ranch. By the time they arrived home both had welts all over them. Mother forbade them to come into the house until they had soaked themselves and their clothes in coal oil. Winnie was hardly rid of her welts by schooltime and wore long sleeves to cover the spots on her arms.

That year I did not return to the Coe school. Mother enrolled me in the new "Baptist College" in Alamogordo where the George Coe family had moved so that their children might receive a better education. I was not very enthusiastic about it, but since Roy and I were good pals the outlook was not too bad. Never away from home before, I needed something as strong as our bond of friendship to help me to go over fifty miles from the ranch. While Mother kept talking about all the educational advantages I would have, I was thinking of all the good times Roy and I would enjoy. That was important to a boy not yet twelve.

My departure was set for around Christmas time when Red Ketchum, one of our ranch hands, was going to Alamogordo with a load of Ben Davis apples. When the actual moment for leaving came, I began to wonder whether my friendship with Roy was important enough to induce me to leave home. Coe Ranch was my entire world and I loved every rock, tree, and mesquite clump on it. Besides, I wanted to be a cowboy and I could not see why book learning was so necessary if all a fellow wanted to do was to ride and rope.

There was an awful lump in my throat when Red pulled up in front of the house and I went outside to climb up on the wagon seat beside him. I tried to get rid of it by biting off a piece of apple, but that made it bigger. All I could do was give Mother a bear hug and climb on the seat as quickly as possible. When we reached the main road, Red took out a red bandanna and told me to blow hard and be careful not to catch a cold. It is a wonder that I did not catch one for sure because that night we had to sleep under the wagon in the bitter freezing weather. By the time we reached Uncle George's next day several inches of snow had fallen.

The following day I enrolled in school and began to look around for all the advantages Mother had talked about. There were several teachers instead of just one, and I was in a room with only two grades rather than eight. Even though I did not think it was such a big improvement I put more than my usual effort into studying so that I could make good grades to take home to Mother and Dad. Chiefly I lived for the end of classes so Roy and I, after our chores were done, could get together and play marbles. Our usual companion was Lonny Buck, a little older than we and the son of the local livery-stable owner. We three formed a sort of syndicate. Before long our pockets bulged with winnings and we had extended our territory to include some of the town boys, whose marbles we eventually pocketed.

Unaware that our sport was being frowned upon by anyone, we put in extra time as the spring days lengthened. We wanted to crown our success by challenging a bunch of experts from the other side of town to a game at recess one Friday in the schoolyard. When the time came a gang of five toughies sauntered boldly on to the grounds. They showed their contempt for us in every swaggering step. Bragging they could beat us mama-boys, they knelt and started to do some fancy flips. Soon Roy, Lonny, and I began to compete our best shots with theirs as some students gathered around to watch the contest. We placed a heavy strain on our knees as we got down in all sorts of positions to make classic shots and then rake in the winnings. Never had our luck been better. We were so flushed with success that we paid no attention to some teachers who were watching us from the school building. They must have looked shocked when they saw the company we were keeping and the pastime in which we were engaged.

When the bell rang we pocketed our winnings and our adversaries skulked off toward the town. Happy with some marbles that were exceptionally pretty, I held out a handful of agates to show a lady teacher as I entered the door. It was then the trap was sprung. She took my marbles as evidence and herded us all into the principal's office. He was a lean, bespectacled, sober-faced man who asked us whether we had been playing marbles. We all told him we had and wondered why he looked so solemn over a game in which we had not had a fight or even a bad argument.

Then he came to the point. "Were you playing for keeps?"

We said that we were. Then he went on to repeat the question and added something about having in our possession property taken in a game of chance. We had not heard marbles called that before, but we readily admitted that we had.

For some time the principal reflected on the seriousness of the situation. Then he asked, "Don't you boys know it's a sin to gamble? And besides being a sin, it's against the rules of the school."

Since we did not know what he was talking about, we did not say anything. When he saw that we were not repentant, he became more angry and told us we had to stay after school and receive our punishment. When he said that, he pulled a strap from his desk drawer. In the meantime he said we would remain out of classes. Then he escorted us down the hall to a dusty storeroom, which smelled of wet mops and kerosene. In it were stored some broken desks, mop pails, brooms, and an empty coal-oil can. He took one of the mop pails and told us to empty our pockets into it, after which he stalked out of the room, locking the door behind him.

We certainly did not waste any time repenting. We were too angry. Instead, we began to look for a way to get out of the place. High up in the wall was a small window that swung out on hinges at the top. If we could get to it, we could drop to the outside. But there was the problem of getting away before someone caught us. The odds were against my being able to run fast enough to escape, so I begged Roy and Lonny to go on without me. They would not hear of such a thing. Then Lonny came up with an idea that sounded all right; he would slip out, hurry to the livery stable for his pony, and come back after Roy and me.

We lost no time in putting this into action. By boosting Lonny, we were able to get him high enough for him to catch hold of the ledge. The rest was easy, and in seconds we heard him hit the ground and run from the building. Roy and I waited tensely. Just when we were about to give up hope, we heard hoofbeats clicking down the street. A soft whistle told us Lonny was outside so Roy gave me a boost and I pulled myself to the window ledge. By propping one of the broken desks against the wall, Roy was able to get to the ledge. In no time we were on the pony behind Lonny and flew down the street with me holding on to Lonny and Roy to me.

Later when I thought about this ride, I recalled how Billy the Kid had made his escape from the courthouse in Lincoln. When Mother was not around, our old cook, who had worked at the jail in Lincoln, would tell me about how the Kid had escaped the hangman's noose awaiting him behind the court-house. (Goss, the cook, was a native of Germany and had come here to escape conscription.) At Billy's behest he had chopped off his big irons and had brought him a deputy's horse to ride. I doubt that the sweet breath of liberty smelled any better to the Kid on that day than it did to me the time I rode from the school with Roy and Lonny.

At the livery stable Lonny's dad, a burly Irishman, vowed that the first one to get licked would be the principal. To make good his word, he rode off at once to find him. After taking a good look at the muscular frame of Lonny's father, the principal must have decided the boy had not committed such a great crime after all, for he assured him his son would not be punished. Roy's fate furthermore would be determined by his own dad.

That left my own still in the balance. As I believed I had done nothing wrong, I did not want to take a whipping. I spent the weekend pondering the matter. My parents had brought me up to be self-reliant so I knew that if I got into trouble I would have to find my own way out. Obviously I would be expelled if I did not accept punishment of some kind, so I decided I did not want to stay at the school any longer, however close my friendship with Roy was. It could never take the place of my pony and my family.

Later in the week Red happened to bring in a load of mohair, so I packed my things and returned to the ranch with him. If Mother was disappointed to see my education at the school come to an end, she did not show it. Dad did not try to hide his disdain for the incident or his amusement at our escape. The first thing I did was to get on my pony and go for a ride. With spring in the air, apple blossoms spreading their fragrance, and the winds of April fanning my face, how could I not be brimful of happiness?

CHAPTER VII

Going to School in Roswell
and Vacations on the Ranch

S MUCH AS SHE WANTED ME to get an education, I think that Granmaw was also glad to see me back. I was her favorite so she did not punish me as often as she did my sisters. Her presence was felt in many ways and we all loved her. Whenever we would hurt ourselves we would run to her room so she could rub us with her soothing salves or ointments or give us some little sugar pills she always kept on hand. We would go out of our way to find excuses to take these.

In sports as well as in music Granmaw encouraged us so long as our fun did not involve too much risk. She could never forget the tragedy that took the lives of Fred and Edith. Especially did she caution us about going too near the water. For her own amusement and exercise she sent away for a croquet game, which she set up on a level spot near a chokecherry tree behind the house. There was one bad feature to the arrangement. The wickets had been lined up on a direct route to the backhouse, and if it was dark or we were in a hurry, there was a good chance we would catch a foot in one of them and go tumbling head first into the ditch or the backhouse. Even Granmaw herself took some spills.

Eager to keep up with her cultural pursuits, Granmaw practiced on the piano and on an organ that she had bought from a mail-order house. She spent many hours poring over the *Étude* magazine. I have heard Dad say that she tried her hand at writing magazine articles, but what she did with them I do not know.

Since the matter of my education was of deep concern to her

as well as to my parents, she heartily concurred with Mother and Dad when they decided to send me to school in Roswell. With the arrival of the fall term Dad took me to board with the Hugh Miller family, who lived on East College Boulevard.

I was homesick sometimes and lonesome for the ranch, but one thing I could always do to amuse myself and to pass the time was to talk over the fence at the Billy Matthews place to their yardman, "Laughin'" Joe, the one who had been sent with Zebrioen Bates to dig the grave for John Tunstall at the McSween home in Lincoln. In his later years "Laughin'" Joe carried with him an affliction supposedly put on him by drunks and bullies back in the old days when they would pull out their six-shooters, pump lead at his feet, and order him to "Dance for us, Joe, or get your toes shot off." And poor, scared Joe would jig and laugh until he was exhausted. This prolonged nervous laughing grew into a trait that habitually took him over. As I would pass by he would prop himself against the fence or lean on his rake waiting for someone to come along and say something to make him laugh. He would beg any passer-by to tell him a funny story. Even if it was not funny, he would throw back his head and laugh anyway.

After the Lincoln County War he and Bates stayed around the town. Joe eventually went to work for Billy Matthews in Roswell; Bates made his home at the George Coe ranch. Born Zebrioen Bates of slave parents, according to his own recollection, he possessed a musical talent which was early recognized by his mistress at the plantation house. Subsequently she gave him music lessons as well as teaching him to read and write. He progressed so well that she allowed him to accompany her at the piano with his violin at the social gatherings. Dad had first heard him play at a saloon in Lincoln and had remarked to Uncle George at the time that it was the sweetest violin music he had ever heard. At a later time Mrs. McSween hired him to work for her, and there it was that Uncle George found him one day suffering from an agonizing hangover.

Bates, it was well attested, could not resist whisky, which kept him drunk or broke or both most of the time. On this occasion he begged Uncle George to take him up to his ranch away from the saloons. In exchange for a place to live, he would help with the work and give music lessons to George's children on any instrument they wished. He would never frequent the saloons again, or so he said. Uncle George promised "Mr." Bates, as he always called him (believing that anyone who could play so well was deserving of the title), that he would talk it over with his wife. Not long after, Uncle George came to Lincoln with an extra horse for Bates to ride back to the ranch.

Except for the drinking part of the bargain, Bates kept his word. Only on infrequent occasions did the temptation to visit the saloons get the best of him; then he would fail to return to the ranch, so Uncle George would ride over to Lincoln, sober him up, and bring him home.

In music Bates was a fine artist and a perfectionist. He took the young Coes one by one and gave them half-hour sessions in which he patiently explained the scales, notes, tempos, and chords. In addition to the George Coe children he taught all seven of us. If I ever entertained any doubt that I wanted to be a cowboy, it was when I wanted to be as good a fiddler as Zebrioen Bates. Long before I had developed sufficient skill to play in the family orchestra I bribed him to let me play with it by sneaking some whisky from the bottle in Mother's cabinet and hiding it out at the woodpile. During the evening he would make frequent trips there, caring less and less about my sour notes though normally he would hate them. But not so with Agnes. She would glare at me and threaten to put me out if I did not play correctly.

Seeing "Laughin'" Joe would make me think of Bates, and then I would feel homesick for the ranch. Schoolwork did not leave me much time to improve my music, but I always managed to find some time to practice. It was not long before I was a member of another marble syndicate which congregated on Saturdays in a vacant lot next to the old post office, where the White Building now stands. Before the season was over I had collected several cigar boxes full of marbles. However, I missed the final tournament of my first year because of an unexpected trip to the ranch.

Since Dad had written me to take the stage to Picacho, forty miles west of Roswell where he would pick me up, I packed a few clothes and reached the stage stop downtown early on a chilly morning. In my haste and excitement I had not brought a coat and I stood shivering in the cold morning air waiting for Jim Gonzáles, the stage driver. Jim made the run from Roswell to Lincoln, which required a day each way, carrying the mail and any passengers there might be.

Shortly before the stage arrived another passenger walked up so we both climbed on the back seat when Jim came. My traveling companion was a solemn, dignified gentleman of middle years who seemed also to feel the rawness of the morning air for he spread over him a laprobe he had carried over his arm. He gave me a questioning look as I sat down beside him, barely able to keep my teeth from chattering. My shaking became so obvious climbing Six-mile Hill that he tucked part of his robe around me.

Thus far he had not said a word, but as we enjoyed the warmth of the robe he began to talk some. He asked me my name and where I was going. When I told him my dad was Frank Coe, he smiled a little and said he knew him well. Then he told me his name was Francisco Salazar. He was the husband of Sara Baca, who had witnessed the slaying of Sheriff Brady. After that he lapsed into silence, leaving me with nothing to do but think how hungry I was. I had rushed off from the boardinghouse without my usual big breakfast. It was a bothersome thought too, for I knew there was little hope for food at the Diamond-A Ranch, where we would make a brief halt so Jim could change horses.

When the sun rose higher overhead we pulled down the robe and I looked over the endless rolling land hoping to spot a herd of antelope or maybe a lobo. But it was hard to get my mind off my stomach. The continual bouncing of the hack made it worse, for Jim in order to keep his schedule drove as if the devil were after us. My rump ached from the jouncing of the worn springs of the seat, and as I squirmed about trying to relieve my discomfort, Salazar gave me a searching look and asked me whether I'd like Jim to stop the hack for a minute. I blushed and explained that I was just tired of sitting still so long. He settled back in silence. After a while Señor Salazar reached down at his feet, opened a leather satchel, and pulled out a paper bag. Then looking at me, he asked, "Tienes hambre, muchacho?"

I replied, "Tengo mucho." He seemed pleased that I knew even that much of the language. He reached into the sack and pulled out an orange, which he cut into four sections with his pocketknife and then handed to me. Then as he prepared his own I began on mine, chewing slowly to make it last longer.

As we were approaching the stage stop my companion asked me whether I had brought my lunch. When I told him I had not he looked very concerned. I did not feel any better when he said the old Mexican at the shack might have a pot of coffee on the stove. Old man Gonzáles, he said, was too stingy to feed his horses, let alone provide enough for his stable helper. Shortly the driver pulled up at a small shack near a corral. There was no protection for the horses and little for his worker. We climbed down, rubbing our rear ends. Miserably I followed Salazar into the hut, hoping for at least a cold tortilla. The stove had two legs propped on rocks and on it was a coffeepot with the lid wired on. Salazar poured some into a couple of tin cups on the table. I noticed that he had brought in a sack and the most I could hope for was another orange. Instead he brought out a big ham sandwich and handed it to me. I have been hungry many times, but nothing ever tasted so good as that. In the bag was another for himself and he washed it down with the bitter coffee.

We had hardly finished when Jim stuck his head inside the door and yelled, "Vámonos. No hay tiempo pa' perder." When we reached the stage he slapped the reins over the backs of the horses, shouted at the team and we lurched forward on the last leg of our journey. This was a rougher stretch because much of the road was over rocky ledges. At Border Hill we had to slow down, and to make the grade, Salazar and Jim walked beside the hack. The worst of the drive was downhill the last few miles before we reached Picacho. As the stage dropped off the ledges, we were jerked from side to side. When the back wheels slid, the hack pushed the rumps of the ponies until their neck yokes pulled their collars up around their ears. They stayed there until they outran their collars. At the foot of Picacho Hill the horses jumped ahead three times before the collars slipped from behind their ears back to their shoulders. From there on the road wound through the mesquite and sand dunes, which often caused the carriage to tilt dangerously. Nothing stopped the tireless trot of the wiry little Mexican ponies Salazar and I had dubbed "rats." They knew they were getting near the end of their run because at Picacho Jim changed teams again.

A German named Klein ran the store and kept the post office at Picacho. I asked for my dad, who was to meet me there, and found out he had not arrived yet. But I was not too concerned. The proprietor placed a coffeepot, crackers, and a can of sardines on the counter and Salazar carefully counted out fifteen cents. He then asked me to share his supper. Jim bought a nickel's worth of cheese and put it between pieces of tortilla from his pocket.

When we finished eating and Dad still had not arrived, I began to get worried. I did not have money for a night's lodging. Not knowing what to do, I explained my predicament to my benefactor. There was no time to talk it over, for Jim was already hustling the mail sack to the stage. Salazar advised me to get back on the stage and ride on down to the Picacho bridge near which the Miller family lived. He was sure they would put me up for the night. I followed him to the hack and got in again, hoping the wind would be in our favor this time, for Jim had bought a fresh plug of tobacco and was cutting off a big hunk.

After a short ride we reached the bridge and I told Jim to stop. But before handing me my suitcase, he asked me to pay my fare. As Dad had told me he would take care of it on my arrival in Picacho, I did not have the money. All I could do was to assure him my father would pay him the next time he went to Lincoln. But that did not satisfy Jim. He wanted his dinero and he wanted it now so he could continue his trip without any more loss of time. During this exchange Salazar listened with an annoyed expression. After Jim had told me for the fifteenth time that he wanted his dinero and his boss did not allow him to give free rides, Salazar asked impatiently, "How much money do you want?" Jim told him the amount and he reached inside his coat and pulled out a long wallet from which he took a bill of large denomination. Jim did not have the change and began yelling louder than ever. By the look on Salazar's face, I felt sure that he would be glad to get rid of me at any price so he promised Jim that he would get the bill changed at Lincoln and pay him. I thanked my traveling companion and assured him Dad would pay him on his next trip to Lincoln, after which Jim handed me my suitcase and yelled at the team.

It was getting dark as I stood watching the stage disappear, and I felt very forlorn. In the dim light I could barely make out the Miller place across the river, so I began to hobble over the bridge. The weight of the suitcase dragged at me so I put it under some brush. A dog ran out and barked at me as I drew nearer the house. He was followed by a man who, on seeing me, sent the dog back and came to meet me. When I told him who I was and how I happened to be there, he took me into the house and told me that he was a friend of my father and I was welcome to stay there until he came. His wife was already putting some cold biscuits, jelly, and milk on the table, and before we sat down we heard the dog barking again, followed by the sound of a team and wagon coming up the road from the bridge. It was Dad.

After he and Miller had put the team up they came into the kitchen and we all ate. As we did so Dad told us why he was late. It was because of a rambunctious horse he was trying to break. The bronc, disliking the strange feel of the harness on his back and the pull of the wagon, had run away and broken the doubletrees, which Dad then had to have repaired.

Next morning when we started out I was afraid to cross the rough log-plank bridge with a skittish horse. I was so preoccupied that I forgot my suitcase until after we had passed it. While I went back after it, Dad stood at the bronc's head and talked to him to calm him. With the suitcase in the wagon, we approached the bridge, but he only pricked up his ears and looked from side to side. Dad's soothing words and his firm hands on the reins kept him going straight ahead and enabled us to make a safe crossing. By the time we arrived home in the afternoon he was well broken in.

When Mother found there was no way to get us properly educated except to go to Roswell herself and make a home for us, we moved there for the school months. Because she would never live in a house she did not own, Dad bought us the only three-story home in Roswell at that time at 109 North Kentucky Avenue. This house stands now in the center of the city. To help pay our expenses Mother converted the upper two floors into apartments and rented them. We used this house until we finished high school. When Dad sold the house he bought a duplex at 405 North Kentucky Avenue. Mother rented one side and kept the other for her own use as long as she lived. When we moved to Roswell Granmaw went to live with her son, Jim Tully, who owned a ranch about three miles up the valley from our place.

Our religious training, like our education, had always been a big problem to Mother. Brought up in the Episcopal church, she had returned to her native Toronto, Canada, as a young girl to attend Summer Bible Vacation School. On the New Mexican frontier she had to improvise as best she could, hoping in time the community would grow into "church size." But as the three Coes, Dad, Jap, and Uncle George, owned so much land up and down the river, there was little hope the settlement would grow enough to justify a church. Jap could not be counted on for support because his particular brand of religion included a lot of hellfire and brimstone. On the other hand, George and Phoebe worked with Mother to attract whatever they could to fill our religious needs. At far-spaced intervals the circuit-rider preachers helped carry to the settlers a little of the inner glow their souls craved. Mother always welcomed them to the ranch. But when the Episcopal minister came she threw back the big doors of the living room and invited the people up and down the valley to attend services.

The circuit riders were roving ambassadors of God's word. They carried their Bibles in their pockets, ready to read a wedding ceremony, a burial service, or a christening. In their saddlebags they carried Bibles, hymnbooks, and religious literature which they distributed wherever they could get a few people together. Sometimes they carried on revival meetings and Jap Coe once allowed them to use his front yard for a service. No matter what faith the minister represented or whether the people shouted their praises to the Lord or worshipped in the quiet manner Mother preferred, she attended the meetings and saw that we children sat quietly. Dad, who was a Methodist, went along with whatever was the preacher's faith.

The camp meetings at Nogal, Ruidoso, and later at Johnson Spring (now Ruidoso Downs, the site of a million-dollar race track ten miles from Coe Ranch) were the greatest religious events of the time. In the relaxing air of the mountain tabernacle under the pines, the preacher praised the Lord and the ranchers delighted in the rains that fell almost daily. Nothing dampened the spirits of the worshippers as they sang the old-time revival songs "Bringing in the Sheaves," "Shall We Gather at the River," and "Softly and Tenderly." The test of a good voice was whether it could be raised above all others. Sometimes, I thought the singing made an awful racket, but it was the spirit that was important. Those who wished to do so came to the mourners' bench and received special prayers from the minister. Later they were baptized in the Gavilán Creek or in the Ruidoso River.

Spending all day out of doors, sleeping in tents, and cooking in the open gave the people big appetites. Also, numerous guests popped up from nowhere at mealtime. The women were kept busy at Sister Perry's cookstove or Sister Humphrey's Dutch oven where the light bread they baked disappeared as fast as it was ready to be eaten. The most popular food was a quarter of beef Dad had brought from the ranch wrapped in a wagon sheet. After the outside had dried in the rarefied mountain air, it kept fresh for four or five days. When the meat supply was exhuasted, the men would go out and round up a nice steer, which they butchered. There were so many cattle grazing in the area that I don't suppose we ever knew or cared about whose beef it was. However, it was safer to select the V-V brand, because they had so many cattle that they would not miss one. After a good meal we were content to sit and listen to the services. For those who wished it there were study groups. The minister conducted a sunrise service for the grown-ups, after which the men went fishing and brought in enough trout for everyone.

As I grew older I needed extra spending money. I was around fourteen when the idea hit me of working during summer vacation. But I kept quiet until just before camp meeting time.

My money-making scheme began to take place the day before we went to the camp meeting. After we packed all our camp gear and food in the wagon, I confided to Annie what I had in mind; she approved and went with me to our trading post at Capitán, about twenty miles away. There I put before G. A. Titsworth, the proprietor, my proposition, which was to get some soda pop, candy, and other supplies on credit and pay him back after the camp meeting. As we entered the store, he was busy at a ledger. Looking at us over his spectacles and pulling up his black cambric oversleeves, he asked what he could do for me. I told him I planned to put up a cold drink stand at the camp meeting, and needed some supplies on credit. I promised to pay him when the camp meeting was over. He asked me how much credit I thought I would need. Without waiting for me to answer, he started to stack some cases of strawberry, lemon, and orange soda near the door. To these he added two buckets of gumdrops and a big sack of mixed cookies. When I saw so much merchandise heaped on the floor, I began to worry about how I was going to pay for it all, so I asked him to stop a minute while I went outside and talked to Annie. "Sure, go ahead, get plenty," she advised me. Encouraged by this, I went back and told Mr. Titsworth I guessed I'd take a few more things, after which he brought cans of sardines and a bag of crackers. Finally he knocked the dust and dead flies from a box of old, dry "three-fer" cigars and added this to my purchases. When he handed me a carefully itemized bill for twenty-five dollars and sixty cents I gasped. I was afraid I was going to be in debt for the rest of my life but there was no backing out now, so I folded the slip and put it in my pocket. By the time the merchandise had been loaded, there was barely room for us in the carriage. Just as we were about to leave, Mr. Titsworth gave us a bag of peppermint.

At the camp meeting grounds I got my pal and cousin, Roy, to help me. We put the stand near the river where we could put the pop into the water to keep it cool. Before we were ready for business, hungry cowboys were waiting to buy things. It was not long before my pants were pulling at my suspenders from the weight of so many nickels, dimes, and quarters, so I found a squirrel hole under some rocks to hide them.

We really did not need a come-on for the stand, but we played an early-model Edison phonograph with cylinder records that Dad had bought at Fort Stanton. As the records did not have cases, they were worn and scratched, but whatever sounds came from the big horn were enjoyed. Our favorites were kept spinning time and time again—"The Blue Danube" and "The Preacher and the Bear." For Mother we would play Caruso singing *Rigoletto,* but his powerful tenor voice sounded frightful with the worn needle and scratchy record.

The Indians were the least appreciative of our music. They listened with disbelief. But they were among our customers and to them we sold most of the cigars, especially after one of the squaws walked away from the stand puffing on one. The Indians were not profitable customers, though, for they wanted to barter, and I knew I could not take beads and buckskin back to Mr. Titsworth to pay for my goods. I would need cold cash for that.

Long before the camp meeting was over I had sold everything. As soon as we reached the ranch I loaded up the empty cases and drove over to Capitán to pay my bill. Mr. Titsworth welcomed me when I walked into the store with my cigar box under my arm and emptied its contents on the counter. Arranging the coins in stacks of one dollar each, he counted them twice to be sure there was the right amount of twenty-five dollars and sixty cents. When I left, he patted me on the shoulder and told me my credit was good with him for any amount, at any time, and for anything. I was pleased about that, but what made me even happier was the other twenty-five dollars I had in some Bull Durham sacks stuck in my favorite hiding place in the low loft over the milkhouse.

I ran this stand at a few subsequent meetings, but over the years I outgrew my interest in selling and took on a new one—girls. When Minnie and Madge Bourne began to spend more time than money at my stand one summer, I started to think of things besides profits. They were pretty sisters who were working for the summer at the Prude Trading Post on the way to Mescalero, near the Indian Reservation line. To get ahead of a handsome fiddler named Grover Hightower, I gave Minnie a bracelet I had traded for with the Indians. At the time Roy was spending more time with his pony than in helping me, but when the girls began to stop by he became interested in the business again. We were trying to work up enough nerve to ask them to a dance at the Coe schoolhouse after the camp meeting. If there was a way to their fickle hearts, it was through dancing and parties. But as we lacked the courage then, we later got on our ponies and rode fifteen miles up to the Prude place to see them. We pretended we were looking for some stray cattle.

The girls were busy with their chores, and Mrs. Prude did not give us very friendly glances for interrupting them. She reminded them several times they had better get on with their sweeping and bedmaking. We were all still killing time when the dinner hour came, so there was nothing for the Prudes to do but ask us to eat with them. We helped them churn, wash dishes, dust, and do other things. We liked especially to go to the spring for water, as this got us away from the watchful eye of Mrs. Prude.

Suppertime came and found us still there. The invitation to eat was less cordial this time. It was more of a complaint. "Since you boys ain't gone home yet, I reckon you'll have to set and eat with us again." The broad hints of the Prudes fell on deaf ears so we talked into the early evening, the girls giggling at our wild stories. When we heard Mr. Prude's boot hit the floor in his room with an awful thud, we decided we had better leave before the other one came sailing in our direction. In our haste we almost forgot to invite the girls to the dance; they gladly accepted.

Before Saturday I had to break the news to Dad that Roy and I would need the hack and a team of horses to take the Bourne girls to the dance. He thought we had lost our senses to drive fifteen miles each way; however he consented with the stipulation we would drive a wild horse and a tame one because it was a good chance to get a bronc tamed. At the time I didn't realize Dad was being crafty. He knew there would be no dropping the lines over the dash and letting the horses jog along. Though to be with Madge and Minnie, Roy and I would have agreed to anything.

Early Saturday morning we roped out a raw bronc and hitched him to the hack with a gentle mare. The trail was rough and having a bronc did not make the going any easier, for he had to be kept under constant control all the way. We crossed the Ruidoso several times, and at each crossing Roy had to take off his shoes to wade and lead the bronc. In our hurry to get there we drove the team faster than we should, so by the time we reached the Prude place, the bronc had worn himself out. Because of this we had to unhitch the horses and let them rest. The girls were rushing about to get their work done early and did not look like much in rag curlers and buttermilk-smeared faces; it was thought that buttermilk could clear the complexion, remove brown spots and freckles, and make the skin whiter and this treatment was popular among the young girls of that day.

But when the time to go came we were dazzled by the change in their appearance. From their pompadoured hair to their high-button shoes they were a pretty picture. As Roy and I had already flipped a coin to see who would get in the back seat, Madge sat there with Roy as I had lost the toss. We all talked and laughed as the carriage rocked on the rough road. I did not have too much time to take my mind from the team as it was downhill most of the way. Roy was busy too looking after the bronc, leaning over to the side of the seat ready with his rope. I had to hold the reins in a tight grip with my right foot pushing on the brake. It was not until we had almost reached the schoolhouse that I could slide my arm on the back of the seat behind Minnie, and Roy could lay his lariat on the floor. We were sorry to reach the schoolhouse for we knew we would not have our girls to ourselves much longer.

In fact, we hardly saw them at all. All the cowboys rushed them, giving Roy little chance to dance with Madge. I did not see Minnie even during the intermission. I hung around the musicians most of the time, wishing for twelve o'clock to come. Roy and I realized we had been a couple of chumps. Two thirty-mile trips just so our girls could dance their shoes off with the other fellows.

The horses had tired so much on the first trip that we had to get a fresh team for the second. It was bright moonlight, so while we struggled to get a new bronc and another tame mare hooked up Minnie and Madge stayed in the house and talked to my sisters about the wonderful time they had at the dance —dancing with the other fellows, I suppose. Roy won the toss again so I had to drive back, taking off with a lunge that jerked our necks. When we reached the middle of the first river crossing, the bronc stopped dead still and proceeded to enlarge the riverflow. We were all full of laughter and chatter all the way there as the bronc jerked the hack back and forth, enjoying every bump, chug hole, and twist in the road. It was almost sunrise by the time we reached the Prudes, so while we took care of the team the girls went inside to make coffee and fry eggs and make pancakes. It was Sunday and the girls didn't have so many chores to do so we hung around until the Prudes began to give us that I-wonder-why-you-don't-go-home look. Then a little later Mrs. Prude hollered to us in the kitchen, "If these boys are going to stay all night, make them up a bed." We could not ignore such a broad hint and left shortly after.

Although my friendship with Minnie lasted for a while longer, I never went courting her again in the hack. My last date with her was some time later when I was on my way back to college in my sophomore year. I met a friend, Ralph Dow, on the train from Capitán to Carrizozo, and he suggested we take in a dance that night. At that time the Bourne sisters were working at a boardinghouse in Carrizozo, where we checked in for the night. After we had eaten we went to the kitchen and pitched in to help with the dishes. I'm afraid there was more horseplay than dishwashing. While I was showing them how to make a bowl disappear from behind a towel, I brought the dish against the corner of the table. There was a sharp crack and before I could bring my hand from under the towel, the white flour sack was stained with blood which was spurting hard from a cut artery in my left wrist. I clamped my other hand over it, but still the blood kept oozing through my fingers and down my arm. While Madge pulled my sleeve up, Minnie ran to the pantry and brought out some sugar, which she patted over the cut. The red stain spread quickly over it so she put on another handful. She kept this up until the bleeding gradually slowed down. When there was no longer any stain on the sugar, she tore an old pillow case into strips and bound my wrist.

By then I did not care much about going to the dance. I was more concerned about my wrist. Nevertheless the four of us went. Minnie had a good time dancing while I just hung around, watching for more bloodstains and wishing the affair would simply hurry to an end. In the parlor of the boardinghouse I later kissed Minnie good-bye, and the next morning I started on the Golden State Limited for California and Stanford.

Later I had many occasions to think of Minnie and her remedy for cuts. When my farm animals suffered deep gashes, I used sugar on them to stop the bleeding. It always worked, too. I never saw a doctor about the cut, and I still have a white scar on my wrist as a souvenir of my last date with Minnie. Few ever knew where it came from; I never told anyone because I was ashamed, knowing I had no business in a boardinghouse kitchen wiping dishes—or performing sleight-of-hand tricks!

After Mother came to Roswell to put us in school, I brought a pony from the ranch and kept it in the barn. Along with Dick Winston and Claude Boone, I would race up and down the streets, kicking up the dust and getting disapproving looks from people. One day a cowboy named Sam Miller from the Diamond-A spread heard me bragging about how my pony back at the ranch could choke the other boys' horses at the end of a fifty-foot rope in a race. So that I could prove my boast, he offered to make the 130-mile round trip to Coe Ranch to bring my pony Fleet to town. Sam was as good as his word. In a couple of weeks he led my pony to Roswell, and I made it known to all the kids that we were going to have a horse race after school on a smooth dirt road lying due north. Each evening I would brush and curry Fleet and give him an extra ration of oats. I had bet five dollars against Dick's pony, and I did not want to lose it, while Sam put twenty-five dollars on my horse and held the stakes for the others. It took the whole crowd to cover Sam's bet.

As I sat my pony waiting for the starting signal, I wondered why Professor Cottingham looked so displeased. And what on earth, I wondered, was he writing in a little notebook? We soon found out. After Fleet had come in an easy first and I had collected my own winnings, I sat astride him proudly while the fellows admired and petted him. The professor still kept putting down things in his notebook. By Monday morning I had forgotten all about the race—but he had not. As soon as the tardy bell rang, the three of us were called into his office and told to remain after school. At that time he questioned us about the exchange of money. For punishment he told us we would have to stay in every day for a week and put our noses in circles drawn on the blackboard, which seemed pretty silly to big fellows like us.

After a session of straining our necks to reach the circles we went to find Sam. He had dropped out of school early in life and scoffed at education of any kind. He promised us he would try to get the principal to change his mind, but he did not say how. Knowing Professor Cottingham, we did not expect much. Like Lonny's dad, Sam thought there was only one way to settle an argument, so he told the principal that if we had to put our noses in circles one more time, he would thrash him properly because betting on a horse was not a crime. His argument must have been convincing because the professor backed down on the punishment, conceding it was a matter for our parents to handle.

I had been struggling with ponies ever since I was big enough to be hoisted up on one, but when I came to the study of *Caesar's Gallic Wars* in my second year of Latin, I found a stony adversary. I had gotten through the first year with its case endings and conjugations, but the translations of the second year baffled me completely. Over the struggle with Caesar, Palmer Bradley and I formed a close friendship. Yet even with the two of us working together to look up words and put them together in sentences we did not get the kind of grades we wanted to take home to our parents.

We were in our lowest spirits when a fellow came upon us one noon hour when we were poring over our assignment and asked us what we would give him for a "pony." We had heard about this mysterious book but we had never seen one. We did not have much money, but he was willing to take the dollar and twenty-six cents we raked up. From inside his shirt he pulled a soiled, worn, backless translation of *Caesar's Gallic Wars* and handed it to me. From then on we sailed through Caesar and his conquests from the Rhine to the English Channel and beyond, not caring whether a noun was in the ablative or accusative case. When our grades came out on the next report they were considerably improved.

As our dishonesty weighed on our consciences and fear of being caught with the pony haunted us, we became shaky. We knew our offense was a grave one—to sass a teacher, break a window, play hooky—these were minor compared with being caught with a Latin pony. Neither wanted to keep it in his desk or carry it around with him so we took turns. When it was my day to take care of it, I was miserable. The harder I tried to hide it, the guiltier I felt. If we hadn't been so dependent on the translation, we would have burned it. I even had nightmares about it.

One day I almost let the pony slip from among my other books in front of a teacher in the hall. I made up my mind right then that I could not take care of it another day. As I rode my pony to school the next morning across the barren stretch a great idea hit me, so I stopped in the middle of the prairie-dog town and studied it. Sure that it would work, I hurried to school and found Palmer. He listened to my plan and agreed to it, so early the next morning he met me at the prairie-dog mounds. I selected a fair-sized hole by one of them and remained at it while Palmer counted off the steps to a prickly-pear cactus. We each noted the direction and made maps of the place. Then I wrapped the pony in some oilskin from an old slicker, put it inside a molasses can and shoved it down in the hole. Thereafter we hurried out each morning to the spot and sat on the ground while we copied our translations. Our tests were always poor, but without too many pangs of conscience we passed the course. Our teacher probably suspected our deception because it must have been written all over our other-wise-honest faces. Perhaps he felt sorry for a couple of dummies like us and let us get away with it.

So much worry over the Latin pony made me happier than ever to return to the ranch for summer vacation. With my sisters, who were all good riders, I helped tame broncs, rode, and watched the cowboys brand calves, break colts, and sit on the corral fence and brag. It was during this summer that a fellow named Joe Kerley worked for us. Anyone could see he was stuck on Annie, who did not have much time for beaux because she spent it all with the horses. Annie was eight years older than I, but we were good friends and loved to gentle broncs together. After these wild ones were tamed they were sold for a good price and were an important part of the ranch income.

However, instead of the method of hitching a tame horse and a bronc together, we would put two broncs to the wagon. While I scrambled up on the seat, Annie tried to hold them by their hackamores. When she let go they would take off with a jerk that snapped my head back. As I whirled by in the wagon Annie would make a grab for the back end and pull herself over the tailgate. We would fly out of the barnyard giving the horses full rein; there was little else we could do. We stuck with them when they headed for ditches, fences, arroyos, or a haystack, and jumped only if we though they were going into a barbed-wire fence.

When we tried to tame Cloudy, a spirited bronc with a wild

look in his eye, Joe happened to be watching. Annie and I finally managed to get the mustang to the neck yoke and hitched up, except for the last tug, which I was trying to fasten so I could climb on the seat. Annie was holding his hackamore. Just as I hooked the tug Cloudy reared and Annie, unable to hold on, was pawed down under him. She just lay there and I feared she was dead or badly hurt. If she was still alive, another blow of his front hoof might be fatal. I swung to the halter with all my strength and prevented a second thrust of his hoof, giving her time to roll out of range. Joe hurried to reach her, but Annie got to her feet without any help from him, brushed the dirt off, and walked up to Cloudy to calm him so she could try it again. This time I was able to hook the tug and climb onto the seat. Annie made her lunge as we passed and caught the tailgate. Most of the time we were on two wheels as we circled the mesa, stopping only after Cloudy had run out of breath. Joe looked relieved when we made it back to the lot.

Joe wrote down many impressions of Coe Ranch. He recalled one morning when Annie came to him with a lariat in her hand and said that she had a new job for him that day. She took him out to the corral, threw her rope over a pair of work horses and in a few minutes had the team harnessed and hitched to a mowing machine. She told him to follow as she drove the mower to the alfalfa field, where she cut a few swaths to show how to lower and raise the sickle bar. Joe said that he felt very lucky, as a few days before he was sweltering in the heat at Roswell, and now he was riding on a mower enjoying the fragrance of new-mown hay. Annie feared that he might have some trouble so she went to the field ever now and then to see how he was getting along.

Joe recounted that they do not grow Annie's kind any more on ranches. Besides being a good cook, pianist, guitar player, and smooth dancer, she was one of the best ropers and bronc riders in the Southwest. He said he would never forget one

Sunday morning when the family was all dressed up in their Sunday best on their way to church. Annie rode ahead on a black horse. She wore a long black divided skirt, white blouse, and her hair piled high on her head. Those were the days before girls wore levis or shorts, at least to church. The rest of the family followed in a two-horse carriage, paying little attention to Annie until she reached a small irrigation ditch and her frightened horse started to buck viciously before she could rein him up. The flopping of her skirt scared him still more and he gave her all he had, furiously pitching and plunging in an effort to unseat her. She stayed with him although her hair came down and a pin fell from her blouse. When the horse had done his damnedest to throw her, she got off, picked up her brooch, tidied herself up, and remounted. Such a performance in Annie's stylish make-up was about the most thrilling piece of riding he had ever seen. Frank Coe was proud of his daughter, but his only comment was that the horse had made her pull leather.

When the summer was over Joe left us to go back to school, loaded with memories of his days on Coe Ranch.

The summer of 1910 was a memorable one. I had caught a ride to the ranch with a cowboy who came to Roswell for supplies. Before school closed I was contemplating some money-making schemes. At seventeen I needed more cash. At that time Dad's income came chiefly from his crops of grain and hay, and livestock. The fine corn yielded one hundred bushels to the acre. Our apple orchard was still small, but Dad continually experimented with fruitgrowing and expanded it gradually. He usually kept a little cash on hand, and since there were no banks the Mexicans in the valley would come to him for help when an emergency struck their families. Dad would make them small loans and take their notes, secured by a cow, pig, or horse. Some of the notes were paid by labor, but many of them were paid by turning in a cow on the account. This helped to build up our own herd.

Not long after I arrived home I found we were going to have a boarder for the summer, which gave me an idea for a summer project. This boarder (and my possible partner in business) was to be Charley Fraley, the nephew and ward of Colonel Pritchard, an outstanding Santa Fé lawyer and Dad's attorney. Charley was attending the New Mexico Military Institute and his uncle, not knowing what to do with him at vacationtime, asked Dad to let him come to the ranch where he could get some practical experience in an ideal summer climate.

When the Institute closed for the summer, Charley took the stage to Lincoln, arriving late at night. He went to the hotel and began trying to reach the ranch over our tree-line telephone. When Roy and I were kids we had rigged up a telephone unit from my house to his. For the line we used the top wire of the barbed-wire fence with insulators made from the tops of beer bottles. The receivers were tomato cans. We would talk to each other and imagine we were receiving answers. This was the forerunner of the tree-line telephone, the equipment for which we got from Montgomery Ward. It reached seven miles over the mountain, at first from Lincoln but was later extended to the George and Jap Coe places. Storms damaged the system, as did livestock and deer tangling in the wire in the low places. Nailholes weathered out, sometimes causing the two-by-four supports to give way, so the service often was not dependable. People traveling over the trail repaired the line when possible or put it back on the trees if they found it down. Our service was improved when a telephone company in Capitán built a more efficient system, which was a private one that gave limited service over the county. This was a big improvement over the early days when Dad kept a pony saddled and tied under the cottonwood tree for emergency. If a traveler came along and failed to stop, he would jump on the pony and overtake him to find out the news of the country. If the traveler was interesting enough, he invited him to come back and camp under the shade of the trees and stay a spell while Dad "simmered" him. He would find out where the stranger came from, where he was going, and what he hoped to gain when he got there—all items of interest to a pioneer family. From these visits he gained much valuable information in a place where there were no long-distance telephone services, newspapers, or radio.

Charley had to crank the telephone for some time before he made a connection with the ranch. The next morning a cowboy rode to Lincoln with an extra horse to bring back our guest, who arrived with his suitcase tied to the back of his saddle. As they approached the house, they received a mournful greeting from old Gloomy, the jack. At the time Dad was beginning to breed mules for the United States Army and you could set your watch by the braying of Gloomy. He sounded a curfew at nine every night and disturbed the cowboys. Old Gloomy's morning call came at about five o'clock.

Charley and I were about the same age and got on well together. The companionship of a boy so daring and pleasant was welcome. His finances were strained also so he readily agreed to my money-making scheme, which was to open a blacksmith shop. We began by making a sign in Dad's workshop that read: "Coe and Fraley Blacksmith—No Job Too Big or Too Small." This we nailed in a conspicuous place to a tree along the road.

Since there were few people passing we did not have much business, so this gave us time to do things outside the shop. If Mother wanted a chicken for the table, we would go out with a .22 rifle to get it because they were so wild we could not get our hands on them. The biggest job we did was to help Dad dig a well. After we had gone down as far as we could with shovels, Charley volunteered to descend into the hole and set off a dynamite charge. This took a lot of courage. I helped pull him back up, pale and shaky. I lost some of my color too just watching. When the windmill ordered from the Jones Brothers in Kansas City arrived, Charley and I went to Capitán to get it. We drove an outlaw horse and a sedate old mare and the bronc spooked at everything along the way. He pranced and shied so much at the "boogers" that he wore us both out and himself as well. With the wagon pulling much harder on the return trip he gave out, so we stopped for the night at Winnie's home in Devil's Canyon about three miles from the ranch. She was now married to Orville Hunt, the nester's son. The bronc was still tired the next morning and by the time he reached the ranch he was as docile as the old mare. The following day Charley, thinking he was still subdued, got on him and was bucked off before he could get set.

Dad gave Charley and me the job of putting up the windmill and the 200-gallon galvanized storage tank which he had on hand. With the help of two Mexican hired hands we set the tower and mill over the well. When our helpers looked up at the fifty-foot tower they were afraid to go up to put on the wheel and the fan. One of them said, "Ay, por Dios, me falta valor." To get the job done I climbed up, strapped myself to the tower, assembled the wheel section by section, and bolted the fan in place. This was a feat Charley and the workers had thought impossible. We secured four large poles about twenty feet long and cemented them in the ground. On top of these we built a platform on which we put the storage tank and anchored it down with heavy wire. We connected the main pipe so that the water would run into the tank, attached the sucker rod to the mill, and the windmill began to pump water. Our workers dug the trenches for the water pipes to the house and the barn. When the pipes were laid and properly connected, we opened the faucets and the water began to flow. Old Gloomy was happy to get a cool drink fresh from the well and showed it by letting out a loud bray of thanks.

There was plenty of entertainment during the summer with box suppers and dances at the Coe schoolhouse. Charley liked to dance with Annie and to get her artistic box with some of Mother's good fried chicken and caramel cake. He also took Annie to the dances at Fort Stanton. With her hair piled high on her head, her puffed sleeves, high collar tied with velvet ribbons, and long full skirt drawn into a small waist, she was a contrast to the girl he was accustomed to see in a divided skirt and boots astride a horse.

In addition to the windmill project we helped Dad build a cement walk and an arched bridge over the ditch in front of the post office. The Roswell paper in an article described it as perhaps the only cement walk in Lincoln County. It did not prove very practical though, for when a big rain came it brought debris rushing through the ditch which plugged up the bridge and caused the overflow to go over the banks and into the house. Charley and I were sleeping in a tent house where the drizzle, when the rain fell, was so thick we could not see each other so we would take off for the haymow.

Occasionally Charley and I did get some work to do in the shop. Chiefly it was shoeing horses, patching up broken-down buggies, and repairing mowing machines and other farm implements. Where we could we used bolts and baling wire, but broken rims and some parts of farm machinery had to be welded. One of our first customers was Manuel Sanchez who drove up in an old rickety buggy, sitting on a goatskin over a board across the seat. His brake was wired on and he wanted a welding job. We had not done any of this kind of work yet so we had to hustle around to mix a welding composition of ashes, sand, fiddle rosin, soda, and borax. Manuel watched us skeptically. Then we brought the two ends of the iron to a white heat and stuck them into the compound. While each held a piece on the anvil, I pounded them together. Only after we put the iron into a barrel of water and saw the metal did not come apart was I sure the compound had worked. We used it thereafter for that kind of repair work.

In the long intervals when there was no business Charley

and I sometimes experimented on various gadgets. I hammered out my first pair of spurs and gave them to a Negro named Charley Glass, one of our bronc busters. Often Dad would come in to help us figure out things that were too tough for us. He was a real expert at making his own tools. One was a machine that he ran wagon tires through to give them the proper curve after they had been shrunk. This was hard to do by measuring with the eye. At Fort Stanton he had bought an anvil, a drill press, and a vise; much of this old equipment is still in the shop today gathering dust, for the dominance of the horse on Coe Ranch is now a thing of the past.

Our main business was horseshoeing and in those days it was a tough job. The shoes had to be sized and then the nail holes made in them. To get them to fit right, we had to fire the ends to a red heat and cut them off with a chisel and hammer. One day Uncle George brought in a mare to be shod, so to help Dad he held the hot iron while Dad chopped off the calks with a chisel. George was wearing a pair of heavy brogans that were flapping open at the top, and a red-hot chunk of the shoe landed inside one of them when Dad swung the hammer. Ordinarily Uncle George moved slowly but when that happened, he moved fast, jumping up and down and screaming for Dad to do something. He stopped jumping long enough to try to fish it out with his fingers but only managed to burn them. Finally Dad made him stand still long enough to rip open the boot which allowed the hot piece to fall out. Dad hated to see his cousin in so much pain, but was somewhat amused to see him move so quickly.

Sometimes we just lazed around the shop. It was during one of these dull spells that I saw a caravan turn off the road. I called to Charley, who was putting some axle grease on the back wheel of a buggy, to tell him we had a lot of business coming up the road. There were two covered wagons and a carriage. At the head of the party was a young man. After bringing his team to a halt he stepped down and introduced himself as Carroll Holland from Roswell. He had seen our sign down the road and wanted to know if we could shoe his mules. They had come barefoot all the way from Roswell and their hoofs were worn to the quick. We told him it was a pretty big job that would require a lot of time so he had better pitch camp under the cottonwoods.

As we talked, Charley and I were stealing glances out of the corner of our eyes at the rest of the party. We could see some pretty girls. Before Carroll had time to introduce Charley and me, Mother and some of my sisters came out, so he presented us all to his sisters, Inez and Louise, his cousin Nona Clement and her mother, his Aunt Ivey, and a brother John. Charley and I did not see anybody much but the girls. As we helped the men unhitch, Carroll told us they had started a few days before on a camping trip to the tall pines of the upper Ruidoso in the White Mountains. They had spent two days at the Diamond-A Ranch, where they were royally entertained. At that time the Diamond-A was operated by the Bloom Cattle Company and had among its horse breakers a Bob Boyce, an expert bronc rider, who later married my sister Edith. Jim Decker, who had learned to ride broncs on the Coe Ranch, had risen to foreman of the Diamond-A.

Right away Mother insisted they stay over at the ranch and camp near the ditch. So while Charley and I inspected the mules, Mother became better acquainted with the Holland family. We saw it was going to be a tough job to put shoes on the badly worn hoofs of the animals, especially since they had never been shod before. As we would have to use rough tactics, we did not want our guests hanging around watching. We suggested they go riding and hunting. I was not strong enough to catch a mule by the foot and hold him, so we had to tie them up, throw them, and cross-tie the front and back feet. In this position we could get on with the shoeing. The worst they could do was to kick a little so we had to be careful not to get hit. We did not like to let the mule lie on its side in the hot sun while we shaped the shoes, punched the nail holes and hammered the shoes to fit their small hoofs, but that was the only way we could do it. We tried to be as careful as possible with their tender feet and finally got the four of them shod. Nona and Louise were watching as we let the last mule up and laughed at them mincing about and lifting their feet peculiarly, wondering what had happened. We felt rich when Carroll paid us eight dollars for the job.

For the remainder of the Hollands' visit Charley and I did no work in the shop. We showed our guests some of our fancy riding and roping and then at night there were music and dancing. I was trying all the while to decide which girl I liked better—Nona or Louise. Both were beautiful in my books, but Louise could play the piano, and Nona could only make big goo-goo eyes.

I had my own fiddle then, which I had recently acquired from Roderick Johnson, son of Dr. S. M. Johnson, a minister from South Carolina who had bought the old John Hale place twelve miles up the valley. He built a two-story house and moved there with his family. Dr. Johnson was instrumental in securing the routing of coast-to-coast U. S. Highway 70 through the Ruidoso Valley. Roderick was about my age and took in the dances at Coe Ranch and the Glencoe schoolhouse. He liked music and his mother wanted him to learn to play the violin so she bought him a very fine instrument. Roderick was more interested in learning how to ride and rope, and he spent a great deal of time at our ranch watching the operations in the corrals. He liked one of my saddle ponies so much that he offered to trade me his violin for him; I quickly took him up. Roderick delivered the violin and rode the pony home. When his mother found out about the trade, she was furious. She complained that the horse kept her awake at night with his neighing and of course she also knew that the violin was worth ten times more than the pony. However, Roderick liked the deal and persuaded his mother to let him keep the animal; I still have the violin.

"Mr." Bates would have been proud of me had he heard how well I played on my new fiddle trying to impress Louise. I hoped that some of the fervor of my music was transmitted to her as she sat with Nona on the steps in the doorway between the parlor and the post office.

After the Hollands left, Charley and I felt lonely, and as the summer drew to a close our blacksmith shop went out of business. Charley returned to the Institute and I went back to Roswell to school. The fun we had riding, roping, branding, and attending the dances became happy memories, and I will not deny that Louise was foremost among mine.

CHAPTER VIII

Taming WILD COWS
for the V-V Ranch

MY EDUCATION extended into the automobile world that year when my brother-in-law Orville Hunt, who had been operating a stage line between Roswell and Carrizozo, left his old Reo with me. Orville ran the Tri-Weekly Stage Line—as they said, you'd go up one week and try to get back the next! I was supposed to sell the car, if I could find anyone crazy enough to buy it. I was always interested in mechanical things, so I spent more time trying to get the Reo to run than I did riding in it. It had to be cranked on the side with a thirty-inch crank. A special skill was required to give it the necessary quick jerk. Otherwise the crank might backfire and break your arm. I caught onto the knack and could start the motor when men bigger and stronger than I had failed. But I had sore muscles, skinned knuckles, and bruised fingernails. My knees were calloused from changing tires so often. It was a lot of fun to show off around town, though, where there were no more than a couple of other automobiles. Most of the time I got stuck somewhere and had to have my sisters bring my pony and pull me in. Between the stalled motor and flat tires, there was little time to take friends for a ride.

When Orville left his auto with me, I had hoped no one would want to buy it. One day, however, a fellow named Pynch showed up just after I had spent an hour getting the motor to run. He lived a short distance from town and wanted transportation in to Roswell to the picture show he operated. When I did not appear to be interested in selling the Reo, he upped his price to an irresistible three hundred dollars and gave me a check for that amount.

As it was Saturday afternoon the bank was closed and I had the weekend to worry about cashing the check before Pynch found out too much about the Reo. Bright and early on Monday I was in front of the bank waiting for it to open. The doors were no sooner unlocked than I hurried to the window to cash the check. After I received the money and pocketed it, I turned to leave and saw Pynch standing just inside the door. He wanted his money back because he had already had so much trouble with the auto he had decided that he did not want it. I promised I would give him all the help I could, so he finally agreed to keep it. I rode my pony to his place at once and spent the rest of the day cleaning sparkplugs, filing the points of the coils, pulling a casing off the rim, and patching a tire that had flattened by the time he got the car home. After we had both cranked a while, the motor finally gave a few spurts and caught. For a long time after that I stayed out of Pynch's way.

When summer came I was glad to be among horses again. I was tired of dodging Pynch, too. Riding broncs was easier than keeping the Reo running so I worked hard at becoming a good cowboy. I had never been one to give up easily when I set out to do a thing, and it took a lot of self-discipline to be a tough-ridin' bronc buster. In spite of my handicap, I set out to be the toughest man in the outfit. My ruggedness and endurance came chiefly from the hard fiber of my Scottish blood and from the extraordinary strength in my arm and shoulder muscles.

To compete with the old-time, wind-bitten cowboys, I would risk my neck to stay on a wild horse. I was determined to break a bronc one day; yet I realized that my legs were not strong enough to grip the sides of the pony and stay in the saddle. I then conceived the idea of tying my stirrups together with a strap under the horse's belly. This was dangerous, if the horse fell on me, but it was one way of staying on. If he did not pitch too hard, I could keep my feet in the stirrups. I made a special leather strap for this purpose and could snap it on before I mounted. I always wore chaps to protect my legs from the brush and because most cowboys in that day wore them. Edd Amonett, the best saddlemaker in Roswell, made my chaps, saddle, and bridle, which are still in good condition.

Mother's influence was a great help to me in this as everything. She fought the temptation to overprotect me, especially when she watched me do the things around horses that were dangerous even for kids with good legs. She had complete faith in Dad's judgment and in his training me to take care of myself in the saddle. Pleased with me when I swung on the back of a spirited horse and stuck there when it began to pitch he would say, "You made it that time, son." Or, "Remember you have to be smarter than the horse."

For a good workout at riding and roping I teamed up with Roy that summer and worked on the V-V spread as Mr. Cree was selling out and needed help to round up his "mulies" and other wild cattle. Upchurch, boss of the outfit then, was glad to take us on for a dollar a day and our chuck so he put us to work at once. For our first project Roy and I went after some of the wild cows over in the Felipe Thicket between Eagle Creek and the Ruidoso, an area of about eight square miles named for Felipe Gómez, who worked for the V-V Ranch for twenty-two years. There was not another thicket in the country to compare with it. The pine saplings grew so thick that the sun never reached the ground. Cattle hiding there couldn't be seen or found except by combing the thicket foot by foot. They hid in the timber and became wild. When mixed breeds of "mulies" and longhorns ran wild for a long time they became rough customers. Sometimes the cowboys had to go after them with trained dogs and even then could not scare them out. The dogs came away beaten and bleeding. In some cases the only thing to do was to let them stay in the thickets.

Roy and I had not gone far on our first trip out when we jumped a bunch, so, pulling down our hats tight and holding our ropes ready, we took down a ridge after them. After a short chase they came to the rim of a deep canyon where they stopped, scared and bunched together. The drop was in front of them and Roy and I were riding for them fast from the rear, our loops ready. Suddenly they turned and doubled back, mad and fighting, and as they did Roy and I each roped one. It was a poor location so we knew we were in for a tough time.

Finally I managed to get my rope around a tree, and with me going one way and the cow the other I got the slack out of my lariat, which placed me in a better bargaining position. While I was struggling with mine, Roy was tugging and pulling with his own in order to subdue it and give me a hand. All I could do was to hold on to my rope while the cow came around the tree and made her first charge. Missing me, she tried another pass. By the time she had made three trips around the tree, she had anchored herself to it. This gave me a chance to try to help Roy. By holding on like a bulldog he had finally busted his cow, so I grabbed my hogging string and made a tie around her feet.

We had the cows now, but they were a considerable distance from headquarters ranch. Roy suggested we cut a couple of cedar poles four feet long and four inches thick and tie one across the horns of each to blind them and cut down their speed when they made for the brush. This we did and, uncertain whether we would be able to head them away from the thicket and up the ridge, we went to report to Upchurch. When he saw them, he said it was hard to believe that a couple of boys like us were able to subdue the cows and tie them.

Upchurch placed two of his men so they could steer the cows into the open country. Then he told Roy and me to turn them loose. When we did, they ran over the cowboy in front of them and headed down the ridge. With the poles across their horns they mowed down everything in their paths. Too surprised to do anything, we all stood listening to the snapping of branches until the sound died away. After we had heard the last crackle, Upchurch looked at our disappointed faces and said, "Never mind going after them, boys. We'll get them in the spring roundup." But the cows and our ropes were never seen again. Roy and I could only figure that they had snagged the poles and broken their necks.

Two weeks later while we were on another ride we became separated and I found myself riding through a glade of scattered piñon and cedar trees over a clearly marked trail. Suddenly I saw a black object dart out of the brush. Thinking it was a dog, I trailed along behind, hoping that when it jumped a cow I would be there with my loop. For some distance I continued to follow, but before long I could see that it was a black bear. I sized him up excitedly and decided he was not too big for me to handle with a rope. I knew that he was probably as scared as I, so he would not attack. My horse shot forward and I cast the loop right around his neck, causing him to run for a tree at the side of the trail. I was going too fast, though, and when the bear ran around the tree, the rope came taut and broke his neck. I was sorry because I wanted to take him alive.

When I showed Roy the bear, he could hardly believe it. As it was too large to take up on a horse, we skinned it and took the hide home. My uncle Kivas Tully, who was visiting us from St. Louis, wanted it for a trophy so I gave it to him. A St. Louis newspaper later carried the story about a young cowboy who had roped a bear, and I received letters offering me jobs and even some proposals of marriage.

The next morning Roy and I were back on the job with the other cowboys ready for another day's work. In level country roundup work was more or less routine, but in the mountains there was always a chance for the unexpected to happen. Riding in the Eagle Creek Lakes country, we figured the cattle would come out of the thickets to water at the lakes, so we schemed how best to catch them. We decided that by going out in the early morning and lying in wait for them when they came to drink, we could jump them.

The plan worked fine. After the cattle came to the water and drank so much they could not run fast, we charged after them, our loops ready. I had spotted a big maverick with his ears standing out without the sign of a mark on them. When the cattle scattered, he headed for an open flat. I made a lucky throw, and when the rope tightened around his neck, it jerked my saddle over to the side of the horse. In the excitement of going after the maverick, I had forgotten to lean over and tighten the cinch. As the saddle went over, it pinched the horse who started bucking and running, causing me to lose my balance and sprawl flat on my face. The horse jerked the steer down and started dragging him, and as he came past me, I swung and grabbed the rope up near his head. I held on until I could get on top of the steer, to prevent him from dragging on the ground. It was his skin or mine.

The horse, who was mad and scared, kept on running until he was out of breath, dragging us behind him. When he stopped, I spoke to him. He turned his head toward me and gave me enough slack to loosen the rope around the steer's neck, for he was all but choked to death. I took my hogging string from my chaps and tied him up. When I turned him over, there was not much hair left on his "down" side.

By this time some of the men rode up, curious to see my half-dead catch. It was a long time before the maverick grew new hair on his side, and when he did it was white.

Later, south of the Ruidoso River, we were riding in the Granddaddy Thicket, which got its name from the fact that only a granddaddy longlegs could crawl through its dense brush and timber. There we spotted a big, ugly, mean long-horned mossback heading deeper into the thickets. Matching strength and wits with a three-year-old cow was one thing, but tackling an old "spoiled" steer was quite another. The Avant Ranch boys who also ran cattle in the area had previously told me they had roped and busted this steer when he was young, just for practice. This had naturally made him wilder and meaner. Every time they had tried to bring him in with the other cattle, he would leave the bunch and take to the dense thickets.

Roy had never seen a cow too tough for him to tackle, so he was impatient to be off. When we rode after the mossback, he made a break for the brush so, with my rope ready, I laid a neat loop over his horns. It tightened around him and he came back, fighting furiously. I got my rope over his hind quarters and turned my horse at an angle needed to bust him. He went down, rose to his feet again, and made another charge at me so I busted him again. After I had done this two or three times, he lay flat enough for Roy to crawl on him and tie his feet.

Once we had him on the ground, we had to decide what to do with him. It was my bright idea to have Roy rope his tail so that when I roped his horns, we would move him sideways with our horses. That way he could not charge either of us. We began to drive him along, with Roy taking care of his end and me looking after my own, leading or pulling him, whichever method it took. Roy had some slack in his rope, and the steer charged at me and broke loose from the tail rope. My horse outran him until we reached the bottom of the hill. Then I turned one way and the steer ran the other. When the rope came tight at a right angle we were all jerked down, the horse, the steer, and I. After I finally stopped rolling, I crawled back to my horse, got him up, and mounted while the steer was still down. By the time I had checked my rope and my cinch, Roy rode up and wanted to know whether to put his lariat back on the steer's tail. After looking the animal over, I said I didn't think he had enough tail to tie it to because the hair had been jerked off with the rope. Anyway I thought I could take him in without Roy's tail hold.

As soon as the steer got up, he made a charge at me in the direction of the corral, which put him closer to where we wanted him. The steer was hot, tired, and mad and he refused to go into the enclosure. When we tried to make him, he charged at me again. I quickly gave my pony the spurs but he did not move, and the horns of the steer raked his shoulder. This caused the horse to give a terrific lunge, and he came down straddling the rope. Then he started bucking. When the rope tightened, the saddle turned and I had to pull leather. This allowed the rope to catch my wrist near the saddlehorn and pin me to the side of the horse. Tied up as I was, I could not do anything to better my position until the horse worked around and gave me some slack.

When I at last freed myself I was near the corral fence so I dropped from my horse and rolled under it right on top of a hill of big black ants. I scrambled up in a hurry, trying to brush them off, hardly aware of the deep rope burns on my wrists. But I did know I was getting some welts from the ants on my back end that would be swollen with poison. Roy got his own horse while another cowboy went for mine. The animal was worn with the heat and the struggle and mad at the rope that entangled him. In addition the steer was still pulling back on it. He stood with his legs braced, sullen, slobbering, and fiery-eyed. It took the combined efforts and wits of us all to put him into the corral. Once there, we yoked him with a tame one.

We drove the pair along with the others to the ranch, enclosed them in the corral and then took off the ropes of the wild one and his partner. By that time the steer was ready to quit. He stood still, his nostrils dilated, his eyes savagely wild, and his body quivering all over. Then his muscles stopped twitching and he fell over dead. Roy and I had risked our necks to prove to the Avant boys that the old mossback could be taken alive out of the Granddaddy Thicket!

Most of the time our attempts to tame wild cattle were successful, but there were occasions like these when all the sweat, cussing, hard work, and all the dragging around in the dust over brush and stones—when all the long hours spent in the saddle under the blistering sun, in the hot winds, or in winter gales—when all the human energy, patience, and ingenuity brought us little or nothing—except maybe a hairless maverick, a steer dead of heart failure, or the skin of a bear to mount as a trophy; or maybe just the hollow sound of a couple of wild cows crackling through the brush down the steep side of a canyon.

CHAPTER IX

TOP HANDS

Ross Coe and Orville Hunt

IF I COULD BE AS GOOD a cowhand as Ross Coe, I'd often say to myself, "I'd not ask more from life." Ross was a top hand and taught me much of what I know about punching cows. An incomparable rider, he sometimes took part in "el corrido del gallo" that the Mexicans played at their fiesta celebrations, such as el Día de San Juan. I would go along with him to watch the daring and skill of the riders.

During the morning of the fiesta day people gathered, talking and passing the bottle. Then in the afternoon all the "valientones" would be "lista pa' el corrido del gallo." This was a game where a live rooster was buried in loose dirt up to his neck. Then a rider would race by, reach down and try to snatch the rooster from the mound alive. If he succeeded the other contestants would chase him and try to grab it from him. Whoever finished with the head of the rooster in his hand was the winner.

Not many cowboys had the nerve to compete, but Ross did, and once he succeeded in beating his opponents to the rooster and grabbed it. Then the tough little Mexican riders came alongside him and tried to snatch it from him. One rider was determined to get the gallo, or at least a part of it, so he slashed at the rooster's neck with his knife. As Ross was clutching the gallo and his saddlehorn with the same hand, the knife gashed his hand. But this was the sport that brought "olés" from the crowd.

At Fourth of July celebrations cowboys had a chance to show off their fancy riding and roping. On one such occasion at the V-V Ranch Ross had a close call. The bronc he was attempting to ride was a real outlaw. He stood straight up and finally shoved his two front feet over the picket posts of the corral. As Ross slid down his back, some men pulled at the bronc's hoofs until they unfastened them. Then Ross got on again. When this happened the horse snorted, pitched, and reared in a desperate effort to unseat him. In trying to stay in the saddle, Ross threw so much weight on the stirrups that one leather broke. As he started to roll off, his spur hung in the remaining stirrup and left him dangling, his chest and head banging on the ground with every lunge of the horse. As the bronc kept swinging him around, George Coe ran out and grabbed Ross and tried to free him. At the same time some other cowboys took hold of George and the whole bunch went swinging over the ground. Old man Avant, who was watching the spectacle, decided it had to be the rider or the horse so he pulled out his gun and stood by ready to shoot the animal. Every time the bronc leaped up or made a swing he bumped Ross's head in the dirt, but still his spur hung in the stirrup. At last the added pull of the other men broke it loose and Ross freed himself. When he got to his feet he was reeling and mad as a hornet. "Bring me that damned outlaw. I'm goin' to get back on him and scratch him from one end to another." With another saddle on him, Ross climbed on again. This time he stayed until he had him subdued.

Later Ross married, had a family, and became one of our solid citizens. He always had a deep interest in the development of the county and he worked hard to get better roads. It was through his effort that the Devil's Canyon road from Bonnell's Ranch (originally the Jap Coe place) to Capitán was constructed.

In July 1956 Ross, who then lived in California, visited us at the ranch, and at eighty-one he was still a handsome man who looked much younger than his years. He still stood a good erect six feet. His eyes were dimmed but his memory was remarkable.

Although his father, Jap Coe, had had no part in the Lincoln County War, Ross had heard much about it from Dad and Uncle George. When I asked him during this last visit what his own father had thought of Billy the Kid, he replied: "My father thought the Kid was all right. A lot of people had seen to it that the Kid and his friends got the blame for things they had not done. When they took the law into their own hands, they were doing no more than people who were considered good, law-abiding citizens. The so-called law at that time did nothing to help the cause the Kid fought for. Not long ago down in El Paso someone asked me at church if I didn't think Billy the Kid was a murderous gunman. I told the man he just didn't know the truth about the Kid. He didn't know it from his friends—people like Frank and George Coe. He admitted that he had never talked to anyone who had really known Billy."

On the controversy surrounding the deaths of Morton and Baker, Ross had this to say: "People talk of the Kid killing Morton and Baker. Well, it has never been proved that he did. But if he did shoot them, he was evening up the score for the death of my uncle, Ab Saunders, who died as a result of the shooting at Fritz Spring. The Kid took it as a personal affront that a friend of Frank and George Coe's was shot down without any justification. Billy never let go of a grudge easy and he knew the Seven Rivers gang had shot Uncle Ab. I was only a little fellow when they put Ab on the train, all shot up, and sent him to California to be with his folks. The boys took up a collection to get his ticket and they told me Billy was right there when the hat was passed." As proof of the friendship of the Coes for Billy the Kid, Ross reminded me: "George Coe went to Fort Sumner and tried to get the remains of the Kid brought to his ranch for permanent burial there."

The years I spent riding and roping with top hands like Ross Coe are dotted with many unforgettable men who had skill, savvy, and good natures—Upchurch of the V-V, Charlie Jones, Aristóteles (Harry) Aguaya, Frank Allison, and others. Cowboys have all kinds of qualities, some good and some bad. If there is one thing they have in common it is bragging—about their pony, their gun, or their sweetheart back home. Many of them bragged so much they actually believed what they were telling was the gospel truth. I never saw a cowboy worth his salt who did not boast about what he could do with his horse and rope.

And about cowboys being bowlegged. They are. Johnny Burns was more so than most. As wagon boss for the Diamond-A Ranch he had a good record. One day in Roswell he hurried from the barbershop and crossed the street to the First National Bank to attend to some business. A bunch of cowboys were leaning against the building and squatting on their hunkers watching him make a beeline for the bank. He did not use the intersection and a fire hydrant lay in his path. The cowboys wondered whether he had even seen it until he walked right over it without touching a hair.

In the Ruidoso Valley interesting and important work on the ranch came once a year when we had to round up the cattle, cut out the strays, and brand the calves. We had the herd inspected by the State Brand Inspector who gave us a bill of health that enabled us to sell. At that time there were no trucks to haul stock to market so we had to drive them by horseback to the shipping point at Capitán approximately fifteen miles away over rough mountain trails. It took three or four days to make the drive and return to the ranch. The calves could not be separated from the mothers until they were in the shipping pens, and it was impossible to drive them by themselves. Only the calves that were in good health and old enough to be weaned were taken away from their mothers and loaded into the boxcar. The cows were then turned out of the corral and headed back to their range. As a rule they gave no trouble on the way back, and as soon as we had put them through the Fort Stanton pasture, which joined our range, we closed the gate and turned them loose. They knew where to go.

In the early years of the cattle and horse business on the open range little or no stock salt was sold in the stores, so the animals had to find saltlicks wherever they could. There were certain places where strata of salt could be found. Occasionally there was a gulch or small stream that seeped from a salty formation which attracted stock and other beasts from miles around. Salt and sugar had other valuable uses in the taming and training of wild unbroken horses.

I remember Saturnino Lara, a bronc buster who worked on the ranch. He could not sign his name but knew a great deal about handling horses. At roundup time he helped brand the colts and tie up the unbroken geldings three years and older who had to be broken for the saddle and harness. In connection with the barn and barn lot Dad built and maintained a round picket corral about ninety feet in diameter made of straight cedar posts eight feet high placed close together and a large, smooth post four and a half feet high in the center of the corral, called the snubbing post.

The horses to be handled were put in this corral. As they were choused around, the roper would cast a loop around an animal's neck, if he was tame, or around both front feet if he wished to "bust 'im" on the ground. This was called "fore-footing." Saturnino was so expert with a lariat that he hardly ever missed a throw. He also knew just how and when to apply pressure on the end of the rope to catch the horse in midair and bust him flat on the ground. He could then tie a hind foot to the front feet that were roped together. The horse could squirm but could not get up. The cowboy then put the hackamore on him and changed his ropes so the animal could get up, but with one hind foot loosely tied so it would not reach the ground. This enabled the horse to stand but he could not move about easily. After struggling and falling some the bronc would give up. The buster would then grab the cheek of the hackamore with his left hand and the horn of the saddle with his right and flip the saddle neatly on the bronc's back. When the bronc calmed down the buster reached for the cinch and pulled it up tight. The horse struggled but soon gave up. The buster then removed all ties and with the hackamore rope in his left hand and the saddlehorn in his right, he put his left foot in the stirrup and swung into the saddle. He then slapped the horse on the head with his sombrero and yelled, "Vámonos." The bronc felt his freedom but, dazed by the treatment of the saddling operation, he lowered his head and started pitching with all his might. Saturnino, aboard with the greatest of ease, fanned him with his big sombrero as the bronc squealed and bucked. When he had enough Saturnino dismounted and let him rest, took from his pocket a handful of salt and put it on the lips of the bronc and spoke to him kindly saying, "You my friend, you no buck me off."

For several years Saturnino broke broncs for us. I never knew him to get mad, beat a horse over the head with the double of a rope or spur him in the shoulders as many other bronc busters did. He handled the horses with care and kindness. As he patted them on the neck or shoulder he talked to them and they seemed to understand his lingo. A lesson I learned from this jinete was that when working with livestock patience and kindness get the best results. In later life when working with people I found the same to be true.

The cattleman was king when Orville Hunt's father settled on the Block range north of the Capitán Mountains. Despised as a nester, Hunt had stuck it out at his ranch, staking his future on a small flock of sheep, a band of mares, and a jack that had cost him a thousand dollars in Iowa. But his mares died from eating locoweed, ruining his hopes for breeding them and building up a mule business. To my knowledge there were few men west of the Mississippi interested in breeding mules at that time. Dad, however, saw a need for them for farm work, freighting produce to market, and perhaps even for riding or packing. For considerably less than the price Hunt had paid, Dad bought the jack and began breeding mules on Coe

Ranch, which proved to be profitable. Some of these mules helped to build the highway from Roswell to El Paso. Most of them were shipped to the Southern states to be used in the cotton fields.

Nesters like the Hunts were not popular with the Block outfit, so Orville at first bypassed them when he was old enough to get a job punching cows. Instead he worked for the Cree Ranch. Orville's mind was not that of the average cowpoke. He was always trying to figure ways to outsmart the cattle and bring them in with a minimum of effort or keep them together on the long drives. One of these drives was to Roswell, the nearest shipping point, for which he once set out with Charlie Jones and Frank Allison, with fifteen hundred cattle strung out for miles. The men were kept busy riding the sides as many of the cattle tried to get off into the unfenced fields or up the side canyons. Coe Ranch was a convenient stopping place so Orville rode ahead to make arrangements with Dad to hold the herd overnight there. After the cattle had been watered and bedded down for the night, the cowboys were invited into the house.

Like many cowpunchers, Orville was bashful. Cowboys, on the whole, loved the freedom and adventure of the open range and shied away from serious romance or matrimony. Until Orville saw Winnie at Coe Ranch that trip he was more interested in some large steaks the Cree boys brought from their chuck wagon for Goss to cook. According to Dad, no one could cook steaks better. He would season them just so and put them into a big Dutch oven in a pit of hot coals outdoors.

After supper we all went into the parlor where Mother threw open the double doors to make room for dancing. Dad took his fiddle from its flour-sack cover and began tuning up as neighbors had already begun to arrive. As soon as Mother sat down at the piano, the cowboys timidly asked the girls for the first waltz. Orville was not too sure of himself on the dance floor so most of the time he stood next to Agnes, who directed the music and criticized those who could not get into step with the tunes. When he dared, he tried to make eyes at Winnie.

Orville stayed through the fall with the V-V outfit and when spring came he asked the Block Ranch for a job. Since they were getting ready to move down on the Pecos for operations, they needed some extra hands and took him on.

At the time Orville hired out to the Block Ranch no boundaries or fences designated the particular limits of ranch outfits. There was the Bloom Cattle Company, owners of the Diamond-A Ranch established in the 1870's, comprising the lower Río Hondo Basin from Picacho to the Capitán Mountains, thence east to the Pecos River and south to the Río Feliz. Its grazing country was different from that of other big outfits because it was composed of rolling hills, rocky draws, and river bottom slopes. Much of it was covered with scrub shinnery and cholla cacti and was so rocky it was necessary to keep the saddle horses shod all around.

The Block Ranch used a vast range extending from the Malpaís on the west to the Pajarito Mountains on the south, to the Pecos River on the east and thence in a zigzag northern line across the Llanos Estacados (Staked Plains). Some, almost seriously, claimed it went to the North Pole. To ride the range for the Block Ranch was to cover a wide area measured by miles instead of acres. The country from the Capitán Mountains to the north was made up of valleys and rolling hills with water supplied from small lakes and buffalo wallows fed by summer rains. W. C. McDonald, later to become the first governor of the State of New Mexico, then owned the ranch. It was so big it employed twenty-five to forty cowboys, each cutting out around fifteen cow ponies for his use. Only the old hands were allowed the regular use of some gentle horses. All others had to break their horses, which were selected by the boss from the remuda. They had to gentle them and train them while they were being used in the regular ranch work. If the job was too tough the horse was turned over to the bronc twister for gentling. "Three saddles" was considered sufficient to tame a bronc. For thirty days prior to the start of the round-up, Block Headquarters was a busy place. Cowpunchers, bronc busters, and ranch hands looking for jobs came in from all parts of the territory and some from Texas. Every cowboy had to provide his own saddle, spurs, "shootin'" tools, and yellow slicker. Many cowboys carried a harmonica to play in the evenings around the campfire. Some old-time Texas cowboys carried a fancy "hawg-leg" with notches on the handle to mark the number of men it had been used to kill.

The Block Ranch raised horses as well as cattle and thus produced their own cow ponies; some they sold to other ranches, and a number went to the cotton fields in the South to pull the plows and cultivators. From spring to fall the ranch had two or three covered wagons operating in the rounding up and branding of calves. Each wagon served as many as fifteen cowboys plus the wagon boss, the cook, and the wrangler. When a rainy spell came along all operations slowed down, and the cowboys were able to wash their saddle blankets, socks (if they wore any), and other clothing. When the sun finally came out again, they had to dry out their bedrolls. Some of the men slept in their boots rather than take them off because they shrank as they dried out. It was then as nearly impossible to pull them off as to get them on again, especially over bare feet.

Men who worked on the big ranches like the Diamond-A, the Circle Diamond, the Three Rivers, the Cree, and the Block were usually good hands. However, there were always some of another stripe—plain drifters, riding the chuck line. Maybe they would stop off for a while with some outfit, pitch in and help in order to rest their ponies and take on some grub. They would make the rounds of the big ranches then start all over again riding the chuck line. Those who bore watching were the rustlers who pretended to be drifters. All they wanted was a chance to get a bunch of cattle headed in the opposite direction from the herd. A fresh cowhide hanging on a fence a long distance from the big ranches was often enough evidence to convict a lot of rustlers.

It was early spring when Orville Hunt took a job with the Block Ranch. They were getting off to an earlier start than the Cree men because cold weather and snow lingered longer in the higher altitude. For a wagon boss the Block outfit had Tom Pridemore. His reputation for being mean was well-known, and when he took on a new hand, he put him through the mill. To try out the six-foot-two Orville, he dragged forth a snorting, mean-looking bronc for him to ride. Orville's own horse had "locoed" and left him on foot. If he had not been too smart to be taken in, Orville would have walked right into Pridemore's trap. Instead, he told the boss straight that he had not come there to ride outlaws. He wanted a job punching cattle, nothing more and nothing less. Few people before had ever dared to stand up to Pridemore and this made him like the kid's spunk and good judgment. After a lot of blustering and cussing, Tom led out a dependable horse rather than lose a prospect with the makings of a good cowhand.

At that time the Block outfit was engaged in one of the biggest roundups of horses in the West. There were forty or fifty men, a remuda of about five hundred horses, and four chuck wagons. Everyone ate together and every day it was beef with sourdough biscuits. The cooks did not bother to take the rocks out of the rice so breaking a tooth was frequent at the camp. Sugar was scarce or nonexistent, and prunes were served every day.

The roundup was getting off to a start when Orville's horse went down and pinned him underneath. The Block boss, Jim Lafferty, roped the pony and dragged him off, and then both started to the remuda to get Orville another horse. On their way back they saw an ominous black cloud which soon plunked hail on them, after which a hard cold wind came up. Three miles ahead at a safe distance from Rattlesnake Cave the wagons had found some small shelter and were waiting for the storm to hit. Soon a black funnel-shaped cloud appeared and began to dip to the ground, heading straight for the remuda. When it seemed that it was sure to hit the horses, it miraculously lifted and passed over them without damaging anything. When it struck the mountainside, it began to suck up the trees in one dip and spew them out with the next. It clawed its way over the Pajaritos, savagely scooping up the trees and leaving a clean path across the mountain, still visible today. So far as I know, this is the only tornado that ever struck in this area.

When this roundup was over, Orville quit the Block. Ever since he had met Winnie and had been smitten by her, he had been looking for excuses to come back to Coe Ranch. Just at this time Dad needed a good hand, and when Orville asked for a job he put him to work. It was not long after this that he and Winnie were married.

Had Orville chosen to remain a cowpuncher, he would have become a top hand. He loved the adventure of it, but the job lacked sufficient challenge for a man of his ability and drive; and the idea of "a million dollars in a million days," as the old saying about a cowboy's income went, had little appeal for him. At the advent of the horseless carriage he deserted cow ponies forever and found a better outlet for his ingenious mind under the hood of an automobile. Since he married Winnie, he no longer needed an excuse to visit Coe Ranch but he often came to see us, bringing sweet, winsome Winnie who had left an empty place in our hearts.

As the owner of the first automobile in the county, Orville attracted attention wherever he went. At Lincoln the whole town turned out when he drove in carrying the mail on the Roswell-Carrizozo run; for the first time in the history of New Mexico the railroads to the eastern and western parts of the state were connected with automobile mail service. Just for the thrill and prestige of it, people would pay him to ride in his auto on such occasions as to and from the baseball games only a few blocks away. Some of the real auto fans walked to the ballpark several times and paid just to ride back.

Along with the mail Orville carried whatever he could get into his auto to help pay expenses. One of his favorite stories was about the time he hauled a corpse in a coffin. At Nogal he had picked up this load, which was to be sent out on the next train from Carrizozo. As he thundered along over the Carrizozo flat, he heard the train whistle at Ancho so he knew he had to pull the gas lever all the way down to make it. For a while it seemed he was losing the race because the coffin bounced so much on the rough road it was in danger of falling off. But fortune favored him and he reached the station in time.

Orville tinkered continually with his machine to keep it running smoothly and he usually knew what to do when it stalled. He started out in his Buick one day and had not gone far when the oil ran dry. After he had filled the cup and started on his way again, he saw a Mexican family coming up the road. When the driver of the wagon saw the auto headed in his direction, he hastily unhitched his horse. The woman and kids fell over the sides of the wagon and took cover like scared rabbits. Holding his arms high and gripping the bridle, the man kept looking over his shoulder at the approaching auto. The horse, finding the bridle loose enough to slip off, ran away and left the man standing there so scared he was unaware of what had happened. He remained there holding the empty bridle and thus Orville found him. Very much amused, Orville asked him if he needed help to catch his horse. "Hell, no," the man replied, "don't bother with the horse. Help me round up my wife and kids."

As mechanically clever as Orville was, he found it hard to keep his Reo running. That is why he decided to leave it with me to sell. But before I got rid of it Orville and I had to attend a trial at Alamogordo so we drove it to Vaughn, where we boarded the train to go to court. There was no possible automobile road to Alamogordo. The trial had to do with a trespassing case against Felipe Sanchez, who was running a thousand sheep in the Forest Reserve. After the Forest Reserve Act had been passed and land allotments had been made, he continued to run his sheep, stubbornly refusing to move them out. Since no sheep permits were granted in the forest, the cattlemen wanted some action taken. Felipe ignored their complaints and continued to run his sheep. At the insistence of the cattle owners, the ranger went to investigate and ordered him out. But Felipe did not scare easily. He patted his six-shooter at his hip and told the ranger how he intended to enforce what he regarded as his rights.

When the ranger reported at headquarters, he was told to get proof that the man had refused to comply with the order. To do this, he had to take some cattlemen as witnesses, so Roy Coe, Nels Bonnell, Orville, and I went along to confront Felipe. We found him out on the range taking care of his sheep. He stood up to all of us and then went off and sat down behind a bush. The sheep had to be counted so Roy, Orville, and I cut them into bunches while Nels did the counting, picking up a rock for each ten sheep.

Since Felipe took such an adamant stand, the only thing to do was to bring the matter to court. Even after we arrived in Alamogordo, there seemed to be no hurry to get the trial going. A week dragged by. Finally we were told there would not be a trial because Felipe had decided he had better move out.

Orville and I boarded the next train for Carrizozo, where we picked up the canvas top of the Reo, which had been stored there previously. We had to figure a way to get some gasoline aboard the train to take back to Vaughn because they did not sell it there. By skillful maneuvering we smuggled a five-gallon can on the coach and stuck it, of all places, behind the stove, where we covered it with our coats. There was a big fire in the stove, and as the weather was very cold, we stood in front of it, with innocent looks on our faces, pretending to warm our hands. The can was well hidden but the odor was not. When the conductor came through, he said he smelled something. I quickly replied that I had recently cleaned my hat with gasoline. He gave me a doubtful look and went on his way.

Pretty soon a porter came through and said he smelled something. Before I had time to tell him about my hat, the conductor came back again and started pushing things around to find out what was causing such an odor. It had spread over the entire coach. The conductor stepped between Orville and me, pushed us aside and pulled the coats off the container.

"You boys know you can't carry gasoline on a train." He threw our coats at us as he said this.

"Yes, we can," Orville answered as if he really thought we could.

"Not any longer you're not." Angrily he picked up the can, handed it to the porter, and told him to throw it out. Orville and I followed him to the rear platform and sadly watched our precious gasoline roll down the side of the embankment. We were in a fix all right with an automobile but no gasoline within a hundred miles.

When we reached Vaughn we went to the shelter where we had stored the Reo and began putting the top on it. We hurried because the snow that had been coming down gently at the time of our arrival was now falling fast. We worried that the gas in the tank would not be enough to get us to Roswell. Darkness overtook us just as we put the last bolt into place, and we returned to the station to spend a miserable night hunched over the stove, waiting for daylight. Every time I dozed off a freight train came rumbling by and shook the building. So between the noise and the cold we slept very little.

At dawn the station door was pushed open and Logan McPherson came in to pick up the mail sacks. He carried the mail between Vaughn and Roswell. We explained our predicament to him and he told us to follow him to the Halfway House about fifty miles out where he had some gasoline stored.

The snow had let up some during the night but was coming down fast again; the road was thickly covered and often Logan could hardly make it out. Orville and I followed close behind him, wondering whether we had enough gas to make it to the Halfway House. In bitter cold the snow continued to come down. When the Reo began bucking, we knew we had run out of gas. All around us was desolate, snow-covered country. When we watched the last little speck of the mail car disappear, our spirits were low and our bodies cold. We put one blanket over the engine and the other over ourselves to begin our wait. We were not too sure that Logan himself could make it through the snow.

Two hours passed, and we waited and wondered, numb with cold. Finally we saw a little speck moving toward us across the wasteland. Good as his word, Logan had brought us a can of gasoline, which, with frozen fingers, we poured into the tank of the Reo. A few spins of the crank and the motor caught so we began following Logan over the tortuous path he had broken. But before we reached the Halfway House, he made too quick a turn and the axle of the front wheels snapped. The right wheel took off across the flat, jumped a barbed-wire fence, and kept going. I don't know whether Logan ever recovered it. It was now our turn to help him, so the three of us loaded the mail in the back of the Reo and continued on our way. At the Halfway House we stopped long enough to eat and later pulled into Roswell to deliver the United States mail to the post office.

Orville later transferred his interest in machinery to other mechanical fields, moving to Wellington, Oklahoma, to be near his people who had given up the nester's life. In nearby Watonga, Oklahoma, he installed a small private electric plant which was so successful that other businessmen hired him for similar projects. Without benefit of much schooling or technical training, Orville put in an electric plant to serve the whole town. Later he and Winnie moved to Oklahoma City, where he bought a laundry. To speed the steam power, he invented a press that was so successful he had it patented. It is still useful today where steam pressure is needed, and one is in service in the large modern Guaranty Laundry in Oklahoma City, which is owned and operated by Orville's grandson.

CHAPTER X

COLLEGE *Days at Stanford*

I MUST HAVE ENVIED Ross Coe and Orville Hunt as much as I admired them; if they wished, they could go on and be cowboys, but I had to get my schooling. After the summer Roy and I spent on the V-V roundup, I entered my senior year in high school at Roswell. My cowboy world lost some of its importance then, for when I could get up the nerve I shyly passed notes to Louise. It was like reaching for the moon, I suppose, to hope for a smile from anyone so pretty. I had thought about her occasionally after the summer of 1910 when Charley and I shod the Holland mules, but in the two intervening years our paths at school had not often crossed. When they did, I would blush and try to murmur a weak "hello." Other girls looked my way now and then but I paid them no attention.

But if Louise cared anything for me, I never guessed it. She was a junior and I always looked forward to history class where I would see her. It was bliss just to sit and look at the back of her head and maybe try to pass her a note. As first editor of our yearbook, the *Coyote*, I had hoped she would notice me, but by the end of the year I had made little progress in reaching the pedestal where I had placed Louise—tall, smiling, shy. Despite my crippled legs I had attained a height only slightly under average, with broad shoulders and muscular arms. But I was still shorter than the stately, brown-eyed girl I liked—and wanted to like me.

Contrary to my usual feeling, I was rather sorry to see the school year close. It had been a pleasant one. Palmer Bradley, who had shared the agony and delights of the Latin pony, was a co-worker on the *Cactus,* our high-school paper—a pleasant partnership along legitimate lines. I had attended my first three years of high school in the old Pauley Building, but for the last one I went to the new building. It was the realization of a dream for M. H. Brasher, the superintendent, who had spent years planning the "finest school in the Southwest." Many future prominent persons were among the forty-two of us who were graduated in the class of 1912.

With graduation came the problem of continuing my education. My parents wanted me to prepare for a professional career. All the other fellows went to the University of Texas but Professor W. E. Caroon thought that because of my interest in ranch life, I should go to A. & M. (now New Mexico State University). Dad wanted me to prepare for the law but Mother left it up to me. What I finally decided was the result of my association with Cecil Bonney (no relation to my father's former associate), whose father ran the first livery stable in Roswell. His mother had been Roswell's first schoolteacher. She had boarded at Pat Garrett's ranch and had ridden horseback each day to teach school.

Most boys at some time or other have their heroes to worship. Mine was now Cecil Bonney. He had finished high school two years before and was attending Leland Stanford University in California. We kept up a correspondence during this time and I decided that my choice would follow his. Being a plain cowhand seemed the logical course to me, but I wanted to please my parents and they wanted me to study law.

So Stanford and the law it was. Cecil knew the ropes and had put me wise as to how to get along on the least money possible. This was essential for both of us. He had gone to college to get an education, not to join a fraternity and waste a lot of time and money in "society." In Palo Alto he had found a cheap rooming house run by a widow with two pretty daughters. Cecil's tips on how to save money appealed to my sense of

Scottish thrift and to my business acumen inherited from both my parents.

When the fall of 1912 came, I caught the Golden State Limited at Carrizozo for Los Angeles, where I had to change for San Francisco. My first lesson from Cecil in how to make my money go a long way was applied when I boarded the train. "It is foolish," he had written me, "to spend money on the surcharge made by the Pullman Company. The way to get around it is to buy the straight coach fare and sit tight until night. Then when bedtime comes, saunter back to the Pullman cars, get hold of a porter, and explain that you are a poor boy traveling a long way and you are very tired. As soon as you see you have impressed him, tell him you will give him a dollar to let you sleep in an unoccupied berth."

I was tired all right when bedtime came. Ten hours in the daycoach had taken care of that. I was excited too about going so far away from home on a train. Mother had cautioned about watching my valise so no one would steal it or take it by mistake. I was as green as they come and a good prospect for any tinhorn crook. I kept close watch on the time, and a couple of hours after dark I decided it was all right to head back through the coaches to the rear of the train. There was so much jolting and jerking that I could hardly stay on my feet as I went through the littered aisles. I ran into a porter at the first Pullman. He had just finished making up the berths so he had time to listen to my proposition. He looked over a list of some kind on file in the vestibule. Then he went to the other end of the car to see whether the conductor and brakeman were still dozing there. He returned, picked up his little ladder, and motioned for me to follow him down the aisle between walls of green curtains. In front of number fifteen he placed the ladder and boosted me through the curtains into the upper berth, which contained a blanket and a pillow without a case. There were no sheets. Then he stuck out his hand into which I put a dollar.

By the time I had taken off my shoes and coat and stretched out I was not too sure I had made such a good bargain. I felt boxed up and had a choking feeling when whiffs of coal smoke drifted back from the engine. About the time I began to feel a little sleepy, the train came to a screeching stop that knocked my head against the berth. There were, in addition, the constant puffing of the engine in the distance and the relentless clickety-clack of the wheels on the tracks. Even though a kindly lady had promised to look after my valise, I could not help worrying about it. I turned on the light by my head and checked my wallet for the hundredth time. Most of my money, however, was pinned up inside the inner pocket of my vest. I checked that too to see that the pins were secure. Lulled at last by the sound of the wheels, I stretched on the green mattress and slept.

It seemed I had no sooner closed my eyes than the porter tugged my arm saying, "You sho'd better hurry up, suh, fo' de conductor gits in here to check de tickets." In a sleepy daze I almost fell out of the berth. Remembering Cecil's advice, I stopped by the Pullman dressing room where there were plenty of hot water, soap, and nice fresh towels. After wading through three coaches of sprawling humanity I found my own seat, where a man was jackknifed into a position trying to sleep. He got up grumpily and wandered back to his own, shared with another person.

It was early and I was hungry. About that time the conductor announced there would be a twenty-minute stop. When I asked him about getting some food, he told me I would have enough time to eat some ham and eggs at the station if I sprinted fast enough. But that cost money and besides I might miss the train. I settled for some candy I had stuffed in my coat pocket. It was a temptation later when the dining-car waiter announced breakfast. But Cecil's warning rang in my ears. "Above all, don't go to the dining car. Money flies faster there than anywhere. They charge you for even looking at the menu.

Besides there's the tip." So for the entire trip I chewed on caramels and ate sandwiches washed down by coffee. For the most part I ate candy, for I found it killed my appetite.

By the time we reached Los Angeles I was good and hungry. At first in the excitement of the busy station I passed up menus pasted on the front windows of eating places. The weather was sultry and humid. Thanks to the Pullman I had been able to wash the train grime from me, and with a fresh shirt my morale improved. I still had the worry, though, of getting on the right train. When I found it, I sank back on the seat relieved. Just to be sure there was no mistake, though, I stuck my head out of the window and yelled to a brakeman with a long-spouted oilcan, asking him if this was the train to San Francisco. He assured me that it was, and as he was the third person I had asked I was satisfied. I always felt better after I had checked and rechecked such information.

At the station in Oakland, I had to find out how to get the ferry which I knew I had to take to San Francisco. The trip across the Bay was exciting because I had never been on such a big boat and I had never seen so much water. Soon the penetrating cold and dampness of the Bay area enveloped me. I was so hungry I could no longer postpone spending some money for food. At the ferryboat lunchroom I spent twenty-five cents for half a cantaloupe.

Disembarking in San Francisco, I lugged my valise outside the station and stood on the corner watching the sights of the city just like any other country boy. I wondered whether I would ever be able to get across the street in so much traffic and noise. A few taxis and other autos were blowing their horns, streetcars were clanging and jangling their bells, and heavy horse-drawn brewery wagons, bread wagons, and milk wagons set up their clatter. I enjoyed watching the large Percheron and Clydesdale horses of powerful build and broad sleek backs pulling beer wagons.

Remembering that I had to cross the city to another station, I recalled Cecil's instructions: "Don't take a taxi. Those birds know how to charge. Ride the streetcar, go slower, and save money." As I was thinking about this warning, a taxi drew up to the curb and before I knew it the driver was out of the cab, throwing my valise in the front seat and pushing me into the back. As he closed the door behind me he asked, "Where to, Sonny?"

I answered that I didn't know I had said I was going anywhere. "Oh, sure'n you're goin' somewhere. Everybody is. People don't go around carryin' valises if they ain't goin' somewhere."

"All right then. I am going somewhere, but I happen to be going on the streetcar."

"On those rattle-trap things? Look, Sonny, I can take you where you're goin' a lot faster. Just name the place and I'll show you."

Seeing that I couldn't get rid of him any other way I put it to him straight and told him I was riding the streetcar because it was cheaper. I didn't know why I should spend twenty-five cents for a taxi when I could ride the streetcar for a nickel.

At that he laughed good-naturedly. "All right, you win. You may be a hayseed but I'll bet no one skins you out of anything. Come along. I'll show you Joe Mulraney's heart is in the right place." With that he picked up my valise and threaded his way through the traffic to the other corner where I was to catch the streetcar. He then slapped me on the shoulder and said, "Good luck."

Soon the streetcar he had told me to take came to a clanging stop. I boarded it, making sure that the conductor understood I wanted to get off at Third and Townsend. At three thirty I arrived at Palo Alto and just to be sure, I asked the station agent there if the university was in this town. He smiled and assured me it was, offering to keep my valise until I could find a place to stay. Unfortunately for me, Cecil, who had done all he could to get me to Stanford, was unable himself to return because of strained finances. Anyway I did not particularly want to go to his boardinghouse where there were distractions. I wanted lodgings to myself where I could study hard without getting involved socially.

When I had left, my dad had handed me two hundred and fifty dollars. He did not have to tell me to take care of it and make it go as far as possible. I knew that Dad and Mother were making a sacrifice to send me to college. Few boys in those days received a college education, and parents were sometimes skeptical about the benefits of one. College boys were generally pictured as a rowdy bunch of rah-rah fellows with curve-stemmed pipes, striped blazers, and shallow-crowned felt hats with the brim turned up on the side. They swung tennis rackets and sang "Boola-boola." The madness of goldfish-swallowing, the Charleston, or coonskin coats had not arrived, but my generation still found it easy to spend their "old man's" money. With girls in long, tight hobble skirts slit daringly to mid-calf they danced the turkey-trot and one-step or romanced to the tune of "By the Light of the Silvery Moon" or "Meet Me Tonight in Dreamland."

I wanted to make a go of my career and avoid the pitfalls of the college campus. I began by finding living quarters. I will admit that at the time I felt lonesome and forlorn and wished I could scuttle the idea of going to college. Just being a plain cowboy back on the ranch was good enough for me. But here I was and somewhere I had to find lodging. It would be risky to pay tuition before getting a place to stay.

On reaching the college campus, I got off the streetcar and stood for a moment just looking up and down the street at the nice-looking houses. I flipped a quarter to decide in which direction to go and started walking. At the end of a block I asked a student I met where the frat houses were. So far as my savvy about the college campus was concerned, frat houses were where college boys lived. They were just like boarding-houses. All I had to do was to walk up to one and engage a room. The boy told me I was smack in the middle of a bunch of them so I went up to the nearest one, which had a "Lazy M-N" brand above the door. The house was so fancy looking I doubted whether I could afford to pay the price they might ask.

Lifting the heavy brass hammerlike thing on the door and letting it fall with a thud, I waited. Soon a very motherly looking woman opened the door and said something about my being one of the fraternity initiates, a new student. She added that they were not expecting anyone so soon.

"They're not exactly expecting me, ma'am. I just got in from New Mexico and I'd like to rent a room from you if your price isn't too high. A fellow down the street told me this is a frat house. That's the reason I stopped."

I wondered why she had so much difficulty keeping her face straight when she answered, "I think what you want is a regular boardinghouse or dormitory like Encino Hall. Now if you will just take the streetcar and go back six blocks, you'll be right there."

I thanked her and went to the corner to wait for the streetcar, a little put out because Cecil had not wised me up to the fraternity house business. I was dog-tired and good and ready to call it a day. At Encino Hall I was given little encouragement. There was a long waiting list. But I was told I could sign up and await my turn if I wanted to. The clerk made it plain, though, he could not promise me anything—maybe next semester if a vacancy turned up. I signed up, little caring at the moment whether I ever got a room there. I was still hungry so I went into a little café nearby and ordered pie with ice cream on top. Just as I started to put a forkful in my mouth a friendly, nice-looking boy about my age sat down alongside me at the counter and said, "Howdy. Is that pie worth the price?"

With that question we began to get acquainted. He was in the same predicament as I. He told me he had looked over two or three places to live but had not settled on any one. He favored most of all a small hotel a block away, adding that the place was full but the manager had promised him accommodations of sorts he could fix up for him. In the meantime he had introduced himself as N. J. Mittenthal from Fresno. He felt sure that the manager of the hotel could put me up too, so as soon as we finished our pie we left for the hotel.

The room that had been promised N.J. turned out to be the lobby. The manager agreed to put up cots for both of us until a room was vacant. I hurried back to the station to get my valise, but as we could not go to bed early we killed time until the rest of the guests turned in. I do not know whether any of them came through our sleeping quarters; I was so tired I wouldn't have heard a streetcar clang through.

Within a couple of days we were given a room and remained there the entire semester. Later on in the year I met a fellow named Earl Dykes, who had come to California with his mother because of her health. His father was to follow soon and take up medical practice at Redwood City. I found a nice rooming house near a cheap café in the vicinity where they lived and later moved there. I had to keep close watch on my expenses. For twenty cents I could get dinner, the main fare being soup, potatoes, cabbage, sauerkraut, and beans cooked German style. Although the food was palatable and nutritious, it was always a welcome change to be invited to the Dykeses. I saved the price of a meal, too. I especially enjoyed myself when Mrs. Dykes made fudge; I supplied the muscle to beat it and a big part of the market for it.

As soon as I enrolled and arranged my schedule of classes, I began to study. Because of low grades on my entrance exams in English, I had to work extra hard to keep up the pace expected of me. Financially I was getting along all right. By the end of the semester I was able to lend Cecil money to return. By charging him interest I found a way to improve my own finances so I set up a *sub rosa* loan agency and lent money to fellows who received checks regularly from home. When I wrote to Dad I explained that with the help of the interest I was receiving on money lent to college boys, I was getting along all right. I added in a postscript that if he could send me some more funds, I could expand my activities. Since he had faith in my business ability, he sent me the money. I knew that if I became involved in any difficulties with my project, I would have to find my own way out.

College was not all boning and figuring finances. While Mittenthal and I were still in our small hotel, a hazing party hunted us down and administered us the rites that made us full-fledged college boys. Although the trustees and faculty had not yet banned freshman initiation, it was frowned upon by them. Whatever was done had to be carried out on the sly. About the time N.J. and I were beginning to feel smug about escaping from it, a gang came to our hotel room and knocked on the door loudly. Without waiting to be told to come in, they burst into the room, picked us up like a couple of sacks of potatoes, and took us out to the square in front of the hotel to a large watering trough. With a warning to us to say our prayers, they dumped us in and sloshed us under the slimy moss on top. We did not try to resist. After they made sure we were thoroughly soaked, they let us crawl out, dripping like rats. Then they told us we were good sports and gave us ten minutes to put on dry clothes and meet them at "Sticky's" (which was our nickname for a little soda fountain nearby) for some pie à la mode "on them." By the following year initiating freshmen was banned so all we sophomores could do was to send them on errands or make them shine our shoes.

During my sophomore year my number came up on the reserve list at Encino Hall so I moved at once into Room 13, which I shared with R. S. Ring. One of our windows opened onto the porch and made a handy entrance and exit. Under the porch I parked my motorcycle, a luxury made possible by an increase in my allowance from home. For two years I shared these quarters with Sid, a brilliant and ambitious fellow who finished college in three years.

During my fourth year I roomed with John Holland, Louise's brother. After receiving a degree in business administration, he settled in Los Angeles and later served as councilman from the Fourteenth District for twenty-four years, from 1943 to 1967.

Valued friendships made during high school and college days have been lifelong, among them Palmer Bradley of Roswell who received a law degree from the University of Texas and became a successful lawyer in Houston as well as vice-president of the Trans World Airlines. Through the years Cecil Bonney has been president of the Chaves County Savings and Loan Association, Roswell's oldest and largest business of that kind. N. J. Mittenthal was graduated with honors in electrical engineering and was later selected by the National Park Service to install the elevators in Carlsbad Caverns, New Mexico. R. S. Ring became an outstanding businessman in Los Angeles, and Earl Dykes, a dentist in Oakland, California. Since graduation these old college friends and their wives have visited Coe Ranch and we have shared many happy memories of Stanford.

In the pleasant company of such fellows as these I kept plugging away preparing myself for law. I had considerable interest in Spanish because of my closeness to it on the ranch. In high school I had studied it, hoping to converse better with our ranch hands, but I found out book Spanish didn't match the ranch kind. Under Dr. Aurelio Espinosa at Stanford, my instructor in Spanish, I showed considerable ability. Hoping that I would keep up studying the language, he secured for me an assistant professorship of Spanish at the University of Colorado, but law was my major field so I continued with it. After receiving my B.A. degree in the spring of 1916, I returned in September for my J.D. (Juris Doctor). But because by then the United States had entered World War I, and Dad had been left short-handed on the ranch, he offered me half interest in the cattle when I came home for Christmas. Since I had never wished for anything except ranch life and had proved that my affliction was no hindrance in pursuing it, I accepted his offer.

At the time there was little incentive to enter the law. Young attorneys who had hopefully hung up their signs were starving while they waited for clients. It is true a good criminal lawyer could make money, but he was not too popular with the people (except perhaps his clients). So with only a gentleman's agreement with Dad I left my postgraduate studies and went to work on the ranch.

CHAPTER XI

Breeding and Shipping
LIVESTOCK

SINCE DAD had gone in for breeding mules on a large scale, we both gave considerable attention to providing plenty of them for the Southern market. On the farms of the South they were used extensively in the furrows of the cotton fields. We already kept two jacks, a couple of stallions, and a number of range mares on the ranch. With the current demand for mules so great, Dad wanted to send as many as possible to the market as fast as he could. That is why I was considerably interested in an advertisement I saw in a newspaper one day not long after I returned from college. It announced the beginning of a new term at Graham's Scientific Breeding School in Kansas City, where artificial insemination, a new thing at the time, was to be taught.

Anything about livestock has always interested me. As a young boy one of my favorite books was *The Illustrated Stock Doctor and Live Stock Encyclopedia* by Dr. J. B. Manning. My father consulted it often. There was no disease of horses, cattle, sheep, poultry, swine, or hogs that it did not include. By studying it, Dad became a very good veterinarian and was often asked to neighboring ranches to treat livestock. Had there been a section in the book about rabbit breeding, perhaps I would have foreseen the outcome of a previous experiment of my own in animal husbandry.

It all began when a doctor at Fort Stanton gave me a pair of beautiful white rabbits. No one around had ever seen anything like them. Thinking that they would be nice pets, I put them out in the storehouse, which was partly underground, and I tended them carefully. Greatly to my delight there soon were some baby rabbits, so I began figuring how I could produce a pinto specimen from them. That was my favorite marking. So I got a black buck from the doctor to start my experiment in crossbreeding.

Dad did not pay much attention to my operations until he noticed that the rabbits were undermining the storehouse. Eventually they began to burrow under the other ranch buildings, so Dad told me to clear them out. I pleaded with him so much that, for the time being, he relented. As the rabbits multiplied, the foundations of the buildings started to weaken. Dad's patience was wearing thin. Finally, when he discovered that the green vegetables in the garden were disappearing, he laid down the law. The rabbits had to go.

This ultimatum came just before I had to return to school in Roswell and so I had to leave my experiment. When I returned to the ranch for Thanksgiving holidays, there was not a rabbit left on the place. Dad (with his tongue in his cheek) reckoned they had hightailed it to the hills to live with the jack rabbits. Thereafter as I rode the range I kept my eyes peeled in the hope that maybe some day I would see a spotted rabbit with blue eyes jumping around with the jack rabbits. I never did.

Improving our production of mules would pay off well for the ranch. Dad found the breeding school's ad of interest and offered to enroll me at Graham's. So I went to Kansas City. The weather was cold and damp but the people were friendly. The students were from the Middle West mainly, and when they learned where I was from they asked me all about conditions in "Mexico." They were surprised that I spoke English so well and wondered why I had come to a place like Graham's. I told them that we raised mules and horses on our ranch and I wanted to learn scientific methods of breeding.

On the first day of school Dr. Graham came around to greet us personally. He had two other instructors who assisted him with the classroom work, which went on all day; evenings were for studying. Toward the end of our term we went to the stockyards and performed experiments on dead animals. I thought our course was very thorough. At the close of the session we were given certificates stating that we had completed the course. I purchased the equipment we would need for artificial insemination, which included a seventy-five-dollar microscope with which to determine the activity of the semen. The price seemed steep, but later ten capsules did the work of a single service. This paid off well in extending the usefulness of a stud or jack. Mule production on Coe Ranch reached its maximum after we started using the reproduction methods taught at Graham's.

The drives to get our stock to the markets were long and involved very hard work. The distances (from fifteen to sixty miles) did not wear out the animals enough to subdue them or accustom them to going with the herd. Half a dozen cowboys were kept busy riding the flanks and trailing the drags. Our nearest shipping point, Capitán, was about fifteen miles from the ranch, and at the time we began making shipments from there it was a coal boomtown. A fine grade of anthracite had been discovered in the Salado country three miles west of the town. This brought a rush of prospectors, which caused a tent city to spring up overnight. People slept in wagons, under tents, and in cardboard shacks. Through the efforts of Charles B. Eddy, the great New Mexico promoter and financier, the El Paso and Southwestern Railroad built a spur line from Carrizozo to Capitán. At the Capitán end of the line a depot and store were erected.

Completed before the turn of the century, the railroad was a masterpiece of engineering construction for those days. The rough high country it had to go over presented many problems. From Carrizozo to the foot of Nogal Hill the slope was gradual, but after that the terrain was broken and rugged with high irregular ridges separated by deep narrow canyons. The relatively "easiest" way to get there still involved two formidable problems: how to climb the first hill and then immediately cross a deep canyon, and from there how to get up a second hill, really a small mountain.

The first climb was accomplished by building a long switchback that started up a deep canyon and then cut back again until it finally reached the top. Then a high trestle was built over the canyon, and so the next mountain was reached. It seemed too high and irregular to go over on a grade tolerance. According to local legend, the railway hired an Indian scout who took his cow to the end of the trestle and turned her loose. By trailing her up the ascent, he located a grade possible for the railroad. In any event, this summit is still called Indian Divide. On the other side a steep cut was made that put the trains on a downward slope from the Coalora Mines to Capitán. All the work was done with pick, shovel, ax, and dynamite, plus the brains and brawn of men.

Going up the switchback was a novel experience affording ample time to enjoy the scenery, for the climb took more than two hours. Crossing the high trestle and making the switchback down were frightening, but I never could resist hanging my head out of the window to look at the view. Sometimes they had to put sand on the tracks to keep the engine wheels from slipping. The downhill ride was even noisier, for the brakes on the flatcars screeched and squeaked. The runs were made on Tuesdays and Fridays; I doubt that the train crews could have stood up under more than that.

On one of my trips we were shipping a carload of cattle from Capitán to Kansas City. After we had driven the stock to the shipping point we waited at the stock pens for the train to back in so we could get on with the hard chore of loading them. This done, I decided to ride on top of the cattle car to be nearer the stock. The cows, jammed together, often became restless and began to push and fight. As the stops were so numerous and jerky there was always the possibility that some of them might be knocked down and trampled. I climbed the cattle car without anyone seeing me and flattened out so I would not be discovered by any of the train crew.

Soon a burly brakeman came along and said, "Boy, you'd better get back to that passenger coach where you belong. The conductor has been looking everywhere for you. He's holding the train on your account." "Please tell him that my cattle need attention and I am here to look after them," I asked. In a bad humor because he had to climb after me, he snorted and went on across the top of the cattle car and down the ladder.

In a short time the conductor walked over the narrow planks down the center of the car. "What in the hell do you think you're doin' up here, cowboy? Don't you know there's a rule against ridin' on top of trains?" I explained that I had ridden worse things than a cattle car and that my job was to be near enough to watch over "those damned old wild cows" and try to help (when we stopped) or at least be able to report if any got knocked down or trampled. Partly convinced, he turned to leave, saying, "Well, if you get your danged neck broke it'll be your own fault."

Alone again, I began to think it over. Evidently the train had really been stopped on my account, for as soon as the conductor left me, it started up. I held on for dear life when the rough jerks began and thought about how dangerous it was. But there was nothing I could do for the moment but grip the planks because we were beginning the slow grind up the Indian Divide. The higher we climbed the less I cared to look at the view. It was a relief to reach the switchback with its long stops because then I could climb down to stir the cattle and look more closely at them.

There was no definite schedule that made it possible for carlot shipments of fruit or livestock to hook on neatly to the main-line freighters at Carrizozo. We loaded at Capitán when we could and waited at Carrizozo to be switched on to the main line. A carload brought there at three in the afternoon stayed on the siding in the burning heat or the freezing cold while the shipper passed away the hours at the two-storied railroad eating house known as the Beanery. This accommodation was a gathering place for tramps, bums, shippers, and anyone else who wanted to escape the cold by huddling around the potbellied stove. They sat, if there was anything to sit on, or stood close to the stove with their hands in their pockets to keep them from getting too hot or too cold, depending on how much coal there was in the stove.

The upper floor of the building contained a string of bedrooms filled with dust, soot, cobwebs, and the accumulated odors of years. Cracks in the walls and floors provided enough ventilation. Each room had a coal-oil lamp with a smoked chimney, a chipped enamel slop jar, a washbowl, and an iron bedstead that guaranteed company—if you cared for bedbugs. I always preferred to sit out the wait in the lobby but had to be careful not to fall asleep and get rolled by some bum.

The whistle of the mainliner steaming up the tracks the next morning was a welcome sound. After the load of cattle was hooked on to it, I went back to the caboose. Except for the worry of unloading the cattle at the pens en route to water and feeding them I enjoyed the trip.

When I reached Capitán on the way back I killed some time around the Titsworth store. It was a place with an interesting history. Shortly after the railroad opened this big mercantile establishment, it enlarged their commissary at Coalora and moved in as manager an energetic young man named George A. Titsworth. He took care of the Capitán business, which was flourishing because of the local coal boom and the wide area the store served.

When Titsworth came to manage the company store he saw a great future there for the mercantile business. Nearby Fort Stanton had become a United States merchant marine hospital and a large market for wholesale goods while rural people traveled many miles to get their supplies in Capitán also. He began to look for capital to open his own store and so he went to El Paso to consult his good friend and former employer, E. W. Welch. Welch knew that Titsworth was a man of high integrity with a lot of drive, and he not only lent him money but also went into partnership with him, calling their concern the Welch and Titsworth Company.

Anyone who opened a business in Capitán was bound to run into some tough competition and rough tactics from the company store. But the twenty-by-forty-foot building that Titsworth put up across from it was well-stocked, and with his policy of long-term credit he drew a large number of customers, including many from the company store. His slogan, known all around the country, was: "Come in and load up." And the people did. From a small beginning financed with borrowed money he built up a business that later made him a wealthy man. Ranchers whose stock or crops failed to hit the markets in time to make payments due at the store welcomed his long-term extension of credit. Titsworth renewed their notes and told them to load up with a six month's supply of food, clothing, stock remedies, tobacco, and other necessities.

In the fall when the produce was ready to sell he sent out circular letters reminding people to come in and settle up their accounts. Along with this notice was a cordial invitation to load up again with bargains in shoes, calicoes, flour, coffee, and implements needed on the farms and ranches. If because of continuing unfortunate circumstances a man was unable to meet his long-overdue obligations, Titsworth did the only thing he could to protect his investment—he annexed a bunch of cattle or a parcel of land. When he extended his business into the Hondo Valley, his brother Will came in as a partner, later marrying my sister Annie. For many years my father and I bought supplies for Coe Ranch from the Titsworth Company.

George A. Titsworth was a man of courage and good judgment. He stood firm in his beliefs and never retreated in the face of difficult going. Living out his life in Capitán, through good days and bad, he was as solid as the rocks of Nogal Peak.

CHAPTER XII

Trips to the South to
SELL HORSES

URING MY LATER COLLEGE VACATIONS I dated
Louise frequently, and by the time I went into partnership with Dad our romance had become more serious. As
Edith's guest she had spent two weeks at our house, riding,
dancing, and taking part in our musical activities. Our families
were well acquainted. Louise's father and mother had come to
New Mexico to settle in 1907 on a farm her father had bought
around 1900 when some promoters of the Pecos Valley ran an
excursion train through Texas. They had invited men with
money to invest in this valley. Louise's father was among the
investors, and bought a section of land near the small village of
Dexter, sixteen miles south of Roswell. Not long after, when
Louise's mother was advised to go to a dry climate for her
health, her father sold out his mercantile business in Bartlett,
Texas, and the family moved to the New Mexico farm. The
Dexter school only went through eighth grade so they soon
moved to Roswell. After Louise graduated from the Roswell
High School she attended the University of New Mexico where
she received her degree in school administration. At the time
when Louise and I began to see each other more often she was
teaching in Glencoe's little one-room school. On my way to
Kansas City to attend Graham's I had stopped there to tell her
good-bye.

The days following my return to the ranch were busy ones.
Dad had previously worked mostly cattle, but now we were
trying to breed mules and build up our herd of mares and
horses. Since I knew a man who had some good-quality range
mares and horses, I made a deal with him to buy some. In all

he delivered forty head at twenty dollars each. Out of this number fifteen were good young ones with special qualities that made them excellent cow ponies and polo horses. I remember selling a dealer one little pony for three hundred and fifty dollars. He was completely obedient to the handling of the rider and had stamina, quick stops, and fast turns. At this time we kept on the range some stallions that sired a good-quality, tough range horse that when mixed with better blood produced a fine-grade saddle pony.

The projected plan to build up a big horse business became threatened by the disappearance of the open range. Fences were coming in and coming in to stay. They spelled the doom of the vast areas of open range land with their grazing for thousands of cattle and horses. We had a few hundred head of horses on the pasture by then and had to figure some way to market and reduce the herds. About 1917 we started rounding them up and shipping them into the cotton states of Louisiana, Georgia, and Mississippi. They were completely wild, tough-fibered mustangs that resisted being herded together for the three-day trip to our shipping point at Roswell. The cowboys had to fan out around them to prevent their breaking out for the open range. I recall a cowboy on one such drive who was riding a black, skittish, half-broken horse. When he wheeled around quickly to chase a runaway, his own horse started bucking wildly. It followed a zigzag path that kept the cowboy leaning heavily on first one side and then the other to keep from being knocked off by the limbs of the trees and by heavy brush. The horse finally dumped him into a clump of prickly-pear cactus. Before he was able to sit on the chuck wagon the rest of the way he had to have emergency "surgery" performed with a pair of pincers. Our drives were often spiced with incidents of this kind.

Once we reached Roswell we had to herd the bunch into the stock pens. Then the train crew helped the cowboys shoo, rope, punch, fight, and cuss until the sixty horses were loaded inside two boxcars. With loading operations over and our two car-loads of horses hooked on to the main-line freight train, Bob Boyce and I settled down in the caboose to sway and rock to Jackson, Mississippi. At various stops the horses had to be unloaded, watered, fed, and allowed to rest.

On one such stop at Sweetwater, Texas, I had to report to the station agent that one of the horses had a broken leg because of negligence on the part of the railroad. I specified that one hundred and fifty dollars should be paid me for the loss of the horse. I was not too sure the injury had been due to neglect but I was playing my cards close, and the loss of a single animal had to be avoided if possible.

The agent argued. "One hundred and fifty dollars is a lot of money for an ordinary horse. I'll get some stockmen to appraise him."

Sure enough, at the next stop three men pondered over the dead horse and came up with an estimate of one hundred and twenty-five dollars, which I turned down. The agent then sent in a claim to the main office for the amount I had named. After much correspondence and a lengthy delay I received a check for hundred and twenty-five.

Bob, I, and the horses were pretty worn out by the time we reached our destination, but there was no time to rest up because we had to get the horses sold as quickly as possible. As I was not selling them directly to livestock dealers, we had to handle them in any market we could find, wherever we could find it. It was important to move fast because feeding that number of horses for very long would rapidly put us in the red.

I met a man around the stock pens and explained my problem to him. He thought the best thing to do was to get them out of town and make direct contacts with the cotton farmers, who needed horses badly at the time. He had no idea how we could get a herd of wild mustangs through the streets of the city, but he was kind enough to offer to go ahead of us with his horse and buggy to show us the road to Pocahontas, sixteen miles north of Jackson. He was sure we could find some buyers there.

Bob and I thought the idea was a good one so we started out. Before we had gone very far we found we had overestimated the tiredness of the horses as well as our ability to herd them through city traffic. Clanging streetcars and other city noises were too much for wild mustangs. Before we had gone a couple of blocks, they were nervous and giving us a hard time. At an intersection a streetcar came around the corner and passed between us and the buggy. We never saw our friend in the buggy again. For a while it seemed that we had seen the last of our horses. When the streetcar headed our way the broncs started running in all directions and then, I am sure, Jackson, Mississippi, saw its first and only real wild horse stampede. Bob rode in one direction to round up what he could of them and I started off in another. Fortunately for us we were near the grounds of the state capitol whose lawn was covered with fine long lespedeza grass.

As quickly as a bunch of grass-hungry horses spotted it, they went in that direction so as Bob and I rounded up the strays, we took them to the capitol lawn to hold them. They remained there without trouble, filling up on the good grass. The exhibition of horsemanship and roping Bob put on that day in the streets of Jackson was better than one could pay money to see. He was handsome astride his pony, and his rope never missed. His uncanny sense of direction helped us round up many of the strays that would have otherwise kept us combing the city.

At first Bob and I were too busy to notice we were attracting a lot of attention. We went about our business, yelling and swearing as only cowboys can do when horses are stubborn. A big crowd gathered as office workers and state officials came from the building and joined the passers-by. We had noticed a policeman among them, but when it seemed he was not going to interfere we both slowed down our pace to give the mustangs as much time as possible to crop the grass. We certainly were a spectacle—real Western cowboys and broncs fresh off the range.

Before we had finished rounding up the last few horses, more policemen joined the crowd and wanted to know why we were causing all this commotion. We explained what had happened and that we needed enough time to round up eight more horses that were still loose. The policemen were understanding and obliging and at once scouted around the town to look for the strays. Bob and I followed a hunch he had and returned to the stock pens where the horses had been unloaded, and we found them there. Knowing that we could not overstay the hospitality of the Jackson officials, we then headed the horses out of town, the policemen helping us. I did get a chance to do some free advertising when I was asked numerous questions by different members of the crowd. I made it clear we were going to take the horses to the edge of town on the way to Pocahontas. If anyone was interested in buying I would see him there.

On the outskirts of Jackson we were able to get an acre of enclosed land for a corral. I left Bob there and went into town to make contacts for the sales. I had little trouble starting conversations with the friendly Southerners. In a short while I spotted a man in front of a grocery who looked like a prospective buyer. When I stopped he came up to me and wanted to buy my nice gentle pony. I told him that back at the corral I had just what he was looking for, so we went there to look over the pony I had been riding the day before.

I had been schooled well by Dad in the art of horse trading and was quite qualified to handle "slickers." However, with this particular customer I did not have to dicker. The minute he saw the pony he wanted to buy it. When I named sixty dollars as the price he took out his wallet and handed me the money. Bob and I were encouraged and felt sure we would not have too much trouble getting rid of the others. As I stood counting the money the purchaser was running his hands over the neck and ears of his new horse to make friends with him. Suddenly he pulled his hand from behind the left ear and looked at something he had in it. "Look here, cowboy, what's this I've found on the horse you just sold me?" he asked.

I didn't have to look any closer, for I knew what he had probably found. When he handed it to me I turned the mite over in my hand. There was no doubt it was a tick of some kind, and I knew that livestock men over Texas and the Southern states were fighting the fever tick. Quarantines were being slapped on livestock wherever ticks were found. To have this happen to my broncs would mean weeks of confinement for the horses and regular dips in the community vat. It would be ruinous for me if word leaked out that my mustangs had ticks.

I had to say something so I answered with, "Oh, I guess that's just a rabbit tick. My horses don't have the worse kind."

"Now, how can you be sure your horses don't have any of the worse kind? It sure is taking a chance to buy a horse with ticks."

"Well, I am sure of one thing, and that is if my horses have ticks, they picked them up after they left New Mexico. Probably in the boxcars or in the stock pens around the South." I was nettled because the man thought I had purposely sold him a ticky horse. I wanted to convince him my horses were tick-free when they left the West. "I don't see how such a thing as this happened. Those horses were given a clean bill of health when they left the yards at Roswell. I couldn't have moved them an inch without it. I'm certain too that I would not have sold you a horse with ticks if I had known about it."

I saw there was no way to change his mind about the tick, but perhaps I could get him to keep quiet long enough for us to sell the horses and leave. I felt absolutely sure it was a rabbit tick and he was making a lot of fuss about nothing. By knocking a substantial amount off the price of the horse, he agreed to keep quiet. It would be cheaper to destroy the others than to put them under quarantine for weeks with the prescribed dips in the vat.

As soon as we got rid of him Bob and I began to look for another place for our operations. When we found one I hired a couple of husky Negroes to help us take what precautionary steps we could to handle the situation. I bought five gallons of creosote, a couple of galvanized tubs, and a spray and we all went to work. As Bob cut out the horses one by one we drenched them from nose to tail with a solution I knew would kill any kind of tick the horses had. As we worked I kept thinking about the man I had sold the horse to. In the back of my mind was the thought he was going to do some talking.

My premonition was correct. No sooner had we finished spraying than the local law officer paid us a call. He wanted to know whether we had any ticky horses. If we did all the animals must be placed under quarantine. I explained what we had done to kill whatever ticks the horses might have and assured him that we did not want to risk spreading tick fever any more than anyone else. I ended by inviting him to examine a few of the horses. He agreed to do this at once.

Bob roped several, threw them, and tied their feet. The official looked them over and came up with two dead ticks. Since they were dead, I argued, the creosote would take care of any others that might be around. Still he was not satisfied. He said that he was a town official and had his duty to carry out. At that kind of talk I began to get very worried. Finally he told me that because the matter was so serious, it could not be decided by him. I asked who could make a decision. When he answered that the only way to get positive identification of the ticks was to send to Washington, D.C., for a government expert, I knew there was no use to argue further. I was aware, too, just how costly this wait was going to be.

Our immediate problem was the close quarters in which our

horses were confined. To bring an inspector from Washington would require considerable time. If he discovered no dangerous ticks, we could get on with our sales; but if he found some, we would have to keep the horses under quarantine for the prescribed period. Bob and I were a couple of glum cowhands after the law officer left. Keeping the mustangs in this close corral and buying feed for them would eat up all the profits.

The constable had not been gone long when a man came up to us and introduced himself as a former resident of New Mexico who loved its blue skies and sunshine so much he hoped to go back there to live. I did not blame him, for I had already had enough of this humid, sultry, mosquito-ridden place. He had heard about our predicament, as had almost everyone else, and he wanted to help us. We told him we could surely use some assistance and were open to suggestions. He then asked us if we would like to drive our horses out to his place and turn them into a pasture of fine lespedeza grass. Desperate as we were, we knew we did not dare move the horses and told him as much. That, he said, was nonsense—pure nonsense. Keeping them in such close quarters just was not good sense. We were quick to see it his way, and later on, when we were sure the constable was not around, we drove the herd out to his little farm and turned them out to pasture in the tall, succulent grass. While they feasted on it Bob and I enjoyed fried chicken, yams, hominy grits, and other delicious Southern dishes. Our host would take no pay for our meals; nor would he accept money for the keep of the horses.

Three days later an inspector arrived from Washington with his little black bag. By that time the whole town knew where we were staying; many people had already come to look over the fence at the horses and stared curiously as the inspector talked to us. He started out by saying he understood we had horses with fever ticks. I replied I did not think we did, but he was welcome to come and look them over, provided we could find the space needed for the examination. I went on to explain that because the horses were wild and hard to manage, it would be quite a job to inspect every one of them. But he was not to be talked out of it so all we could do was to rig up a place with a runway in the chicken yard. I went to work at once cutting them out of the herd, one at a time, while Bob forefooted and threw them. After he had flattened the first horse, two Negro boys rushed on top of it and held it for the inspector.

With the horse ready for his inspection, he opened his black bag and took out a fine-toothed comb and some other paraphernalia and started feeling over the animal. After running his hands around over it and using the comb, he found only two or three dead ticks, which he placed in a small box. He kept this up, horse after horse, making no comments about his findings. With his loops flying in the broiling sun, Bob readied the mustangs for their examinations. His rope sang through the air and never missed, despite the fact that he was becoming tired, hot, and short-tempered. Even the poor yield of ticks failed to discourage the inspector. The horses were also suffering from so much roping and throwing. Finally I asked the inspector whether he thought he could judge the situation by what he had already found. He said he did not think so. He had come a long way to look for ticks, and it would be a pity to stop too soon and maybe miss some. Then I wanted to know whether he had found anything that looked serious. So far, he had not. Well, if he had not found enough evidence by now, I wanted to know why we had to go on with the examinations. My cowboy was all in. He explained he had a job to do and he would have to keep on with it. With that he took up his inspection work again.

At last when there were only ten mustangs remaining, Bob walked off and sat down under the shade of a chinaberry tree and fanned his face with his hat. He said he was through. If no wrong kind of ticks had been found by now, he was not going to bust another blankety-blank horse. That was that. I thought the inspector would be angry, but instead he smiled broadly and began to put the things back in his case. "You know," he said, "I've been dead sure for a long time that you don't have any fever ticks, but I've been enjoying watching that cowboy rope so much I didn't want to stop until I'd seen him throw his loop over every last horse in the bunch."

Bob did not appreciate the compliment and what he said to the inspector had better not be repeated here, especially after we found out the dead ticks were rabbit ticks. While Bob cooled his temper I inquired as to how soon we could get on with the sales.

"Right away," he answered. "I'll give you a clean bill of health and you can sell them anywhere at any time you choose."

When I heard that good news I climbed on a post, waved my hat, and let out my biggest cowboy yell. This got the attention of the people, and then I made clear that an agent of the United States government had declared there was not a fever tick in the entire lot of horses and I was now ready to sell them.

Immediately a Negro man came up to me and said, "Ah sho' does like that one, mister. How much you want for him?"

"He's yours for forty dollars."

"How about that one?" another man inquired. "Is he tame?"

"He's a little skittish now, but when you get him away from the crowd here, he'll be all right."

Word had spread in advance that the buyers would have to bring their own ropes to lead the horses off so they were prepared. After the last transaction was made, the purchaser pulled the horse along while his friends shooed him from the back, and what with the shoos and the pulls I guess they finally managed to lead him home.

The following day I happened to meet one of these buyers and I asked how he was getting along with the horse. "Oh, he's gittin' on fine. He sho' is a fine-lookin' horse."

"Have you hitched him up yet?"

"I ain't had time yet. But next week when I gits around to haulin' some fat pine around town to sell, I'll know how he gits along in the harness." By then I hoped to be on my way back to New Mexico.

Our host had spread the word around about the fine horses from New Mexico so our sales went fast. The tick scare had helped to advertise them too. Some buyers came hoping to hear the worst about the ticks, which would make it necessary to abandon the horses rather than sustain the cost of quarantine. Others were eager to make deals for them. We took in a few scrub ponies in trades, which accounted for the fact we were always riding a tame pony. Even though I was young for the horse business, the slickest traders found that I could not be taken in. After a few days only about half a dozen remained, so we sold them to a horse trader when we left for home. Our host gave us each a big bag of pecans and told us any time we wanted to ship horses to his place to sell, we could use his farm for headquarters, free of charge.

On our way back we rode in high style in a chair car. When we had crossed the Mississippi on the way to Jackson, we had to go on flatboats a few cars at a time. Bob and I, wishing to see all we could, had ridden the cowcatcher of the locomotive. At El Paso on our return we went on a shopping spree at the White House, at that time the most famous store in the Southwest. As Louise and I by then had made definite plans to marry, I bought a blue-serge suit. Both Bob and I purchased presents for our best girls. Since I had already given Louise a diamond engagement ring, I bought her a string of pearls that set me back considerably. She still wears them. But I was well supplied with funds and was thankful for our good fortune. For a while it had seemed the ticks were going to put us out of business.

To get our livestock to the best available markets I found it necessary to make additional trips to the South. On one occa-

sion Kirk Johnson, a Roswell real-estate man, bought two car-
loads of mules from us to ship to Mississippi and asked me to
go along with the shipment. His father-in-law, Mr. Montgomery, lived near Jackson, and would help me on that end of the
line. It was short notice but I told him I would go.

I took with me Lon Baker, a homely-looking cowboy with
fiery-red hair. Lonnie was a drifter and had bummed around
the country on freight cars with some pretty rough characters.
He was good company though and a fair hand with the rope
and the dice. Lon was happy to be on the move again, riding a
train instead of the rods, even though we rode the caboose
with its hard seats and rough starts and stops. The biggest
problem was to get something to eat. At the stops the train was
usually on some desolate siding in the country or at a spot
where we had to take a long hike over the railway ties to the
freight yards. This was difficult at night when we could not see
the ties. It was risky too and we often had to go hungry rather
than take the long walk and maybe miss the train when it
pulled away from the siding.

When we drew up at last at Jackson Mr. Montgomery was
there to meet us. I don't know who had the greater shock, for
Lon and I were accustomed to the way the farmers and ranchers in our locality dressed, and I am sure Mr. Montgomery had
never seen real cowboys before. He must have spotted us at
once because he came up and introduced himself, wearing a
frockcoat, black string tie, and wide-brimmed straw hat. We
hardly knew what to say when he asked us to be his guests
during our stay. We were not dressed fit for anything but some
cheap lodging house or hotel. Lon nudged me, so I mumbled
something about being pleased at the invitation. He then
called a Negro boy who was waiting in the carriage to drive
over and get us. Lon whispered something about the colonel's
"undertaker coat" as we followed him to the curb and got into
the back seat of the fancy carriage with its polished brass-
trimmed lamps on the sides. We felt rather silly riding down

the street with people looking at us curiously. A short distance outside the town Henry turned the team into a pleasantly shaded driveway that led up to a plantation house with Grecian columns supporting a wide front veranda. When I saw that I began to have doubts as to how we would fit in such a place. I was more worried about Lon, who had never known anything fancier than a chuck wagon or bunkhouse.

A servant met us at the door and showed us inside, where we were introduced to the family. They were friendly and polite and did not stare too much at us as we sat stiffly in their best parlor chairs. Lon could not say much so I carried on the conversation as best I could. After what seemed a long time the "colonel" pulled out a big gold watch and said he had to see someone at the cotton gin before dinner and would pick up our suitcases. Lon and I looked at each other, and when we told him we did not have any with us the family looked surprised. At his house, Mr. Montgomery went on to explain, everyone always dressed for dinner and it would not do for Lon and me to appear without coats and ties. Then he rose to leave the room, saying that he thought he could remedy the situation.

Henry came in about that time and showed us to our room, at the end of a wide hallway upstairs. Inside was a large four-poster bed and other old walnut furniture. Over the fireplace was a portrait of some ancestor who I assumed had once occupied the house. When Henry brought us hot water, we began at once to try to remove some of the grime of the train ride. We were beginning to think that Mr. Montgomery had forgotten all about the coats and ties when Henry returned with some clothes folded over his arm. He was grinning as usual, but this time it must have been in sympathy. As soon as he left we rushed over to the bed to look at the things he had brought. Lon held in his hands a frockcoat, the kind the "colonel" wore. The other coat was of the ordinary type, but narrow in the shoulders and skimpy. Lon took a look at them and put on his hat. He said he would crawl out the window and over the back porch roof and jump to the ground before he would be seen in either of them. I argued we could not do a thing like that and hurt Mr. Montgomery's feelings. We would have to go through with it somehow. Reconsidering then, he made a grab for the coat I held and we almost ripped it apart before we decided to flip a coin for it. I lost and would have to wear the one with tails. When I tried it on I almost lost my nerve. Lon could hardly stop laughing and I did not blame him. The sleeves came down over my hands while the tails dragged down in the back to my boots. The shoulders slid halfway to my elbows. I did not feel any better about it when Lon told me I would "booger" the tamest mare on the ranch in that outfit.

It was my time to laugh when he tried to get into the other coat. He looked like a Chinese laundryman in his Palm Beach jacket from which his arms dangled from the sleeves almost to his elbows and with shoulder seams so tight he hardly dared move. "Look, Wilbur, it ain't worth it. We both look like we belong in a circus. Let's slip out the window. I'd rather pay for lodging and grub."

I knew we should not do a thing like that, so I finally convinced him again that we must go on with the dinner in our borrowed clothes. I knotted his tie for him and we both put on our coats about the time a bell tinkled downstairs. When I took a final look in the mirror at my rear with coattails brushing the tops of my boots, I all but changed my mind. Two more funny-looking people, I am sure, never went down that graceful curving staircase. Yet if the family thought we looked ridiculous, they did not show it. I remember that beautiful silver and china were on the table and a large family Bible was at our host's place. As soon as we were seated he began to read from it. I found it hard to keep my mind on the Scripture with so much tempting food in sight and hoped he would hurry and finish. He did not though, much to Lon's discomfiture also. Finally he closed the Bible, began serving us a big portion of roast beef, and then handed our plates down to the other end of the table where his wife heaped on rice and gravy. By the time we had helped ourselves to vegetables there was no room left for the beaten biscuits. In the enjoyment of so much good food, we forgot about our coats and ties, especially when we were served large cuts of blackberry pie with whipped cream.

After dinner Lon and I did not talk long with the family in the parlor, for we were weary and could hardly keep our eyes open. Before going upstairs we told Mr. Montgomery that we would leave early in the morning to get the mules and drive them back to his pasture. He said that he would have horses ready for us. We were to leave them at the stock pens when we no longer needed them. We were both glad to get this done and start on our way back to New Mexico. By then we were able to laugh about dining in such high style.

A waterspout had flooded some of the tracks between Clovis, New Mexico, and Portales, leaving a stretch of the roadbed under three or four feet of water. As the land around there was an old lake bed, the water stayed for some time. Clovis, a large railway junction of the Santa Fé, at the time had little except the handsome Harvey House, a few stores, a cluster of houses, and the stock pens. We were lodged comfortably at the hotel as guests of the railroad and ate well at a cost of about a dollar a day. Among those marooned with Lon and me was the distinguished governor-to-be, Mr. Hinkle from Roswell, who had just been nominated to the office. Also in the crowd was the friendly Colonel Bujack, a famous criminal lawyer from Carlsbad, who, dressed in fancy cowboy clothes, entertained us all with his stories.

After two days we were told we could get through even though the water had not entirely gone down. Several of us were taken over a makeshift passage to the edge of the water and put on a handcar, a few at a time. By pumping on the handles we reached the other side where a train was waiting to pick us up and take us on to Roswell over the spur line of the Santa Fé.

Having hit it off so well with Lon on this trip, I took him with me later to Shreveport. On arriving there, I left him at the pens to feed the stock while I went up the street to try to make contacts with possible buyers. My efforts were fruitless so we drove the stock to a pasture at the edge of the city, owned by a man I had met at the pens. Before we finished the job I began to feel very sick. As it was the winter of the disastrous influenza epidemic of 1918, I had grave suspicions about my condition, which was growing worse all the time. Since the weather had been sultry, warm, and humid, the chance of picking up flu germs was excellent. By the time Lon and I had finished pasturing the horses, I had no choice; I had to see a doctor and I had to see him in a hurry. I explained the situation to the fellow whose pasture we were using and he promised to look after the stock while Lon went with me to see the doctor.

The doctor took a look at me, shoved a thermometer into my mouth, and after reading it, told me to get to a hospital while I was able. I sent Lon back to look after the horses and I went to the hospital. At the office I asked for a bed, explaining that the doctor had sent me. I was told there were no beds available. Then I tried to explain that I was a stranger in town and had no other place to go; if necessary I would sleep on the floor. The admitting clerk asked me the name of the doctor I had seen, and after talking with him she sent me to a ward already crowded with other miserable people, where I remained about two weeks until the fever left me and I could get back on my feet.

While I was in the hospital, I was too sick to think about anything much, but I could not help but wonder why I had received no word from Lon. At the end of a week the man from whom I had rented the pasture came to see me, wanting to know what he should do with the horses left in the pasture. He told me that for the first few days Lon had been in charge he had sold a number of them. Then one day he hadn't turned up at all. As I was still too sick to leave, I asked the man to take care of the sales until I could get there.

As soon as the hospital would allow me to go, I hurried down to the pasture to find that Lon was still missing as was about a thousand dollars of my money. Knowing that it wouldn't remain with him long, I went to a lawyer and filed a complaint against him. Not long afterward I found him broke and with a hard-luck story about becoming sick and wanting to be near his folks. His hard luck, I was sure, had been at a gambling dive where they had picked him for a sucker and taken my money. He did appear repentant, however, and promised to repay every cent. Since I reasoned he would have a better chance to get the money if they did not jail him, I took his notes endorsed by his father, who had to mortgage all he owned to cover them.

Back at home I kept in touch with Lon, but no payments ever came in. When I saw his father, the worried man confessed "the boy was no account and never had been." For me to force him to stand good for his son's notes meant the loss of all he owned. I did not need the money that badly, so I just charged the experience to profit and loss. It had not been all loss, for a contact I had made at Shreveport later brought three carloads of horses off the range, paid for in cash, relieving me of the work and bother of selling them myself.

But we sometimes had fun on these trips. On another one to the South, Bob Boyce and I were caught out among the scrub oak and pine trees of Louisiana with a bunch of horses and no place to corral them for the night. We had progressed some distance without seeing a fence of any kind, so when we arrived at a dilapidated slab house with a sagging clapboard roof, propped off the ground with a large rock at each corner, we spoke to the owner, who was sitting barefoot in a rickety chair on the porch. We had seen that he had an enclosure large enough for our stock. In fact the horses had better prospects than we, if we were to judge by the outside appearance of the house.

I tied my horse to a sapling pine and walked up to the porch; I noticed a woman in a sunbonnet in a patch of garden between the house and the barn. When she saw me, she put down her hoe and joined her husband, wiping her perspiring face with the dirty apron she wore over her shapeless dress. She was barefoot too, and from the corner of her mouth the frayed end of a snuff brush stuck out. A trickle of brown juice ran down the lines around her mouth. They both just stared at me in an unfriendly way and said nothing, their native-born suspicion of "furriners" showing clearly in both their faces.

I spoke to them in a friendly manner, saying something about the nice place they had in the clearing. The man looked me over as if I were an inspector and said laconically, "I reckon so." As they stared at me from my Stetson to my spurs, I explained that we needed a place to corral our horses to keep them from straying. Bob was already having a devil of a time with them by now, I was sure. Could I have a place there to pen them up for the night? And in addition, could they put Bob and me up and feed us? The woman started to say something but her husband silenced her with, "Shet up, Flory, I'll take keer of these here fellers."

Apologetically I said we weren't very hungry and that we would sleep anywhere. As I said this, I pulled out two dollars. At the sight of the money, the man reckoned they could feed Bob and me, but he'd have to have "extra" for the horses. When I brought out a couple more and handed them to him, he rolled them up with the others and stuck them into the watch pocket of his bib overalls. Then we went to a small clearing behind the barn where Bob was herding the horses and drove them into the pen. At a nearby well our host dropped the bucket in the well and brought it up full several times and poured the water into a wooden stock tank. After that he pitched some hay from the barn into the pen while Bob and I went to the kitchen where Flory was putting dishes of cold, greasy turnip greens, corn pone, and some cured ham on the cracked oilcloth of the table. The coffee had been placed close enough to the hot embers of the stove to warm up. Then in order to show her growing friendliness, she brought out a jar of elderberry jelly and some cold biscuits. As Bob and I had nibbled on cheese and crackers at noon we found the meal surprisingly tasty.

It was dark by the time we finished eating, so we all went out to the porch to cool off. Once our host and his wife no longer felt inhibited, they proved to be quite talkative. I do not recall just how we ever got around to the subject of books, but Flory asked me if I had ever "heerd of a book called the alminack." Pretending I did not know much about such a book, we listened as she told me about it. The "alminack" had everything in it—when to plant "taters," what to do for hives, what time the sun comes up, when it's going to rain or snow, how to get rid of bedbugs, and all the latest "news." Besides, Dr. John's Special Liniment could cure anything wrong with a person. Evidently Flory pored over her "alminack" because its pages were well worn when she showed us by lamplight some more of its wonders.

By the time she closed the book Bob and I were glad to stretch out on our corn-husk mattress on the floor of the breezeway until dawn. As it was a dry spell, the mosquitoes did not bother us. But at daybreak the flies swarmed over us, so we jumped up and went to the stock tank to wash our faces. Flory was up before we were, cooking hominy grits, eggs, and coffee, which we fortified ourselves with before driving off our string of horses. Before we had gone far, Bob rode alongside of me and soberly inquired, "If that durned 'alminack' of Flory's has so much information in it, why in the blazes didn't you find out for us where we can sell these pesky horses at a good price?"

CHAPTER XIII

I Marry LOUISE

FTER WE BECAME ENGAGED Louise taught school at
Capitán and whenever I could I would drive to see
her in our Buick roadster. I was hurrying there one day, and
instead of stopping as I should at the Hondo toll bridge to
pay the fee, I drove on through. Jim Gonzáles, who had
been the stage driver, operated it and when the gate was
down and he was not around, young fellows liked to slip by
him without paying. Jim had put up the bridge at his own
expense so we could either pay his toll or ford the Río Bonito
where there was danger of bogging down in quicksand. On this
particular day Jim had gone back to his store, a large two-story
building at the Hondo junction where they also held fiestas and
dances.

Jim saw me race by and ran after me, yelling for his dinero.
He must have known that the engine would get too hot on the
hill toward Lincoln because I drove too fast up the grade, and
he soon overtook me, mad and puffing hard. I could not blame
him for being in a bad humor; beating him out of his toll was a
shabby trick. When he got his breath he started hollering at
me, demanding his money. I told him I had not heard him yell
when I was coming up the hill and that I had forgotten all
about the toll. But I could not talk him out of it. People two
miles up the road at Spring Ranch must have heard him. He
was in a better frame of mind after I gave him his fifty cents.
He told me I could get a bucket of water from his rain barrel to
put into the radiator. I forgot about Jim, though, as I drove on
to Capitán. I could think only of Louise and how lucky I was to
have won her.

As our interests came together more and more, my future with her promised to be a wonderful one. I asked her one time what she saw in a cowboy like me and she named some of the things that counted a lot with her—sincerity, character, unselfishness, ambition, and some other traits of mine I had not even noticed. Having similar backgrounds drew us together too. She admired my mother's musical gifts and cultural background as well as my dad's kindly manner, courage, and keen sense of humor. High principle was important to her, and she made it plain that when she married it would be to a man who could measure up to her standards. I felt bold and cheeky when I asked her to marry me. Yet my father had won a beautiful, cultured, and talented girl from Chicago at a time when many condemned him for having been an associate of Billy the Kid and a participant in the Lincoln County War. Our situations in no respect were parallel, but I have always enjoyed a challenge and winning Louise was the most inspiring one of my life.

Louise and I were married in Roswell on December 18, 1918, in a simple ceremony at the Holland home. I was too nervous to remember much, but I have never forgotten Louise in her white satin and georgette dress with her veil bound around her head with lilies of the valley and smilax. After returning from our wedding trip we went to live at Coe Ranch, as my folks were staying in Roswell for the winter. I had bought a farm adjoining Dad's and the construction of our new home had already begun.

In February of 1919, not long after we started living at the ranch, Louise and I found ourselves in a situation reminiscent of Billy the Kid days. It was during a cold snap that Dad, Johnny Mackey (a Spanish-American who was irrigating for us), Louise, and I were eating dinner. As a special treat there was ice cream which I had made in the gallon freezer that morning after I had found ice frozen in the horse trough. We had finished the main course of Swiss steak, brown gravy, and mashed potatoes and waited while Louise went on the back porch to the freezer to fill our dishes. She had just returned with a trayful and had sat down with her back to the kitchen door. On her right was Mackey, opposite her sat Dad, and I was in the chair on her left.

We had no sooner picked up our spoons when we heard a man's voice at the outside kitchen door. Before we had time to move, he was in the dining room door with a six shooter in his hand pointed at Louise's back. He commanded, "Put your hands up. Get a rope and tie yourselves." Then he leveled his gun at me and stated, "This is what you get for not giving me work yesterday." I was too astonished to be afraid. I stood up and said, "I'll give you work, anything you want. Put your gun down and eat some ice cream with us." Louise got up and began urging him to put the gun down saying that we would give him work, automobile, money, or anything he wanted. He kept his gun pointed at me and as I moved closer to him he backed a few steps into the kitchen. I followed him, looking into the barrel of his gun. This was a sensation I had always wondered about. I was gambling on being able to talk him out of using it and could see that he was fast losing his nerve. Mackey still sat with his hands in the air. Dad had kept silent but when he had a chance he told Mackey to slip out the door and bring him his gun. Mackey eased outside but we did not see him again for a week.

As the gunman glanced over his shoulder he saw a phone on the kitchen wall. He raised his gun again pointing it first at me then at Louise, saying, "Don't you call the police." Louise hurried to say that we could not call the police as we were sixty miles from town. I kept insisting he lay his gun down and eat dinner. He must have been hungry because he finally began to unbuckle his cartridge belt and laid it and the gun on a chair. When Louise brought him a plate of steak, potatoes, and gravy, he failed to notice that I had picked up the gun.

Now he was at our mercy. We began to lecture him, reprimanding him sternly. "Yesterday when I talked to you I told you to come back if you couldn't find work elsewhere." Unable to look either of us in the eye, he stammered something about wanting a riding job and I didn't have one for him. He said he was broke and wanted to get some money in a hurry. His story was that he had drifted in from Montana. With little cash he had come as far as New Mexico only to lose everything to some card sharps in Carrizozo. After several days afoot, he had thought about stealing a horse and getting out of the country, but on the previous day as he walked up the valley he had changed his mind. When he reached Coe Ranch he figured there must be some money around the place and he was going to get some even if he had to use his gun. He said, "Yesterday when I talked to you out at the windmill, I didn't have no idea of takin' a job even if you offered me one. All I wanted was a chance to look the place over. That's why I asked you for a drink of water. I wanted to get a look inside the house. After I left you I sat up there on that hill in front of the house for about two hours and watched everything that went on. I seen who was working. I knowed when you and the others stopped for noon chuck. I even figured where you'd be settin' when I came to the back door."

At this point I interrupted him and inquired, "If you had your mind made up to kill us and get money, why didn't you do it?"

"I guess I got cold feet mainly. It was in my mind all right when I aimed the gun at you and your missus. But I just couldn't pull the trigger when you was treating me like I was company . . . asking me to sit down with you and eat ice cream."

After we had finished lecturing him, he looked like a whipped pup, but we were ready to get rid of him. We were far from the sheriff's office and didn't want to take the time to get an officer and go through court proceedings. We considered also that he could have killed us and he didn't. During our talk with him we decided that he was not a hardened criminal and he had learned his lesson.

About this time Roderick Johnson from up the valley came tearing down the road driving his Model T version of a hot rod. He skidded in the dirt as he came to a stop in front of the house to visit us for a few minutes. He said he was on his way to Roswell. This seemed like a solution for us so I told him I had a passenger for him. I gave the boy five dollars for his gun and cartridge belt and with relief Louise and I watched him bounce off with our neighbor. We never heard of him again.

(This holdup has always reminded us of the experience that my mother and father had with desperados the night they were married as told earlier in this book.)

For several days afterward Louise and I were uneasy, but soon I had all but forgotten the incident. Not so with Louise. She relived the scene many times, wondering how she had had the courage to face the gun in that shaky hand and say calmly, "Come on, sit down and have some ice cream with us."

Even though building materials had to be hauled long distances and our workers were slow, Louise and I were able to move into our new home in about five months. By that time Mother and Dad had returned from Roswell, where they had spent the winter. By going around to sales we had accumulated quite a bit of furniture. Louise was especially proud of the piano I had bought her from Ben Ginsberg, who still owns the Ginsberg Music Company in Roswell. At the time Ben had just opened his store and had a fine piano that had been purchased for a ranch. When he quoted me a special price of three hundred dollars, I bought it—but not until Louise went in and tried it out to make sure she liked its touch and tone. The same piano stands in the music room of Coe Ranch today and many have sung and danced to its accompaniment over the decades.

When we moved into our new home it was a modern house with running water and a bathroom, a true accomplishment for the Ruidoso Valley in 1919. Any house in those days with better than a backhouse was considered modern. We introduced Coleman lanterns into the valley, but I was not satisfied with that kind of progress. I wanted electricity, so I began experimenting with an old automobile generator attached to the windmill. With the power it generated, we could burn twenty-five-watt bulbs, providing we did not turn on too many at one time. One day Frank English, who was in the hardware business in Carrizozo, came along with a Delco plant he guaranteed would make all the electricity needed for all our household requirements. We then added steam heat, which made us about as modern as we could get.

Our new improvements had made us comfortable inside our home, but we still had to drain the water from the radiator of our Model T auto and truck on freezing nights. To get rid of this nuisance I built a double garage with thick adobe walls and snug-fitting doors. This helped but it was not a positive guarantee against a burst radiator when the temperature dipped to zero and below. Salt water would not freeze but it did rust the radiator. I didn't care to try Dad's suggested solution of honey and water with its predictable results.

Proud of our new home, Louise busied herself taking care of it and cooking my favorite frijoles, steak, and apple dumplings. But her dynamic nature and abundant energy lacked sufficient scope within the four walls of a house. When we were married she wanted to think her teaching days were over, yet she could not remain indifferent to our educational needs. Her friendly nature had extended itself to the people of San Patricio, among them Leopoldo Gonzales, a prominent Republican politician and an outstanding, progressive-minded leader. Single-handed, almost, he was trying to keep the Gonzales school open long enough for the children to receive at least a minimum of learning. As he knew Louise's musical talent and teaching capabilities he suggested she take over the school in San Patricio. He was deeply distressed because the teachers

WILBUR COE

Portrait by Peter Hurd
1955

never stayed there more than two or three months. The last one had remained only thirty days. In Louise he hoped to find someone who would challenge the apathy of the students, encourage their attendance, and maintain discipline. Leopoldo dreamt of a full nine-month school year with all the children in regular attendance.

After thinking it over Louise agreed to apply for the position and the board, headed by Leopoldo, gratefully accepted. She made it clear in the beginning that she would take the teaching job only on the condition that before she ever opened a text-book, Leopoldo was to come to the school and give the students a good talking to. In it he was to specify unconditionally that the presence of knives, slingshots, paper wads, rocks, and other weapons would no longer be tolerated. If chasing the teacher off had been good sport in the past, those days were over.

As good as his word, Leopoldo appeared on the first day of school with a very sober face and lectured the students until the worst of the overgrown bullies hung their heads. To back him up, he brought along the priest who raked them over the coals and laid down the law in a manner they understood well. Thus with the stern board member and the padre to back her, Louise had good reason to believe that education in San Patricio would be able to move forward.

As much as possible Louise used her training in music as an approach to win and sustain her pupils' interest. Her own love for music had been instilled in her when she was no older than some of the younger of her students. Her mother had been eager to have the Holland children enjoy all the possible advantages of education possible. This was especially true in music. Louise and her sister Inez drove in a small buggy with a gentle horse eight miles to Cumberland City to take piano lessons from Mrs. Emily Gaylord Welty, an accomplished musician and composer. Louise progressed rapidly and was hardly tall enough to reach the pedals when she played for church choirs and at the neighborhood gatherings where music was a part of the entertainment. Here at the Gonzales school near San Patricio she put on operettas and other musical programs that enabled the children to work off their energies in singing and dancing. On the school grounds when they played ring-a-round-a-rosy and London Bridge and sang the songs in Spanish, she learned from them. Ride through the Ruidoso Valley today and stop at some store or filling station and mention Louise Coe, and someone standing near may say, "Oh, yes, when I went to school Mrs. Coe was my teacher. She taught us manners and other things we needed to know that weren't in the books."

In discipline Louise met with no more than routine difficulties. Capably and confidently she took over the teaching of forty-five children of Spanish-American descent, ranging from six to eighteen, in grades one through eight. Standing firmly behind her at all times was the imposing figure of Leopoldo, who saw his dream realized when the school remained open for the nine-month term, with the children in regular attendance without benefit of attendance laws. But trying to reach numerous children in so many grades was frustrating and discouraging even to one of Louise's determination. Knowing her task was an impossible one, she prevailed upon the people of San Patricio the following year to consolidate with the Gonzales school and employ three teachers at San Patricio. This was a new and different approach to education, and it was hard to break down old established customs. The people finally agreed and she became the principal of the three-teacher school and a pioneer in the field of consolidation in the state. As a career woman of the twenties she drove down the valley each day in her new Model T Ford to the San Patricio School and used her salary checks to pay our taxes and buy some fine bulls for the ranch. The children rode on wooden benches on the sides of an old open truck which they sometimes had to push on the hills.

Louise worked at her teaching with initiative and enthusi-

asm. Half measures were not acceptable to her. If something
had to be done, it had to be done at once. There is no mañana
in her nature. Sports especially appealed to her. That is why
she happened once to take some schoolchildren to a field day
in Carrizozo, the county seat of Lincoln County. She herself
had been there only twice before, and some of the children had
never been so far away from home. It was a treat for them all,
and they made a great occasion of it. She was particularly
proud to show off the basketball team she had coached on the
outdoor court at San Patricio, where skinned knees and scraped
elbows were a part of the game. This was the first team the
school had put into competition.

Just at the moment when she was sitting on the sideline
yelling for George Romero to "shoot," three gentlemen who
were attending a Democratic convention in Carrizozo came up,
but she was too busy to notice them. To get her attention one
of them tapped her lightly on the shoulder. "You are Louise
Coe from the Ruidoso Valley, I believe?" he inquired.

Even though she did not like having her attention diverted
from the game at such a critical moment, she smiled pleasantly
and said, "Yes, I am married to Wilbur Coe."

The man cleared his throat and continued. "Mrs. Coe, I want
to introduce myself as the chairman of the County Democratic .
Committee. These other men with me are its members."

Louise did not see what possible interest that information
could be to her.

At that moment the shouting of the spectators made it difficult to be heard so the chairman raised his voice and continued, "I won't waste words, Mrs. Coe, for I see you are busy.
We have come to ask you if you will consider running for a
political office."

To such a question, coming at a time when the women of the
United States had been voting for only two years, Louise gave
an answer that was straightforward and honest—nothing was
farther from her mind. Then, assuming the matter was closed,

she thanked them for the honor. The committeemen, however, were unwilling to accept her refusal. They continued to urge her to run against Maude Blaney, the Republican candidate for county superintendent of schools, an efficient and highly respected officeholder who was up for re-election. After Louise had given every logical excuse she could think for not running, she reluctantly accepted and campaigned in the same manner. She subsequently was defeated at the polls.

However, two years later Louise ran again and this time she went out to win. She defeated her opponent and became supervisor over eighty-five teachers in Lincoln County. She entered into her work vigorously and performed her duties capably, making friends and finding that politics could be stimulating, exciting, and challenging. Under an exceptionally fine teacher who lived in Carrizozo, she continued to study music. She busied herself in community activities and made many friends, especially among the Republicans.

Back at the ranch I cooked for myself and managed somehow to have the place neat-looking when she came home on Saturday. I did not like batching, but I realized when I married Louise that I was not going into partnership with someone who would be satisfied with a broom, dust cloth, and pots and pans all day long. Her tremendous energies had to have an outlet elsewhere.

Nevertheless I was happy when she decided at the end of her term that she would not run again. It was a satisfaction to her to know she had served the people efficiently and successfully; she was ready to leave politics and be Mrs. Wilbur Coe, housewife. Or so she thought. When the committeemen again approached her she remained firm. She was through with political office as well as neglecting her husband and home.

But sometime after the campaign of 1924 got underway, out of a clear sky, the committeemen once again came calling at our home. The members were glum and despairing and well they might have been, for in the middle of a heated campaign the nominee for senator on the Democratic ticket from the Eighteenth District, which comprised Lincoln and Otero counties, had withdrawn. When they asked her whether she would run she gave another "no" and repeated the reasons she had given before. The committeemen continued to plead with her on the grounds that the office of state senator would not require her to be away from home very much. It would be just like taking a two-month vacation in Santa Fé every two years, they explained. To further induce her to run for the office they told her that Judge Hewitt of White Oaks, a beloved district judge and a good friend of us both, would pay her campaign expenses.

Louise thought it over. Two months out of two years certainly would not mean a great deal of time away from home. And if she could get to Santa Fé, there was much she could do to further the desperate needs of education, with which she was so familiar. So she consented to run and once again became a reluctant candidate, this time for senator from the Eighteenth District of the state. With her plea to the people, "Vote for my opponent and let me leave public office and return home," she received a send-off that led to victories in four consecutive political contests for the same office.

It was not until she had assumed the duties of her office that Louise knew she was to be the recipient of an historic honor in the annals of New Mexico's political history. The first session of the legislature was called to meet on the second Tuesday after the first Monday in January 1925 and for the occasion she had selected a stylish fawn-colored suit with coordinated accessories. When she entered the senate chamber a ripple of surprise swept over the faces of the twenty-three senators already assembled. They had no doubt expected to see some suffragette in a man-tailored suit, topped with a severe sailor hat. Instead they beheld a tall, distinguished-looking young woman with an original Paris chapeau and a nosegay pinned to her jacket. She smiled shyly as she stood to be introduced as the first woman senator and the youngest person ever to be elected to that office. Several decades later as I write this she is still the only woman who has held that office in New Mexico.

At the time Louise was elected to her first term there were six Democrats and eighteen Republicans in the state senate, and from them she received profound respect and consideration, for she was an opponent to be reckoned with. As she grew more familiar with her work her confidence increased, making her voice ring with sincerity and conviction from the floor as she defended legislation she thought was good; and with equal vigor she debated against measures she judged to be contrary to the general welfare.

On the several committees on which she served, she found herself most interested and challenged when she worked on school matters, for they were closest to her heart. At the beginning of her second four-year term she was appointed chairman of the Education Committee at a time when the Republicans held the majority of seats in the senate, a signal and unprecedented honor which she retained throughout the remainder of her time in office. During the last four-year term she was elected president pro-tem of the senate.

Louise left active politics in 1942 but she has never lost any of her lively interest in local, state and national affairs. In matters of local concern, particularly, she has worked with continuing zeal. We both promoted the Lincoln County Museum, the Lincoln County Historical Society, and the annual Billy the Kid Pageant. Louise has worked consistently in our community for the improvement of schools, and now the one-room schools in the three valleys and the Capitán Mountain area have been replaced by a consolidated system. In 1957 when the National Education Association celebrated its centennial with ceremonies in schools all over the United States, the teachers of the Hondo Valley School unanimously chose Louise as the person in the community who had contributed the most toward education.

It was because of her lasting interest in national affairs that Louise made her first trip to Europe in 1946. When the State Department set up a commission to study government reconstruction plans in England, France, and Sweden, Dr. Goodwin Watson of Columbia University selected her to serve in a group of twenty-four, representing a cross-section of America. Their ages ranged from seventeen to seventy, and there were three Negroes. While they were in England they sometimes visited the House of Commons; this was while Harold Wilson was serving his second term. He was selected to lecture to the group, and at this meeting Louise and he became friends. On later trips to Europe she has visited with him.

In 1951 Louise had an occasion to serve unofficially as a representative of the United States and to do some extensive traveling. She started out on this mission with her good friend Georgia Lusk. As State Superintendent of Education, Georgia had appointed Louise State High School Supervisor in 1931. However, Louise did not keep the job long because it meant maintaining an office in Santa Fé and being away from home. Later Georgia was elected the first Congresswoman from New Mexico, and after serving one term, was defeated for the second. She was then appointed Vice-Chairman of the War Claims Commission with an office in Washington. It was during this service that she asked Louise in October of 1951 to go with her to Manila, the Philippines, on official commission business, provided she would pay her own expenses. Louise spent ten days with Georgia in Manila and was invited to all the official affairs given for Mrs. Lusk. One was a trip to City of Baguio with the General of the Philippine Army in his private plane. On another occasion they boarded a submarine chaser and went to Corregidor with the commander of the Philippine navy.

Since Georgia was on official government business with expenses paid, she flew back to Washington when her work was over. Louise however continued on to visit Japan, Hong Kong,

Thailand, India, Turkey, and several countries in Europe. On subsequent trips around the world she has been to Russia (twice), Saigon, Nepal, Egypt, Pakistan, Kashmir, Greece, and several other nations.

Louise has traveled alone much of the time, but in fact she has never been alone. Through her unerring judgment of people she has been able to make and enjoy worthwhile friendships. Such was the case in 1955 when she and her sister Inez were traveling in Switzerland. In a cable car in the Swiss Alps she had noticed an interesting-looking couple and characteristically just introduced herself to them. They were Edward de T. and Louise Seaman Bechtel. He was a distinguished lawyer, bibliophile and rose grower, she the founder—at the Macmillan Company—of the first of the great juvenile departments of American publishing houses. At the time Louise met them, the Bechtels were in Geneva attending an International Rose Show at which Mr. Bechtel was serving as one of the judges.

No trip has been without its interesting experiences. Louise especially enjoys telling of an amusing incident that happened in Bangkok, Thailand, one that pleases me. She engaged a young Thai to take her in his small launch to see the commerce on the canals near Bangkok. He spoke very good English although he had never been out of Thailand. Louise told him she was from New Mexico and then began to explain its location in the United States. To her surprise the young man said he knew where New Mexico is as he had read about Lincoln County and Billy the Kid!

Louise and I have traveled together extensively in our own country as well as in Canada and Mexico. In 1937 we were among the first American tourists to travel by automobile over the Pan-American Highway from Laredo, Texas, to Mexico City. We made the trip with Louise and Bill Hill during Christmas of that year. Bill was the chief highway engineer for constructing the road from Ruidoso through the Mescalero

LOUISE COE

Portrait by Henriette Wyeth
1958

Indian Reservation and was interested in how they built highways south of the border. Our trip went without any trouble
until we topped the summit of one of the high mountains
between Tamazunchale (pronounced "Thomas and Charley"
by Ernie Pyle, who made the trip before we did) and Mexico
City. There we were stopped by four armed Mexicans who
demanded that we let them ride to the next town. We did not
dare refuse, so they stood on the running boards of our Chevro-
let sedan for the remainder of the way. The drive to the next
village seemed much longer to us than it actually was, and we
were relieved when the Mexicans got off our car.

Later we were among the first Americans to go over the
highway from Nogales, Arizona, down the west coast of Mexico. At the time there had been heavy rains and the newly
constructed bridges were impassable. Our car had to be ferried
over several of these large rivers. The ferry "deck" was nothing
more than two troughs wide enough for the wheels of a car,
and the craft was paddled across the rivers by four Mexicans.
Since 1937 we have had many interesting experiences on our
trips to Mexico, but nothing ever frightened us or prevented us
from making another trip. Of all the places we have visited
there, Acapulco is our favorite spot. Louise likes to swim, and I
like to fish and sit on the beach and watch the pretty señoritas.
After having visited Lake Louise in Canada, Lake Antigua in
Guatemala, and practically all of the beauty spots in our national parks, for a real vacation Acapulco suits us best.

Our first trip there was in 1938. We had gone to Mexico City
by train and had flown from there in a small seven-passenger
plane. There was no airport, so planes landed on the beach in
front of the Papagayo Hotel. We took a horse-drawn taxi to La
Marina Hotel, where we had reservations. It was across the
street from the docks where there were a few small launches
that could be rented for deep-sea fishing. It was also near the
central plaza where hogs wallowed in the mud holes. Our
large, scantily furnished room had a twelve-foot ceiling. The

straw mattress on the wooden bedstead was filled with rolling humps. On the open veranda where we ate, the flies were so thick the mozos were kept busy shooing them with a palm leaf. After a night at La Marina we began looking for another place to stay. When we stopped at Las Palmas Courts managed by an American by the name of Barkley, we met a charming lady guest from Iowa who told us she had been there two weeks, the place was clean, the food good and the rate was five dollars per day for room and board. We registered at once. When Mr. Barkley saw our address he said, "That's funny. We've just had here a Mr. and Mrs. Bruce Griffith from Glencoe, New Mexico." They were friends of ours, but we were unaware they had been in Acapulco. Since then we have met them there many times.

We have seen this seaport resort grow from unpaved, unlighted streets and slums to a beautiful modern city. Almost everything has changed now except its natural beauty, the delightful climate and the warm water in the bay. The many vendors that used to stroll the beach, with whom we enjoyed bargaining, have almost disappeared. The free beach chairs we used have given way to colorful umbrellas and coconut-palm cabañas for which a charge is made.

At the Courts we met Mr. and Mrs. Blank from Puebla, Mexico, and with them we arranged to go deep-sea fishing. We rented a launch for a day for twenty-five dollars, the price including the fishing tackle, bait, and cold beer. The captain and his two helpers took turns steering the launch and helping us with the fishing. We left the docks early in the morning and returned about four o'clock in the afternoon tired and sunburned, but it was worth it because I caught the largest sailfish of the season. It was 11 feet long and weighed 135 pounds. Because of its size and beauty I was given a certificate of honor from the Sailfish Association of Acapulco.

Today, among other things, we miss the open markets, the overloaded burros driven by barefoot peasants, and oxen yoked to homemade carts loaded with bananas or papayas. On our first trips there we saw few tourists from other countries and a foreign ship in the harbor was unusual. But the greatest change has come to the Mexican people brought about by their improved economic conditions.

CHAPTER XIV

Cattle and Horse BREEDING

ROM THE TIME Uncle Lou Coe first breathed the clear
pure air of Lincoln County and warmed himself in its
bright sunshine, this bit of New Mexico was to be for the Coes
a place of unsurpassed climate and natural advantages. It
was because Dad believed the climate there would restore
Mother's health after their first baby was born that he fixed
a makeshift bed in the hack and brought her here from Farmington. Mother lived many years to enjoy Lincoln County
with its wonderful climate and broad opportunities for farming
and ranching.

But it was Uncle George who did the big job promoting New
Mexico's healthful climate. After the Blazer's Mill battle he had
washed the bleeding stump of his trigger finger in the clear
pure water of the Tularosa River and had never bothered to
consult a doctor about it. Fifty years later when Louise was
attending the state legislature she met Dr. W. R. Brown, head
of the Valmora sanitarium for tubercular patients. Long a promoter of the health-giving qualities of the New Mexican climate, he became interested in Uncle George and his finger
which had been healed by sunshine, water, and pure air. That
was just what he needed to advertise New Mexico's climate at
the forthcoming annual Valmora dinner at the Hotel Stevens in
Chicago in November 1931. But when he asked Uncle George
to be the guest of honor at the banquet, George replied that he
was not interested. He had never been on a train and would
not know what to do if he rode on one. He also vetoed the
suggestion that he fly. He had come west in a covered wagon
and had braved the dangers of Indians and outlaws, but at

seventy he did not care to take any more chances. He did promise though to think about the invitation and discuss it with his wife, Phoebe. In the end he reluctantly consented to make the trip, provided that Louise would go along and show them around.

At the expense of the Santa Fé Railway Company the three of them flew to Chicago and registered at the Hotel Stevens. If Billy the Kid himself had walked into the lobby, he could not have caused more of a stir. Dad and Uncle George had worn beards since they were young men, and now the sight of George's long beard caused a commotion among the guests who tried to get a closer look. With genial manner and friendly smile, he soon could call everyone around the hotel by his first name. The hurried life and noise of the city confused him and Aunt Phoebe, but with Louise's help they managed to get into the elevators, across the streets, and back to their rooms. Punching the right light switch, however, remained a puzzle to them.

In honor of Uncle George the dinner was called the Billy the Kid Banquet and gathered to celebrate it were two thousand doctors and chamber of commerce representatives from Chicago's metropolitan area, sporting red bandannas around their necks in Western style. Among other notables who attended was Walter Noble Burns who had lived for a while at the Coe Ranch when he was writing his very popular book, *The Saga of Billy the Kid*. But George Coe was the hit of the evening. Distinguished looking and entirely at ease, he stood before the guests and told them the story of Blazer's Mill. As a promoter of the New Mexican climate he was impressive; to prove his statements he offered the stub of his trigger finger, a reminder also of a spunky little man named Buckshot Roberts, a gunman to reckon with in those days.

What attracted the Coes and others to Lincoln County, to settle in this wild new territory? Why were these men willing to defend their homes and land with their guns if need be? The answer lies chiefly in the climate, the rich farming land along the river, and the vast areas of open range for stock raising. In the early days there were two ways of acquiring this land. One was by the right of pre-emption. A federal law allowed citizens, under certain conditions, to claim and buy a quarter-section of land. The other way was to get land by the use of scrip. This the government issued as payment of bounties or bonuses for services in wars, and it gave the right and authority to certain people to own land. It led naturally to a big land grab. Both ways were unjust in that no consideration was given the first settlers and the native Mexicans. Shootings and killings resulted, for they did not want their farmland, grazing range, and homes taken from them.

The law encouraged rather than prevented a monopoly of public domain. A man claiming his hundred and sixty acres dominated an enormous area because he controlled the water from the streams and springs on his property. When the sheepmen invaded this territory they took up public land with watering places by pre-emption, which gave them, in some instances, control over vast areas. Some cattlemen acquired dozens of other springs and had domain over thousands of sections of public land and could keep the sheepmen out.

Such were the conditions when Dad settled in Lincoln County. The first survey of the land had recently been made and a man had the legal right to file on one hundred and sixty acres. As I mentioned before, Dad had more than this and in order to hold it he sent for Uncle George and his brothers to file claim on some of it. His brother Jap came from California in 1884 and soon after Austin came from Missouri. Three living streams furnished water for the land claimed by them, the Ruidoso, Little Creek, and Eagle Creek. There were also some live springs scattered over the area. Porfirio Spring was one. Named for Porfirio Chávez, a onetime sheriff of the county who watered his sheep there, it is still being used on my range. Goat Spring was a seep spring within the Fort Stanton Reservation.

Another watering place was the Government Spring located near the east boundary of Fort Stanton land. This was used by my father and others during the days of the open range. In Devil's Canyon was the English Spring developed by the Coes, and in the Little Creek country was the Ketchum Spring, named for Red Ketchum, one of our helpers who filed claim to the land around it. The Austin Spring claimed by my uncle Austin lay in the Eagle Creek country. Before the railroad took the water from the Bonito River this spring ran enough water to irrigate twenty-five acres of land. With Austin's claim Dad controlled the range between the Ruidoso and Bonito rivers, an area eight miles long and four miles wide.

With his water rights established and his range ample Dad began to build up his herd. In the beginning, livestock breeding was the main business of the ranch. He recognized the basic demand for horses and our range was right for raising them. Without the right kind of horse the cattle could not be rounded up and driven to the distant markets. The horse had to be intelligent, quick, strong, and accustomed to the rope and to hauling and being ridden. Dad set out to develop this kind of horse. He recognized the Indian cayuse was wiry and tough, but it didn't have body and stamina. To improve the breed Dad imported some good mares from Missouri, among them the Belgians, Percherons, Clevelands, and Morgans. When bred with the native stock, they produced a fine type that had speed, stamina, action, intelligence, and the sure-footedness necessary for the rough neighborhood. They made good cow ponies and workhorses. A team of them could pull the hack or spring wagon sixty miles to Roswell over rough, hilly roads in two days.

We had several hundred horses who grazed over the entire range. At roundup time because of the broken terrain we had to cover, we used a procedure different from the other big spreads. Instead of a wagon and wagon boss, we went out with pack horses. Our provisions and bedrolls had to be tied down with ropes because we had to go single file over the high narrow mountain trails. Sometimes we had to leave the trail and climb a steep hill or go through thickets and brush so heavy that the going was nearly impossible even for a single horse. There were dangerous places on the narrow trails and rims where we had to watch carefully to see that our mounts did not get pushed or crowded off.

In the Pajarito Mountain country eight miles south of our ranch we usually camped at Encino or White Tail Springs to round up the horses there. This was a beautiful area of lakes and grassland. If we were in the Four Lakes territory we set our camp there and worked the stock in that area. We first cut some cedar or juniper saplings to make pickets for the corrals to hold our herd; then fanning out in all directions, we took after the horses to bring them in. In the brushy and thickly wooded places it was rough going for both men and ponies, and we all came out scratched and tired. But we could never find a better way to do a job like that in the kind of country we had to work.

Operations like this would take as long as two or three weeks, and then we had to get the horses ready for the drive back to headquarters. One cowboy rode in the lead of the herd, two or·three covered the flanks, and as many more trailed with the drags. Only skilled men and stout horses could accomplish such drives.

Besides selling cow ponies, Dad also sold polo ponies for Easterners, dray horses, fire horses, and horses needed to take care of the ice, grocery, and milk routes around the cities. Good strong horses were always in demand for freighting, especially at the mines. Buyers for the United States Cavalry also came to our ranch at roundup time; they were careful to select the horses of a dark solid color that would avoid detection by the enemy. The bald faces or buckskins would not do for the military.

As we brought in only from two to three hundred horses

with each drive it usually took all summer to get in the herds. This was a busy season for the "jinetes," or bronc busters, and we kept two or three of them busy breaking horses throughout the season. Each would cut out about nine and put hackamores on them. Then they sometimes tied them to a post. A lot of bronc busters liked to stake them to a log that was too heavy to be dragged away. You would see broncs tied to logs or posts all over the place. A day or two of fighting the rope or tangling in it made the horses less frightened, and after two or three days they became used to the rope. When the jinete thought the bronc was ready, he took the rope from the log and tied it back around a hind foot and up around the shoulder. This hampered the horse when he tried to kick and plunge, but there were still many dangerous moments. Sometimes a man on a gentle horse helped him with his operations, and all day long, every day of the week, the bronc busting went on. The jinete took a lot of spills, bruises, broken bones, and trampling for his dollar a day and board. He had to be extra good to earn forty dollars a month. The rest of the horses brought in on the drives were turned out of the corral, the mares and colts along with the others, and they drifted back to their old range in the mountains. There they remained until another roundup time and another drive back to the ranch.

Dad was proud of his horses, some of which were sold to both East and West coasts and even to England. Around the turn of the century a Mr. H. V. Musgraves Clark of Cottonwood Farm, Lewes, Sussex County, England, bought a fine stallion from Dad and shipped it to his estate. In 1955 Louise and her sister Inez Wilcox had the pleasure in England of meeting Mr. Clark, who greeted Louise with, "Mrs. Coe, I feel I know you from your father-in-law, Mr. Frank Coe, whom I visited fifty years ago at Coe Ranch and from whom I bought a handsome stallion." On another trip Louise visited the Clarks at their country estate and saw some descendants of the Coe

Ranch stallion running over the rolling green countryside of Sussex County.

As dinner guests at Coe Ranch one evening we had our friends Robert O. Anderson and his wife, Barbara, who recently built a home at his Circle Diamond Ranch at Picacho. The dinner was just prior to a trip Bob was making to England to buy some Thoroughbred horses. When Louise mentioned the stables of H. V. Musgraves Clark, Bob told her he had already bought some of Clark's fine horses and was returning there to purchase more. Today when one drives through the Hondo Valley he may see among the handsome high-spirited horses and colts grazing on the green pastures of Anderson's Sunset Ranch some mares whose ancestors may have been sired in England several generations back by a sleek stallion from Coe Ranch, twenty-five miles up the valley.

When Dad first came to Lincoln County, he found the cattle there were as little promising as the horses. They were small and wiry, with long horns and tails and practically no backs. Their hair was of all colors and their frames had little flesh on them. A calf could hardly get enough milk from its mother to live on. At home we had to milk several cows to get enough for family needs. Dad could see that there was plenty of money to be made in cattle. When he and Mother settled on the ranch he began to build up the native breed by importing Durhams and Herefords and mixing these better breeds with the Mexican cattle. There were few registered bulls closer than Kansas and Missouri, and he scoured the country for good ones. These he bred with the different herds to improve them and build up his own. He was interested in quality rather than quantity. The Hereford mixtures were good rustlers and could get a living in the rough places and around the rocks while the Durhams added size and weight to the breed. Dad always had a substantial bank account which he accumulated from good farming practices. He had a ready market for his hay, grain, and livestock. He was an unusually good dealer; traded, bought, and sold when he saw a profit could be made. Thus he built up his herd of cattle, horses, hogs, or goats, buying or trading for young stock and keeping the increase as long as it was profitable.

The cattle grazed over the same land as the horses, but they did not roam so far. An area of about fifteen miles between the Ruidoso and Bonito rivers was their range. All was open land and public domain. This situation continued until the passage of the Forest Reserve Act in 1910. This act gave certain allotments of land to the ranchers that greatly reduced Dad's grazing area. With the allotments came fences and Dad, no longer able to graze his entire herd, had to sell off the greater part of his stock. We rounded up eight hundred cattle and drove them to Roswell where we sold them to Charlie Ballard. This left only a few hundred to graze on our reduced range. Our horses and mules also had to be sold. The Coe, Tully, and Bonnell allotments now bordered practically the entire south side of the Fort Stanton Reservation. Big outfits such as the Block took over areas where we had grazed, and the Indian reservation fenced off the Pajarito country, our best horse range. The coming of fences was the beginning of the end of the public domain.

With his grazing lands and herds so greatly reduced, Dad imported some fine Angora bucks from the East, bought a shearing machine, and went into another kind of stock business. The rough hills were good for the goats. They cared little for grass and ate mostly the brush and wild plants, especially mistletoe. At the peak his herd numbered around a thousand and the shearing season netted hundreds of soft fleeces with long silky hair.

All this time Dad was improving his fruit and grain crops. Alfalfa and grain found a ready market at Fort Stanton and the mercantile stores, but jolting over the roads to distant markets did not make fruit growing profitable.

CHAPTER XV

APPLE *Growing in the Early Years*

WHEN UNCLE LOU COE came to New Mexico in the sixties, he had hoped to set out a fine orchard in Lincoln County. He was a sort of Johnny Appleseed with a six-shooter, for wherever he stayed long enough he planted apple trees. His first were planted in the same part of the San Juan Valley where Uncle Fred Tully had surveyed the land to bring water to the first irrigation ditches. After Uncle Lou left the Farmington area he went to the Pacific Northwest to raise apples. But after the dry climate of New Mexico he found the dampness and cold there unhealthy. He contracted tuberculosis and moved to the milder climate of Arkansas and from there to Missouri, but the disease ultimately killed him.

Coe Ranch saw its first fruit trees when Dick Brewer lived here. His mother and father had visited him and seeing the possibilities of growing fruit had sent him some apple seed to plant. Dick was killed at Blazer's Mill by Buckshot Roberts and did not live long enough to see the trees mature. After my parents moved to the ranch, Dad began to explore the possibilities of raising fruit and sought Uncle Lou's advice. Uncle Lou had worked in a nursery back in Missouri and knew how to graft fruit trees.

Dad sent to Missouri for the seed of his first apple trees because at the time there were no railroad facilities for shipping young trees. He planted the seed in an acre of ground under a ditch close to the house. As soon as the seedlings were old enough he transplanted them to a permanent orchard and set them out twenty feet apart. With ample irrigation water all year and good summer rains, they grew fast. To protect the tender young shoots from the livestock until they had sufficient size and strength, he marked each tree with a sturdy post of cedar or juniper. The result looked like a grove of posts, which caused Dad to get a lot of ribbing from his neighbors about "the fine crop of posts he was raisin'." When the trees were large enough the posts were removed and used to make a picket corral. Some that escaped pulling stood for fifty years.

When the trees reached the right stage of growth, Dad pruned them using the shears, saw, and ax. It took expert skill to use the ax, but he knew just where to lay it and how to swing it to make a good clean cut. From Uncle Lou, Dad had learned how to graft fruit trees so when he was ready for this process he tied graft buds into place with scions and sealed around the cuts with melted beeswax to keep the sap from bleeding. His first experimental orchard grew into trees that eventually bore fine fruit and a few of the trees still stand, among them the rugged old survivor in the west terrace today.

From Dad I learned grafting and at a later time I experimented on walnut trees, and with scions from a California nursery I grafted English walnut trees to our native walnut. The first year they reached seven feet, but the winter was so cold they froze back and stunted. This happened again the following year. The third year they were completely ruined by a freeze. Of the ones I worked with, only a lone survivor near the house grew to maturity and bore a few nuts.

For a number of years Dad did not need to spray his fruit trees, but the insect population gradually threatened the fruit so Dad began spraying. He used a simple and cheap process compared with that of today. Into a barrel filled with ditch water he put Paris green. Then he hauled the barrel on a sled and with a hand pump went among the trees showering them with the solution. Now with our high-powered equipment and our expensive chemicals I doubt the results are any better than they were in those early days. Dealing with insects becomes more complicated and keeps the scientists and fruitgrowers busy trying to keep them under control.

When the trees reached the bearing stage everyone pitched in to help at harvest time. Dad with his seven kids had a fair-sized corps of pickers to begin with, and he did not have to do a lot of hiring. We took much pride in our jobs and competed to see who could pick the most. I remember in about 1910 we had a fine crop of apples that were for winter storage in an underground pit. The weather was nippy and the first freeze was expected soon, so Annie and I decided to get ahead of it. I took the tops of the trees and she worked underneath until, one by one, we cleaned them out. We hardly stopped long enough to eat, but by dark on the night that the killing freeze came we had finished. Our arms ached and Annie's neck had a crick in it, but we saved the crop. Our reward came during the winter when we could reach our arms through a tunnel and pull out a sweet juicy apple. York and Golden Russet were some of the varieties we raised.

To haul apples from the orchard Dad built a narrow sled eight feet long and put old tire irons on the runners. The apples were loaded and hauled to the graders who worked in a shed near the house. They used a table twelve feet long and three feet wide with a canvas bottom for grading. In about 1920 when the orchards began to produce in quantity Dad bought an apple grader and sizer that could accommodate six graders and four packers. One of our best packers was Leo Joiner of Hondo, who could pack one hundred boxes a day. The number-one apples were wrapped and packed in wooden boxes that were labeled and stamped for quality and count. We often shipped five hundred boxes averaging forty-eight pounds per box by railway cars loaded at Capitán. These apples usually sold for three to four dollars per box. The small and second-grade apples were sold locally for fifty cents to one dollar per box, which helped to pay the expense of the crop.

I used this packing plant for several years after I bought the ranch, but with the coming of the carton apple box it was necessary to change the method of packing. About 1955 we installed a modern grading machine and a sizer and an electric machine for stapling the boxes. We began to use large padded wooden bins which hold twenty bushels each. These are placed in the orchard at convenient spots and are filled carefully by the pickers. A mechanical lifter loads them in the orchard and unloads them at the grading machine. Recently we have been selling a great many of our apples packed in cartons to Safeway at El Paso. This is profitable because the Safeway trucks load at our shed.

Earlier Dad had to find his own markets. Before the advent of modern transportation, shipping by carload lots required hauling the fruit in wagons to Capitán. To appreciate what transportation in the old days was like let me quote again from Joe Kerley: "Late in the fall when the apples were all picked, packed, and stored and all the hay was cut, cured, and put in the hay shed, Frank Coe and I loaded apples and went all over the mountain country selling them. Frank drove in the lead with the four-up and I followed with the two-up team. Every now and then he would look back at me and call out, 'Hold a tight line, keep in the middle of the road and watch out for the rocks.'

"It was a valuable experience skinning a team over the rough mountain roads with a load of perishable fruit. We took in every ranch and village for miles around, going to White Oaks, Nogal, Capitán, Carrizozo, following the trails familiar in the old days to Frank and Billy the Kid. We had our bedrolls and chuck box, camped out, and did our cooking over a crackling cedar fire."

We often shipped a carload of apples from Capitán and getting them hauled over the mountain road was continuous hard work. Using two wagons with four horses or mules hitched to each, it took a week to load a car. The wrangler was kept busy roping out new horses, for one trip was all the young ones could take. Dad often took advantage of these hauling trips to break in broncs. The driver had to wind in and out among the trees and up and down the sides of arroyos, sometimes zigzagging sharply and endangering the load. No matter how carefully the drivers managed their teams, an accident sometimes happened. A spill took place once with Manuel Corona, one of our best drivers. He had worn out the foot brakes and when he came to another steep incline he had nothing to hold back the wagon but the harness that came around the rumps of the mules. When this tightened on one of the mules he started running. The wagon failed to make it on a turn and went over a bluff, pulling the mules in on top of it. Manuel jumped before the wagon went over the thirty-foot drop. He was momentarily stunned, but as soon as he could he climbed down to reach the team. Mules, fortunately, will not strain, struggle, or kick when they are in such a spot because they do not wish to harm themselves. They remained in their uncomfortable positions on top of the wagon until Manuel cut and unfastened the harness and released them. Most of the load had broken from the boxes and was scattered over the hillside, too damaged for any use except as food for the squirrels, deer, and other animals. Manuel returned to the ranch a very sad man indeed.

Nelson Bonnell, Bert's brother, was a fine mule skinner. At White Oaks he handled as many as six teams at one time hauling for the mines. After he came to our ranch to work he did many of the hauling jobs. In time he married my sister Agnes and they moved to the "spring ranch," a part of our place called that because it had the largest spring in the area. Nels ran some cattle on the shares and continued to work for my father until he homesteaded and started a ranch of his own about a mile and a half from Coe Ranch where he reared a fine family and lived out his life.

Around Christmas was a good time to hit the road with a

load of apples from our storage cellar, and I remember one time helping Nels get ready for a trip to Roswell. We had to shoe and curry the horses and put them in shape for the four-horse teams, a wheel team and a lead team. We checked the heavy mountain wagon to see whether the brakes were in order with new blocks and ratchet. The wheels were examined for broken spokes or loose tires. If a tire needed shrinking, we did it in the blacksmith shop. After the wagon was in shape we put a thick layer of clean hay over the bottom of the bed and loaded the apples in bulk on top of it. A tarpaulin was tied over the load to keep out the cold and protect the fruit as much as possible.

Nels climbed on the seat and clutched the lines with one hand, cracking the whip with the other. As he whistled to the teams they lunged forward, eager to hit the collar on a cold morning. As there were no county funds to maintain the roads, Nels had to go over places that were rough, rocky, and deeply rutted. By the time he reached Picacho Hill, twenty-five miles away, he was ready to camp out at the foot of the hill where he could get water for his horses and a pail of it to make coffee. He slept under the wagon and was up at dawn cooking bacon, eggs, and coffee to go with his cold biscuits and apple jam. When he had fed and harnessed the horses he hooked them to the wagon and began the climb up Picacho Hill, a challenge to both driver and horses. In places the roadbed was sideling and marked with chug holes, several stretches of it consisting of slanting hard bench rock, neatly packed like the steps in front of the First National Bank building. When the wheels hit them the horses would have to heave and struggle to maintain their balance and hold their footing. After the steepest parts they would pause to get their breath. Once on top of the hill, Nels stopped again for the team to rest while he made a careful inspection of the harness, running gear, and load.

A difficult descent on the other side brought Nels and his

load to the monotonous drive across the prairie where the antelope grazed undisturbed on Border Hill. By noontime he made it to the halfway station where he let his teams rest a while. From the stage station to Roswell the road was smoother, and after a stop at the twelve-mile water hole he reached the crest of Six-Mile Hill west of Roswell just after sundown and continued on into town after dark. Tired, hungry, and stiff from the cold and sitting so long, Nels drove into the C. D. Bonney Livery Stable.

After a night on a hard mattress and a one-sided fight with bedbugs at the rooming house he ate breakfast and went to the stable to check his outfit. While he talked with Mr. Bonney he invited him to pick some apples from the top of the load to give to his friends and neighbors and told him to be sure to mention that a big load of mountain apples had just come in. Nels then removed the coupling gear from the wagon, hitched up old Pet and Molly, and drove to the Joyce-Pruit Grocery at the corner of Second and Main streets. When Mr. Joyce came out to greet him and make inquiries about the fruit, Nels offered to sell him the entire load at a bargain, or for a slightly higher price let him have part of the load. Mr. Joyce was not able to handle such a large quantity and suggested that Nels peddle what he could on Main Street and bring back whatever was left for him to buy.

Nels drove down the middle of Main Street to a place in front of the courthouse where he could start selling. He rolled back the sheet cover, and filled several bushel baskets which he spread around the tailgate of the wagon. The people seemed to smell the fruit because it was not long before they started to gather, some on foot and others in buggies and wagons or on horseback. By noon the load had been cut to less than half. But by then with the increasing cold and the dark clouds hanging over the mountains to the west, the sales went down considerably.

The following day the weather was even colder with snow falling in big flakes. Because the severe weather could damage the fruit, Nels drove back to the livery stable. Many people who had sampled the apples given them by Mr. Bonney came there to buy. Christmas was close at hand and a bowl of juicy red apples would add much to the festivities. By the time the weather had moderated enough to melt the snow Nels had sold several bushels more. The remainder he took to the Joyce-Pruit store and traded for sugar, flour, coffee, bacon, a keg of horseshoes, and other supplies for the ranch. With some of the profits he purchased several packages of Bull Durham and a quart of Old Crow for protection against frostbite on the way home.

As far as it was possible Dad stored apples he was unable to market. Such varieties as the Winesap, Rome Beauty, and Black Twig kept well during the winter months if put away properly, but the Maiden Blush, Bellflower, and the Snow apple were marketed earlier in the season. The first fruitgrower to build an apple house in the valley was my uncle Jap Coe. It was seventy-five feet long by twenty-five feet wide, constructed of native stone. On either side of a breezeway running down the middle from door to door were eight-by-ten-foot bins. The roof was made of adobe mud spread six inches thick to keep the building cool in the summer and warm in the winter. Heavy log beams supported its weight. At regular places high above the bins portholes were made for cross ventilation. Apples stored here kept until late spring, losing none of their original flavor which by more modern methods is to a degree lost.

Using a similar plan Dad built a larger apple house of adobe bricks, which, like Uncle Jap's, is still in use today. This kind of building eliminated the crude storage bins used in the orchards all winter. Later, on the east side of the apple house we built a packing shed where fruit could be graded and stored or sold. After the "dumper-upper" took the apples from the horse-drawn sleds he filled the bins. After they were loaded to the ceiling they were covered with sheeting to keep them fresh and clean. Except for the Jennetons, a hard freeze in the late fall generally put an end to the apple picking for that year; that variety stuck on the trees and became sweeter and juicier as the frost bit into them.

CHAPTER XVI

EVOLUTION *of Apple Growing*

HEN I WAS OLD ENOUGH I began going on selling trips with Dad. I was about eight when we started out in the mountain hack one fall with a load of apples piled loose in the bed and our chuck box and bedrolls carefully placed on top of the fruit. The hack had good springs, so after the fruit settled down we went over the bumpy roads without much damage and bruises to it. Our destination was White Oaks and the Jicarillas fifty miles away. We were prepared for the long trip with hobbles for the horses and a good buggy whip, the hobbles to put on by night and the whip to lay on them by day. The road was only a narrow trail and it took hours to drive from one settlement to the next. In order to protect the fruit Dad had to drive carefully over the chug holes, ruts, and sideling places.

Sometimes when Dad got tired he would hand the reins to me and say, "Here, you try your hand for a while." That suited me fine until we came to a deep gully or a slanting stretch of road. Then I wanted to pass the reins back to him, but he would say, "Tut, tut, you can't do anything worse than turn the outfit over." I learned a lesson that I never forgot from that experience—don't ever say you can't.

When the evening sun was low and the team was getting tired from the hard haul over hills and valleys, Dad said, "Well, keep your eye peeled for a good spot to pitch camp for the night." I watched closely and when we came to a level place where there was a tall friendly tree, I told him it was just the spot we were looking for. We unhitched and hobbled the horses and let them graze on the tall grama grass that grew all over the flat. With dry limbs and pine cones that we scraped from around our campsite we made a fire and cooked our coffee and a nice cottontail rabbit Dad had killed along the way. Dad never went anywhere in those days without his rifle. His eye was keen and his aim steady, and when his trigger finger moved something dropped. But I never heard him brag about what he had done with a gun or what he could do. He had always refused to bet with Billy the Kid as to who was the better shot.

When we finished our supper and took the nosebags off the horses, we rolled out our beds under the hack and turned in for the night. The moon was full and the stars bright and we were tired after our long drive. In the early dawn we could hear the lonesome yip of a coyote and the eerie scream of a panther nearby, which sent cold chills up and down my spine. I huddled close to Dad while he reached for his rifle and settled down with his finger on the trigger. We could not go back to sleep so we crawled out, lit the fire, and filled our lard can with enough water and some Arbuckle's coffee with which we washed down our eggs and bacon. We licked it all up in a hurry and soon were on our way.

We reached Capitán, which was no more than a wide place in the road with the Welch and Titsworth Store, Sebe Gray's livery stable, and a saloon. The road from there was impassable because of heavy rains that had fallen all the way from Capitán to the top of Nogal Peak. The only road left that a wagon and team could get over was from Capitán to Coalora and it was over the bed of the Salado Canyon. Ordinarily this was a dry gulch with a smooth bottom and straight-up banks six to ten feet deep. We knew that it was dangerous to drive over it in the rainy season.

Since we had a perishable load and White Oaks was our destination, Dad said he would risk it. We entered the canyon and found no more than a trickle of water running over the sandy bottom and thus no danger of bogging down. Dad wanted to get over it as quickly as possible so we wasted no time. He drove at a trot until we were within a hundred yards of a place where we could pull out of the gulch. As we made a small bend we suddenly heard a loud roar and, looking back, I saw a great wall of water rolling and churning straight for us. Dad stood up in the hack and began bathing the horses with the lines with one hand, using the whip with the other. With the first slap of the reins the horses sprang forward, and with the flick of the whip they went into a dead run. My hat flew off, but I didn't dare look back to see where it had gone. Just as we reached the turn off I sprang from my seat, grabbed the dash-board and yelled "gitty-up." When I risked a glance over my shoulder I saw big logs, boulders, white foam, and what looked like a cow tumbling over and over. The team had sensed the danger and had run at full speed up the sloping bank of the turn off, out of reach of the raging water that slowed down some as the flood lapped at our hind wheels, seeming to say, "Hey, fellers, what's your hurry?" (A flash flood is the result of a cloudburst, usually over a small area, bringing a wall of water down a generally dry arroyo with great force and speed.)

Dad must have guessed that I was a little shaky as we continued on toward Coalora, which at that time was a new mining camp. As we drew near we could see the coal-mining boom town with its tents, shacks, dugouts, and coffee-box huts. Heavy rains had slowed up the mining operations so the miners were all gathered around the commissary, blowing off about how hard it was to get anything to eat or drink around the place, I guess. Dad had no sooner set the brakes and tied the reins to the brake rod than the hack was surrounded with "lookers and peepers."

One big husky fellow looked at me and grunted, "What yuh got there, kid?"

"Apples, mister. Big, red, and juicy." I was quick to answer.

"Got any samples?" he roared at me and winked at the other men.

"Sure, at a nickel a throw."

While I was making my sales pitch, Dad pulled out our ten-pound lard can we used for making coffee and began filling it up with apples for twenty-five cents a bucket.

One thin-looking miner asked, "Boy, where'd yuh grow them fine apples?"

"On the Ruidoso. That's what makes them so sweet and juicy."

He looked at me doubtfully, saying he was from Kentucky and he had not seen apples in the mountains there that looked like ours. He ended by buying a bucketful and after emptying them in a tow sack he took off, happily biting big chunks out of one.

We spent some time at Coalora and what we sold made a dent in our load. As we had to find a place to camp for the night, we left before the sun was too low. Dad headed the team for Nogal, which is just over the Indian Divide near the east edge of the Carrizozo flat. Here he knew he could get wood and water. We stopped at a good location near there and hobbled our horses. But before getting our chuck ready, Dad counted the coins from the sale of the apples. Every time he would count out a dollar in change I would throw a nickel into a tin cup. The number of nickels represented the dollars received, this was our mode of bookkeeping. At the end of the count we had eleven nickels and three pennies. By that time we were hungry so we hurried to get our supper and crawl into our bedrolls. Before we dropped off to sleep we counted our blessings and thanked the Lord for sparing our lives from the floodwaters of Salado Canyon.

Early the next morning we set out for White Oaks. As few wagons had gone over the trail it was dim. However a few miles out of the town we ran into the ruts of the old gold trail over which many a ton of ore had been freighted by ox team, yoked eight to a string and hitched to a large high-wheeled freighter and trailer. In the 1880's a prospector named Paul Mayer had shunned this road. Over a secret trail known only to him and his Mexican helper he carried a canvas bag with the gold he took from his mine in hunks, chunks, and nuggets. Rolled in a blanket, it looked like his bedroll. On a much longer and more roundabout trail he led his pack horse to San Antonio, New Mexico, about 70 miles away, to have his gold assayed, appraised, and turned into spending money. In the same era another old-timer decided, like Mayer, to take only the pure gold from his mine. But he rode over this old trail Dad and I were now driving over, and to handle his own gold safely he established a first-class livery stable where prospectors and others coming to the boom town could rent a buggy. He operated this with bronc busters from the Block Ranch who were laid off during the winter season, and established a fast buckboard service over the first mail and passenger line from White Oaks to San Antonio. Simpson stashed away his shipments of gold bullion under the mail pouches, and no one ever knew that gold was being hauled to San Antonio this way. When I grew up the gold-rush days of White Oaks were not so far away, and I heard old-timers tell of the days of Mayer, Simpson, and other prospectors. As we rode along in the big comfortable ruts made by the ore wagons I hoped we wouldn't meet anyone and have to pull out.

When we reached White Oaks Dad drove up to the Ziegler Brothers Grocery and left me to hold the horses while he went in and talked to the owner. He soon returned, grinning, with the proprietor who was carrying a wooden candy bucket estimated to hold a bushel. He looked at the fruit and said he would take five bushels if they were cheap enough. He was a good trader, and proud of it. He warned Dad not to do as other peddlers had done—sell him a big order at a high price and then go around to people's houses and sell the same thing cheaper. Dad chuckled at that as he measured out five heaping bushels at a dollar and a half per bushel. This was about 1903.

From there we drove on up to Whiteman and Sons Store and Rooming House. Like the Zieglers they were old-time friends of our family. Mrs. Whiteman, tickled to see us, greeted us in a friendly and hospitable way. While Dad shook hands and talked to the men around the store she led me by the hand to the soda-pop stand and candy counter. Pulling out a strawberry pop from under a wet blanket used to cool the bottles, she handed it to me, saying I must be thirsty after my long ride. Then she reached into a large glass drum and brought out enough mixed hard candy to almost fill one of my pockets. I had never seen such mouth-watering candy, and when she was not looking I could not resist the temptation to snatch up a big red gumdrop also and cram it into my mouth. At that moment she chose to start asking questions about my mother and sisters. To my embarrassment I found when I tried to answer her that my jaws were locked, and I could not open or close my mouth. She saw my plight and popped a finger into my mouth, wrapping it around the gumdrop. Giving a sharp tug she brought it out and a tooth along with it. I had been putting up with the loose tooth for some time because I was too chicken-hearted to pull it myself. A sharp pain and my bloody mouth made me want to cry, but I remembered that Dad had told me if I did not act like a man on this trip, he would not take me again. Seeing that I was a little pale, Mrs. Whiteman, dear lady that she was, reached up on a shelf and brought down a bottle of sugar pills. "Now, you're all right, again, Wilbur." And I was. At the same time I was ashamed because I had snitched the gumdrop.

In the meantime Mr. Whiteman had told Dad that business was slow, and he did not think he could take many apples. But he did concede that if Dad would make a good price he would take ten or fifteen bushels and perhaps we could sell the rest from house to house. What remained he might take off our hands at a reduced price.

After unloading what Mr. Whiteman had bought we went on up the street, and at the first place we stopped we sold two bushels to an old friend, Judge John Y. Hewitt. From there we hurried on to some other places he had directed us to so that we could get rid of as many apples as possible before dark. We then returned to the Whitemans for supper and to spend the night. As soon as we finished eating we got ready for an evening of music with Abe Whiteman, Charley Whiteman and his wife, and their daughter Dora, for wherever Dad went there was musical entertainment. Dad tuned up on a borrowed fiddle, and Dora sat at the piano while the Whiteman brothers readied the banjo and guitar. I was too young to play an instrument, but I was on the job to suggest numbers to play, such as hornpipes, reels, quadrilles, and old favorites like "Sally Goodin," "The Irish Washerwoman," and the "Arkansas Traveler." When we all became too sleepy to enjoy the music Dad broke into the "Home Sweet Home Waltz."

Before going to bed Dad expressed his thanks for a pleasant evening and extended to them a cordial invitation to come to the Coe Ranch for another shindig. Mrs. Whiteman showed us to a couple of cots in a hallway and explained that her rooms were all occupied. After she put on clean pillow slips she kissed me good night and said she hoped my tooth would not bother me. I had already forgotten about it. The next morning after breakfast we made an early start for home with only enough apples left to eat on the way.

Until modern methods of transportation came we depended on railroad shipments to dispose of the bulk of our apple crops. Late in the season one year we loaded a car of Black Twigs at Capitán and I went with it on my first selling trip. Before leaving I picked out three prime apples from the storage bin, so big that I could hardly get them in my overcoat pocket. Then at Capitán I caught the caboose behind the load of fruit.

At El Paso I found a lodging for a dollar on Santa Fé Street where I slept in the lobby rather than fight the bedbugs. Early the next morning I hurried to the market district and stopped in front of a hole-in-the-wall office with Crombie and Company painted above the door. A man sweeping the sidewalk in front sent me inside to wait for Mr. Crombie. I walked around the dingy office trying to keep warm. Soon the owner of the company came in followed by his assistant who shook down the stove and lighted a fire.

I could tell by Crombie's looks he would be a tough one to deal with. His face was serious and his manner abrupt as he inquired about the apples. As I tugged at the ones in my pocket to get them out I told him they were red juicy Black Twigs as solid as could be found. He wanted to know whether I had any more like the samples so I said they were all pretty much the same. To take care of any difference in the size of the others I priced the lot at two dollars a bushel. He took out his knife and cut one through the center and looked satisfied as he wiped the juice from his knife and desktop with his handkerchief. Then he told his helper Jake to go with me and come back with a report.

Jake and I went to the siding and got in the car, and as I opened the boxes he dug into them to pull out samples. I was too busy to pay much attention to him as I kept on opening boxes and he continued to stuff his pockets with specimens for Crombie. We returned to the office and Jake put his collection on the desk. He must have rooted around in the boxes for the smallest ones he could find, for they did not look much like the ones I had carried in my pocket. Crombie looked at me sternly and picked up one of the apples. He did not say a word as he cut it in two and put half of it up against the half of my own sample. Finally he swiveled his chair around and commented that the ones Jake brought did not look like the samples I carried. I admitted they did not. I was getting mad, but at the thought perhaps of having to move the apples from the siding and route them to some other town I did not say what I wanted to. As Crombie made no move to buy the load I knew I was wasting my time so I told him I'd try to find another buyer. He agreed it was a good idea.

I went out disappointed that my first selling job had ended that way. The market district extended another block or so, and as I walked along I figured how I would have to rebill the load to another town. The only alternative was to sell to jobbers in small lots. At the end of the market district I crossed the street to return so I would not be noticed by Crombie. As I walked down the sidewalk across from his office Jake came over to tell me the boss wanted to see me again. I said to myself as I crossed that if Crombie wanted to haggle over my price I was not interested, but I went to see him anyway. The first thing he asked was how much I'd come down on my price. I knew I would not lose on the deal if I knocked off a little so I told him I'd lower it ten cents a bushel. We haggled a little and I finally knocked off another nickel.

"You've made a sale, lad," he said in his thick Scotch accent, "and you're a good trader. But I want to give ye a wee bit of advice. The next time ye go out to sell apples don't carry around the biggest ones. Take some of the large, some of the medium, and some of the small. That way ye'll not be fooling anybody." Then he turned to his office helper and said, "Jake, draw up a check for Wilbur Coe and leave the amount blank. I'll tally that part of it and write it in."

I walked out with the check in my pocket, feeling relieved and happy. I was wiser too, for the experience taught me that to deceive anyone even partially in a business deal is wrong, and I had a canny Scotsman to thank for the lesson. He knew I was not a crook but a country boy who needed to learn a lesson. In the years that followed I shipped Crombie many apples on an open order, and no complaints ever came back to me.

The coming of automobiles facilitated marketing. Long creeping drives over mountain roads ended, and the rattle of wagons and the shouts of the drivers no longer echoed over the hills and mesas. During the early 1920's we made the transition from teams and wagons to trucks. One of ours was a new Model T and the other a second-hand one we got from Bob Boyce. I had to take out a loan to buy the trucks so when I asked Mr. Cahoon, president of the First National Bank of Roswell, what security I should give, he said, "All I want to know is that you are the operator of Coe Ranch and your father's name is Frank Coe." While he counted out the cash in one-hundred-dollar bills I brushed away a tear of delight.

At that time the New Mexico Highway Department had crews working on and repairing roads to accommodate faster travel by automobiles. The road to the mountains had been improved, including Picacho Hill and other dangerous spots. Where it had taken two and a half days of slow going with a team, it took only a matter of hours of comparatively easy riding in a truck, even though some of the hazards still remained and the old road by today's standards would be regarded as nearly impassable! So instead of using the trails, we now kept to the main roads. In the peak of the loading season at Capitán we ran trucks day and night, not without breakdowns that made us sometimes nostalgic for the steady reliable teams.

When we finished a season's loading at Capitán we headed out in our trucks for more distant places in New Mexico and Texas. It was my policy never to return with any apples, no matter to what lengths I had to go to get rid of them. I managed to find some sort of market, but it was not always easy.

In search of better markets I would drive as far as Littlefield or Lubbock in Texas. If no kind of salesmanship worked, I would have some of the load left. Rather than take any back with me, I would find a farmer and trade what I had for some stock feed. If he had no milo maize, I would load up on kafir corn or some other plant used for stock feed by valley ranchers. If I went to El Paso I would try to get a payload coming back. There was always someone in our area who had a piece of freight lying in the freight yards there. Or maybe someone needed some building materials and was glad to get some cement or window sashes hauled. I would even select a piece of furniture someone wanted badly and bring it back with me. This hauling often paid for my gas, oil, and food.

In Roswell I would go from door to door to sell. If I stopped in the street I would not have to wait long for customers, for the grapevine started working right away. Housewives gathered with their baskets and buckets, and while I filled up the containers they munched on samples and gossiped. They usually bought in large quantities, and if there was more than they could carry, they would have the kids bring wheelbarrows or little red wagons. As soon as the sales were over in that block I would move to another, find a nice shady spot, and turn off the engine. Before long I would have an empty truck and my pockets would be sagging with silver.

If peddling up and down the streets was slow and I was left with part of a load I would figure out some other way to sell it. I knew that the best place to find buyers was in the stores, so I would begin looking around downtown for one that had a lot of customers going in and out. Then I would go in and ask the owner about renting a corner of his store to sell apples. "Sure," one of them said as he munched on a sample, "put as many as you want over there next to those sacks of chicken feed." It did not take me long to move in, and for rent I would pay him off in apples. If business was especially good I would give him some cash too. Usually my stock disappeared fast, and it was necessary to hire a helper while I went back to the ranch for another load. This beat house-to-house selling, and for several years I sold apples in this way.

It was not long before Coe Mountain apples gained a reputation among the people. This necessitated expanding the business, so I began to look for an empty store to rent. Louise's father had one he let us use, and I put an ad in the paper and waited for customers to come in. In the front end I lined up my choicest fruit, never for a moment forgetting what Crombie had taught me about showing all sizes. Business reached the point where I could not handle it alone so I hired a storekeeper. People liked the idea of buying fruit that was always fresh from the trees. I promoted sales at Christmastime by fixing up special gift boxes, all top grade, fancy-packed and wired for long-distance shipping with a special foolproof wiring that defied the slickest thief. The idea went over big, and the people who received gift boxes told others. During the weeks preceding Christmas I loaded an express truck almost daily. It was a special pleasure to send some to Washington or Oregon to show the people up there that New Mexico could grow good apples as well as prickly pears.

I decided it would pay to bring in apples to Roswell and put them into cold storage so they would be on hand for the Christmas trade. At times I had as many as five thousand boxes stored, and from them I supplied retail outlets. I branched out to El Paso, where I rented an empty store at Five Points for a dollar a day with the understanding that I would vacate if a permanent tenant came along. The choicest apples I sold from the store, and the second grade to peddlers and jobbers at the City Market. I used the cold-storage method there also. Most of this business was handled by me personally, which cut overhead costs greatly. The fruit was carried to the markets in my own trucks and I did my own selling. There was no keen competition. A few hucksters bought apples from me and resold them, and my buyers included all sorts—the housewife, marketman, peddler, jobber, wholesaler, retailer.

During a good Christmas season in Roswell one year Will Lawrence came around to sell me some life insurance. He told me he would make it so I could pay the premium in apples. That suited me fine, and he wrote out the policy and began sending boxes of apples to his mother in one place, his sister in another, and friends scattered in various locations. At five dollars a box my premium was paid in no time. Lawrence did me a big favor by showing me that insurance is a good investment, for through the years mine has collected dividends. It has also been a convenient collateral for loans.

Shifting from teams to trucks did not take all the hardship out of getting apples to the markets. The old-style trucks were open and the driver had little protection from the cold. I had to generate my own heat by wearing the warmest clothes I could get on and as many garments as I could wear and still move around. But whether it was in hot weather or cold, I began selling apples as soon as I left the shed. The small stores along the way were regular stops, and while I would dicker with Mr. Stover at the San Patricio post office and grocery, I would warm my toes or cool the motor of the truck, depending on the season. A part of my equipment on these runs was a log chain and a shovel. If I was not stuck somewhere myself, there was usually someone else who was and so I would help dig him out of a hole or pull him back on the road.

Later, paved roads and motor transportation changed things, and we found it more profitable to sell fruit at the ranch to truckers from all over New Mexico and from other states. They bought by the load, thus eliminating the cost of grading, packing, and hauling. As long as the apples are firm, clean, and edible, the truckers are not too particular about the size. I have sold many apples off the trees for thirty-five and forty cents a bushel and felt that I was making as much profit as I did on the ones I sold for five dollars a bushel after grading, boxing, and hauling. In more recent years competition, regulation, and market demands have changed the fruit business. Today orchard owners must grow fruit to meet the demands of the large chain stores.

To help take care of my fruit crop I constructed the first modern cold-storage plant in the Hondo, Bonito, or Ruidoso valleys. With the advice and help of W. A. Wunch of New Mexico State University I worked out the details of its construction, sealing and insulating the adobe walls of the building with cottonseed hulls hauled from Las Cruces. When that work was completed I had a cooling system installed. The room has a capacity of two thousand boxes of apples, and I find it valuable for temporary storage of prunes, plums, pears, and peaches as well.

The roadside stands one finds up and down the Ruidoso and Hondo valleys today came into existence with the increase in automobile travel. Back in the early twenties I put up the first one. It stood under a huge cottonwood that sheltered it from the sun, and on a hot summer day it was an inviting place to stop and cool the engine of the auto, and get some fruit to take along on the trip. I built the stand over an irrigation ditch that ran water at all times, and through a trap door in the floor I lowered jugs of cider to cool. But when the paved highway was constructed the road changed, and I had to move my place of business.

Road stands are big business today, and one can count several of them to a mile through much of our orchard country. But when I was starting out in the business it was quite different. Cars were few and far between, and waits for customers were long. I found it interesting, though, to meet people from different parts of the country, and there was plenty of time to talk to the tourists. There was not the pressure to hurry waiting on one customer and getting on to the next, as is the case at our stand at the ranch today. Sometimes all the parking space is taken by people lined up in cars, in a hurry to get waited on and get on their way again. The day is gone when the motorist, hot, tired, and dusty from the road, would turn an apple box on end and pass the time of day for an hour or so.

I recall an incident in the early days that took place one morning when I had just opened the fruit stand for business. A car from New York pulled up and three ladies traveling alone, a very daring thing then, got out. It happened that at the moment I was busy giving instructions to a couple of my Mexican workers. The ladies said they were in no hurry and for me to finish my talk with the men. My instructions in Spanish were somewhat detailed as I was explaining just where I wanted some fence put up and just how I wanted it done. I got down on my knees and drew a diagram of the plans with a stick, and after I finally made it clear I went back to my customers. They told me to fix up a big sack of the best eating apples I had, and as I selected them from some baskets and chatted with them they studied me carefully. After they paid me and got back into the car, the lady at the wheel asked, "Have you lived in this country long?" I assured her that I had, and she added, "Well, mister you surely do speak good English."

From a ten-dollar day at our first roadside stand in 1925 Coe Mountain apples climbed in sales until the business became profitable. In 1940 we began selling from our new fruit stand. While I supervised the picking and hauling of apples, pears, and other fruit, Louise did the arranging and selling at the stand. She is a super saleslady and greets a customer with the same cordial friendly smile whether he buys a pound or a carload of apples.

For more than twenty-five years I have exhibited apples, pears, and other fruit grown on Coe Ranch, first at the Chávez County Cotton Carnival from 1924 to 1931 and at the Eastern New Mexico State Fair from 1931 to the present. During this time I have been awarded more than fourteen hundred premiums. Several hundred of these ribbons have been arranged on a large piece of white felt, fashioned in the design of an Indian feather headdress, hanging in our dining room. This colorful array of ribbons, which I look upon with pride, bears testimony to the high quality of the Coe Ranch produce and of the part it has played in the development of the fruit industry in Lincoln County.

CHAPTER *XVII*

MUSIC *at Coe Ranch*

MUSIC has been a vital part of Coe Ranch. It has been a force that has drawn and kept us together and brought enjoyment and relaxation. A love for it has passed from one generation to the next. I have heard my dad say that my grandfather, Benjamin Coe, traveled many miles to fill an invitation to play at a country dance, usually receiving for his talent what could be collected in the hat. Or perhaps for playing all night he would get a couple of dollars and some apple cider. When Granmaw Tully left Chicago with her family in the late 1870's to live on the New Mexican frontier she brought her piano with her. From Granmaw Tully we Coes learned to understand and appreciate different kinds of music. But for my part, I only wanted to learn to play the fiddle like Zebrioen Bates.

Dad did not take to girls much when he was growing up. And he did not care as much for dancing as he did for music. He loved to listen to his father's violin, filling his head with tunes he longed to play when he could get a fiddle of his own. The only way he could try out his father's violin was to wait until he was sure Benjamin was away from the house and then make a run with it for the corncrib. There he would saw away on the strings until he could play a couple of tunes. With my folks, then, music was not just a pastime; it was an essential part of their lives. Dad said more than once that his fiddle was as important to him as the ax, plow, and gun. I can remember as a kid seeing him, after a hard day's work, reach for it and tune up for an evening of music and dancing. He was happiest when he shared his music with others, and he never accepted any compensation for his playing. All the return he wanted was for others to enjoy themselves, a feeling I have always shared with him.

In the days of Billy the Kid both Dad and Uncle George were widely known as musicians. Whenever they could, they put aside their farm tools and guns and got the neighbors together for a dance. Music helped them to forget the hum-drum of their lives and the struggle to make a living. When they did not have instruments of their own, they played on borrowed ones. Uncle George sometimes played "second fiddle" by beating time on the first fiddler's strings with a couple of knitting needles, an old-time idea of improvising several tones that gave greater volume to the sound of the fiddle strings. It also produced a harmonious tone to the music as Dad sawed out the melody with his bow. After acquiring his own instrument Uncle George played second fiddle (as we now understand the term) to Dad's lead.

My oldest sister, Sydney, was the first of us to learn to play the piano. Once she heard a tune she could play it by ear, and she could transpose with ease. Before starting a number she would insist that all instruments be in tune. As long as she lived she was the pianist of the Coe orchestra, in which she took a leading part. Most of all, Sydney wanted her music to bring joy to others. At seventy she stood behind the scenes at the annual Billy the Kid Pageant in Lincoln and faked the music of Mrs. McSween's piano on her accordion.

Next to be added to the orchestra was Annie. She learned to read the printed note. After Mother moved to Roswell to put us in school Annie spent many of her evenings playing with a musical group. When Brown and Curry, an evangelical team, came to Roswell she took the lead in the violin section of the fifty-piece orchestra selected from the community for song services. After all the souls had been saved and registered in the church of their choice, Brother Curry offered her a steady job if she would join his organization and tour the country and lead the instrumental music at meetings. Annie declined the offer, saying she was not ready to travel for her health, which was about as much compensation as was offered her. Besides, she stated, she had some calves to brand and a bunch of horses to break on the ranch.

Winnie, the third in line, learned to play the guitar and banjo but cared little for other instruments. As she spent all her time with these she became very proficient, especially in fast fandango music. Her solos always brought resounding applause.

Our fourth member was Agnes, who did not play an instrument or sing. But she had a wonderful taste in music and was valuable to all of us as a critic. She could detect any false notes regardless of how much racket was going on around her. And she let the one guilty know about it. She kept the orchestra going in time.

Of all the members of our family orchestra Edith became the best all-around performer. She was my father's special pet, and in her alertness, smiling manner, and sense of humor she resembled him much. She learned to ride a horse before she could walk, and by fifteen she was busting broncs and riding to the roundups with the cowboys. At the county fairs and other community gatherings she won many prizes for her horsemanship. Always on these occasions she proudly wore the beautiful handmade boots Mrs. Cree had given her. She could play the piano, guitar, and zither harp, which she still plays on special occasions.

Youngest of the group of six musical daughters was Zebulah (Zubie) Helena, named for my dad's sister and for my mother. Growing up later than the others, she undertook an intensive study of music after she began her musical training with Mother and Granmaw and took professional lessons in Roswell. In Helena, Mother's musical voice and placid nature live again. She is firm, patient, reserved, and tolerant; all these traits are made more pronounced by her serene beauty. When she was growing up, her innate shyness bothered her greatly at times, as when Dad would say, "Come, Zubie, let's have one of your songs." Embarrassed but smiling she would ask him what he would like to hear. He would ask for "Juanita," "The Old Oaken Bucket," or another of the old favorites my mother had sung earlier in their married life. If her reticence caused her to hesitate or if she stammered around too long Dad would give her a couple of taps on the top of the head with his middle finger, his strongest punishment. Then she would take a deep breath and sing in her clear true tones as Dad sat back and pridefully enjoyed it—and perhaps in memory he heard another Helena singing in a frontier cabin.

Seven of us and every one interested and gifted in music! You might think that I, the only boy in the family, was the pet; but it was not that way at all. I had to practice hard to make any showing with my talented sisters. Before I could ever sit with the orchestra I had to pass muster with Agnes and "Mr." Bates. Agnes expressed her opinions freely and candidly to all and with me she was especially strict. Before I ever played with them she laid down the rules to me, stressing that if I hit a sour note or had poor timing I might not get to play the next time. However if I should get mixed up about the time or fell behind with the changes of chords, I was to keep quiet and merely go through the motions of picking on my guitar. Under no condition was I to interfere with the harmony of the orchestra by hitting sour notes. At all times she kept me under her closest scrutiny. I was happy and surprised when I struggled through my first appearance without a great deal of criticism from her. And Winnie was so delighted with me that she unselfishly yielded her place to me as guitarist while she took up the banjo.

When I grew a little older I was especially fond of Mexican music and had the pleasure of knowing and playing with several early-day Mexican fiddlers around old Lincoln. These talented musicians played for many a "baile" when Billy the Kid swung the señoritas to the tune of a Mexican polka. Among them was Primitivo Brady, a son of Sheriff John Brady who was killed by the Kid during the Lincoln County War. Even though he had never taken a formal music lesson he made his living playing for the dances. In many of his numbers he changed keys from G to C to F and back to G, a skill he had learned from his father and from Salomón Montaña, Zebrioen Bates, and other musicians around Lincoln.

Another fiddler of exceptional talent was the blind Hilerdo Chávez, who learned to play by listening to others. He could push an expert bow on the fast Mexican polkas or draw it softly on the waltzes, often with several changes in key. Unlike most of these early musicians, Hilerdo never took a drink of whisky while playing for a baile, although many times during the late hours he would appear to be sound asleep as he laid his chin on the fiddle and drew the bow. Hilerdo was always in demand for such occasions as el Día de San Juan, el Día Santana, and el Cuatro de Julio, as well as the ordinary bailes.

One time I played with Hilerdo at a wedding dance at Las Chozas, where there was only a dirt floor to dance on. The mothers sat on long benches around the walls, their daughters huddled around them. The men gathered outside where they stood talking and drinking in the dim glow of the doorway The light in the dance hall was furnished by two lanterns and a string of tallow candles placed on a high shelf that ran around the walls. At the far end of the room the musicians sat on a high table where nail kegs had been placed, tuning up and waiting for the ceremonies to begin. By the time the bride and groom with all their family and kinfolks arrived the moon was shining brightly, and the "valientones" standing around the corner of the building had no trouble finding the right end of the bottle to drink from.

At the Mexican bailes it was customary in those days to have a mayordomo conduct all phases of the dances and see that the musicians were seated "comfortably," ready for the grand march. When the time came the wedding couple, their kin, and all their friends who could crowd into the sala with a compañero marched around the room until it was packed. At this point we broke into a lively polka, which was a sign for the valientones to rush in and take the bride for a whirl. She had to go first with one and then another until she was dizzy from swinging around the floor. The fiddlers then obligingly stopped the music. After this the mayordomo allowed as many men as the space permitted to select a partner to jump up and down, part time on their toes, until the music abruptly stopped, after which the señoritas returned to their seats or standing places and the men went outside for another "traiguito."

Unless the mayordomo had some special selection he wished played the fiddler called the tunes. The music and dancing still continued at midnight, and the valientones were getting "muy borrachos." Evidently they thought things were a little dull, for one of them slipped inside the hall and set off a large firecracker under the fiddler's table where Hilerdo, half asleep with his chin on his fiddle, dreamily played "Sobre las Olas." I was picking away on the guitar, very intent on keeping in tune with Hilerdo as he changed keys on his fiddle. Sometimes when I nodded and went off key Hilerdo turned and grunted, "Do, re," for a change of key. As I struggled to make such a switch the firecracker exploded like a cannon under us and almost knocked us off the table.

There was no blaze but the smoke and confusion caused a panic in the dimly lighted room, and the acrid fumes mixed with the odor of burnt-out candles. Outside, the moon had gone behind a cloud and left in darkness some of the valientones who were propped against the wall sleeping off their drinks. At the sound of the firecracker they all snapped back to life and looked with surprise at the people as they tumbled outside and piled on top of each other, receiving some cuts and bruises as they scrambled around.

Hilerdo and I jumped from the table clutching our instruments. When we saw that there was no fire we worked our way through the crowd to tell the mayordomo. I figured the best thing to calm the people was to start some music, and I yelled to Hilerdo to get a tune going. Soon the dancers were back on the floor, and it was not long before the compañeros were choosing their señoritas for the good-night waltz. In the meantime the joker who had thrown the firecracker received some rough treatment from some of the men who had not found the trick very funny. For my part, I was happy when the mayordomo slipped three dollars into my pocket, and it was time to mount my sure-footed pony, Skeeter, and ride with my valued guitar under my arm over the rough hilly trail ten miles to the ranch. What brought me the greatest joy though was the words of the mayordomo as he told me good night and added softly, "Muy buena música, Weelver."

As the years went by and my sisters married and established their homes the Coe orchestra dwindled. Times changed, too. People no longer felt the need for entertainment centering around the home because the automobile changed all that. The old one-room schoolhouse built by the Coes gave way to the Bonnell Ranch. This place, formerly the Jap Coe home, had belonged to J. Landly Pool, and when it was put up for sale Sydney and her husband, Bert, bought it. Bert Bonnell had come to Coe Ranch from White Oaks to work for my dad. After the roundup was over he would help supervise and work on the farm while Nels did the hauling and freighting. At first Bert and Sydney moved to the "goat ranch" where my father grazed some five hundred goats, but Bert continued to work for Dad. The location of Bonnell Ranch made it an ideal spot for a dude ranch because it was situated at the meeting of the Ruidoso River and Eagle Creek at a road junction that connected the settlements of Tularosa, Lincoln, Fort Stanton, and Capitán, at whose two extremes lay Roswell and El Paso. With natural assets of a delightful climate in both summer and winter, and hunting and horseback trails in the surrounding mountains,

Bert and Sydney's place had great possibilities at the time of the transition to the auto. In addition, its facilities were used for community picnics, Fourth of July celebrations, high-school parties, Ruidoso Water Users Association meetings, and live-stock conferences. But above all it was a place for community get-togethers at Saturday-night shindigs.

In the beginning Sydney and Bert established the ranch as a halfway house and stage stop where travelers taking the auto stage from El Paso to Roswell could get tasty home-cooked food and ranch-style lodging. Bert began with a couple of tents in the backyard, but soon they needed more room to accommo-date their guests and so he built a string of cottages in the orchard. When spring rolled around the following year, 1930, Bert put an ad in the Chicago *Tribune* offering room and board for forty dollars a month including a horse to ride. It was not long before letters came from all over the country inquiring about accommodations and the kind of artillery the guests should bring with them in case of attack by Indians or outlaws! In giving them information Bert suggested they bring only an extra pair of patent-leather slippers to swap off to a cowboy for a pair of boots he could wear to the next Saturday-night hoe-down. In the meantime the cowboy, if he so desired, could step out in his patent-leather slippers and cut a shine with the girls sitting on the sidelines and patiently hoping for a partner to dance with.

There could be no better host for such a place than Bert, who came originally from the Ozark country in Missouri where he had learned all about hog calling and square dancing. Ge-nial and friendly, he was a fine caller and floor manager. He knew everybody for miles around by their first names. When the musicians had finished tuning up and were ready to go he would shoot to the center of the floor and call for four or eight couples to "wash their faces and take their places and get set for an old-time square." If another couple was needed to com-plete a set Bert would grab a girl by the arm and skid her into place and then, taking her as his own partner while still doing the calling, would yell out, "Honor your partner. Don't be late. All join hands and circle eight."

I sat on a stool near the piano with my fiddle under my chin, sawing with a bow which was resined to make the loudest and most mellifluous sounds possible. Sydney at the piano beat out the melody and rhythms while she kept an eye on the dance floor. Ralph Bonnell, son of Sydney and Bert, and Harold and Joe Coe were there to pick the guitar. When the hours of dawn came the dancers would come around and say, "It's too late to go to bed and too early to start to work so let's just dance some more." Always the last one to say quit, I fiddled away as long as anyone was on the floor. It took me until midnight to get in my stride, but once I got strung up I could go on indefinitely. Bert once said to me, "I've heard better fiddlers than you, Wilbur, but I have never seen one that could outlast you." In reply I told Bert, "If people get as much pleasure dancing to my music as I get from playing it, I am well paid for my work." My father and grandfather before me had shared the same sentiments.

It was not long before the old-time tunes and dances were pretty much replaced by the one-step, fox trot, grapevine, frog's leg, Charleston, and others of the twenties and thirties. Louise was in great demand to play for these new dance numbers. With our marriage another musical light shone over Coe Ranch, one that added new life to the orchestra. After we were married Louise continued to study music under Miss Lorena Sager, a professional pianist in Carrizozo. However there were some people who liked the old-time dances, so Sydney took care of them and Louise took over with the popular music of the day.

The fame of Bonnell's Ranch spread. In far off Honduras an Englishman, Rowland Cowper, picked up a copy of a magazine and read about it. Liking the sound of the place, he caught the next freighter to New Orleans where he boarded a bus which brought him to the Bonnell Ranch. He stayed there for two years and left in 1939 only because the war had started and he had to return to England. With him went a pretty school-teacher from Capitán whom he had married. In later years Louise visited them at their lovely home in Folkstone.

Rowland Cowper was just one of the many guests at the Bonnell Ranch who enjoyed the climate and scenery along with good food and ample diversion. Another was a young lad by the name of John Frerichs, whom I vividly remember. He came with his father from St. Louis in 1930 to spend the summer and enjoy the outdoor life. He learned to ride well and find his way around the area, catch the stock and help us at the roundups and branding the calves. In the years following—through 1941—he acted as guide for most of the Bonnell guests on their rides. But at the dances he was too bashful to get on the floor. Instead, he put his attention on the music. Next summer he brought along a banjo and a guitar and joined the Coe orchestra. After he had finished college and medical school at Johns Hopkins, John taught for several years at Leland Stanford University, my own alma mater. But he never forgot the Southwest or lost his love for it. About nine years ago he moved to El Paso to make his home, and Dr. John B. Frerichs now is a pathologist there. He is still a young-looking man and the father of a fine family. In a recent conversation he told me that if Glencoe had been served with a first-class hospital he would have settled there right away because he has always loved the climate, the people, and the free way of life which to him is the best in the West.

During the summer months the Coe orchestra played every Saturday night for the guests at Bonnell Ranch. Those who were in any manner talented were invited to join in the fun and take part in the entertainment. One of the summer boarders who never missed a Saturday night, rain or shine, was Louise Bolton, now Director of Musical Education, Isleta, in the El Paso school system. She plays the violin beautifully. Others who were at different times members of the orchestra were Roy and Will Coe, sons of Uncle George. Will had learned to play the fiddle from Zebrioen Bates, and with two fingers he was able to produce smooth and sweet music. His son, Harold, became an expert guitar player and a good singer as well. In addition to these there were Ralph Bonnell, Junior Perry (a grandson of Uncle George), Chester Stockley (fiddler), Aaron O'Neal (bull fiddler), and my friend Louise Massey. Her brother, Curt Massey, who is now a popular television and radio star, enjoyed vacationing here and often took part in the orchestra. Louise Massey is best remembered, perhaps, for her own musical composition, "My Adobe Hacienda," a smash hit of the fifties.

Thus it was that at the Bonnell Ranch people enjoyed some top performers in music, dancing to Sydney's schottisches, waltzes, and squares and to Louise's modern dance tunes. It is to the credit of the Coe orchestra and caller Bert Bonnell that the old-fashioned square dances, which are so popular today, were kept alive here in the valley. For over fifty years the Coe musicians contributed their talent to many benefits—Victory Bond Drives, women's clubs, health and welfare entertainments, highway dedications, Red Cross drives, weddings, and many other civic and social events, large and small.

When Saint Anne's Chapel was built, the most important music in Sydney's life was playing the organ every Sunday for the church service. She and Bert donated the land for the building, which is across the highway from Bonnell Ranch headquarters near the Glencoe schoolhouse. In May 1929 the Reverend F. B. Howden, Jr., rector of the Episcopal Church in Roswell, son of the Right Reverend F. B. Howden, Bishop of New Mexico, began regular services in the schoolhouse and immediately started a fund to build the chapel. Aided by general contributions from the American Church Building Fund Commission and other organizations, the people in the vicinity raised the necessary funds. This little architectural gem is constructed of native stone with a red-tile roof. I hauled the handmade tile in my truck from a small factory in La Luz near Tularosa. The furniture is made of pine from the nearby mountains. Louise and I gave the wrought-iron hanging lamps made especially for the chapel by Scotty Andrews, who lived in Roswell for many years. The church has a seating capacity for about forty persons. St. Anne's Chapel was named for my grandmother, whose patron saint was Saint Anne. It was consecrated on June 4, 1934, by the Right Reverend Howden, who officiated at the service. Several of the charter members of this chapel are still living, and they and their children are among the attendants at the services today.

An event of 1940 gave the Coe musicians another opportunity to contribute their talents to a worthwhile cause. This was the year in which New Mexico celebrated its Cuatro Centennial, which commemorated, among other things, Coronado's march through New Mexico in search of the treasures of the legendary Seven Cities of Cíbola. In Lincoln County it was decided that a performance based on the history of the county ought to be presented in the form of a pageant. Louise was selected as chairman of the committee in charge of getting the pageant into production. She and I helped to acquire a sizable tract of land adjacent to the Lincoln County Courthouse Museum. A large stage was constructed and a concrete seating arrangement was made in the natural amphitheatre of the slope of the mountain. A professional writer from New York wrote the first script for the pageant, "The Last Escape of Billy the Kid," in which Peter Hurd played Billy the Kid. Before a large crowd the pageant was enacted near the very spot from which the Kid made his escape in 1878 after killing his guards, John Bell and Bob Ollinger. The Kid rode away down the street of Lincoln on Sheriff Pat Garrett's horse.

The enactment of "The Last Escape of Billy the Kid" aroused much interest because it portrayed history in a romantic fashion. The Lincoln County Historical Society, of which I served as president for many years, decided to sponsor the pageant and produce it annually. Our good intentions were interrupted in 1941 by the war. The pageant was not re-enacted until 1948 but has been presented every year since.

Ralph Bonnell played the part of Sheriff Pat Garrett many times. From the beginning Dan Storm, our friend and neighbor, has played Buckshot Roberts, the plucky little man who stood up to a posse of thirteen at Blazer's Mill. I played the part of John Chisum, the cattle king of the West, for the first few years.

Louise worked tirelessly each year to organize the pageant, get the rehearsals going, and keep them moving. She served faithfully as director and general consultant, and this covered about everything from getting an old stagecoach moved out from Roswell to hauling lumber to enlarge the stage facilities. She drove down the valley and then back up to Lincoln for rehearsals, picking up along the way people who were taking part. Her enthusiasm was inspiring to those who worked with her. If her energy lagged she took time out to join the actors, stage hands, electricians, extras, narrators, and villagers around the campfire. The spirit of "the show must go on" was shared by all of the participants, who sometimes rehearsed in the chilly mountain air or in soaking, nearly freezing, summer rains.

Music has played an important part in the success of the pageant. It seems fitting that Coe music should have had a part in "The Last Escape of Billy the Kid" because many years before in a wilderness home on the Ruidoso my dad and Uncle George fiddled away lonely hours for their own enjoyment, and for a few months also for the pleasure of another who shared their cabin, a restless friendly kid with a ready smile and a fast gun. His brief appearance on the scene in Lincoln County during a turbulent period in its history was the basis for the first Billy the Kid pageant in 1940 and for the subsequent ones. At this performance and at others which followed I played my violin for another generation and for spectators who watched the unfolding of a part of our historical past, sitting in the

Louise and Wilbur Coe Stadium in Lincoln. Demetrio Peralta, of Capitán, who played the old-time Mexican tunes on his fiddle, was accompanied by his two sons, one on guitar and the other on the bull fiddle. They joined the Coe players to furnish the background music for the pageant. The theme song, "Sleepy Lincoln Town," written especially for the pageant by my friend and neighbor Bruce Griffith, is so popular that it is always used in the musical opening.

Today the pageant receives a grant from the state. It is sponsored by the old Lincoln County Courthouse Museum Commission and is staged the first weekend in August each year. My hope is that it will continue through the years.

Because of a feeling for the historical past of our county Louise and I are deeply gratified that we were instrumental in setting up a memorial in the Old Lincoln County Courthouse Museum which, in a sense, commemorates our early pioneers. More specifically, it is in memory of my mother and father. Through the cooperation of Mrs. Dessie Sawyer, chairman of the Old Lincoln County Memorial Commission, members Will Keleher (noted writer from Albuquerque), Colonel E. L. Lusk (long-time Superintendent of the New Mexico Military Institute at Roswell), and curators Nan and John Boylan, the old jury room of the courthouse has been designated "The Helena and Frank Coe Room." For the dedication of "The Frontier Parlor," invitations that were sent out brought a gathering of almost four hundred people to the museum on July 17, 1960. Here have been placed Granmaw Tully's organ and rocking chair; Mother's walnut clock that graced the shelf above the fireplace in the original one-room adobe house; the bookcase, containing among others Dad's stock reference book, Mother's medical guide, and the family Bible; the mahogany library table with its wide bottom brace where I rode my first "horse" and on which I later whittled a little; two walnut folding chairs upholstered in red velvet; and the sideboard made in our workshop by the carpenter who also built our barn, and two of

Dad's most prized possessions—his single-action .45 rifle and his folding-top desk with pigeonholes. In another part of the museum are Mother's wedding dress and Edith's size-three riding boots given to her by Mrs. Cree.

An exhibition of a different kind took place at the museum on May 28, 1966, when I exhibited some of my "nature sculpture." Under the curatorship of Paul Gardner, who for twenty-five years was the director of the Nelson Rockhill Museum in Kansas City, Missouri, we showed some one hundred pieces from a collection of several hundred. My interest in this work came about through years of riding over the ranch looking after our horses and cattle. In my search for a particular kind of animal it was necessary to keep a keen eye on all parts of the landscape, both near and far, because the stock liked to stay hidden in the thickets and brush, on top of the high hills, or at the heads of deep canyons. In early morning the animals went out into the open glades and flats to graze, at midday they would lie low under trees or in the shelter of cliffsides, and in the late afternoon they would ease out into the openings to graze again. This constant scrutiny of the landscape required a good imagination and often some guesswork. I learned to create in my mind's eye images of objects of all kinds.

On one occasion when I rode out on a high point of the mountain overlooking the valley far below, I spotted an object. I was looking for some horses, and this appeared to be one of them. Yet I hesitated, for I saw the color was gray and the object was shaped like a big bird. When I rode down to it I could see then that it was a juniper stump five feet high. I took another look and imagined that by placing a head on the stump it would then appear like a gray eagle. Later I had the stump brought to the ranch, fashioned an eagle head for it, and placed the finished product on the rock wall in front of the ranch house where it stands today.

That was the beginning of my "nature sculpture," a form of art in which I use twigs, branches, stumps, driftwood, cacti, grapevines, climbing-rose branches, and many other suitable forms fashioned by nature. For tools I use chiefly a good Western pocketknife, an electric drill, a hacksaw, and a hammer. These must be sharp and dependable. In addition I keep handy a bottle of mercurochrome and a box of Band-Aids. I seldom use either of these but would feel insecure without them. I do not, in general, "carve" figures—the Lord has made my material, and I have only to restore occasionally an eye, ear, horn, leg, or tail to bring out the character and appearance of the imagined object. Very often only my perception of the mere object as representing something has brought about very happy results; this is in fact most often the case. I do not consider my work with sticks and stones a hobby. It is an art—a specialized form of it that few other craftsmen have practiced. It is an art that could foster many desirable skills and traits in the minds of those who may care to work at it. Every piece is an individual specimen which I try to make stand alone and hold its identity from any point of view. I have created objects ranging from the size of a gnat to a full-grown giant, such as a twelve-foot image of Billy the Kid. This occupation demands patience and feeling. It also requires research and a keen observation.

CHAPTER XVIII

Coe Ranch TODAY

OU SUDDENLY come upon Coe Ranch today a few miles beyond San Patricio over U. S. Highway 70 going west from Roswell. In its more than a century of existence it has been occupied by Jack Gilliam, the Harrell brothers, Dick Brewer, the Miller family, and, since 1882, the Coes. The house is almost hidden by trees and shrubbery. The warmth of its pueblo-style architecture softens the stately dignity of the Lombardy poplars at each end and of Mount Coe, which rises a thousand feet high to the west. As you draw near the front entrance, you hear the gushing and churning of the main irrigation ditch, which runs across the front lawn and flows a mile down the valley to water the orchards and gardens. As you cross the footbridge, the graceful, sweeping branches of a willow tree over it bow a welcome.

At the back of the house lie the main gardens, landscaped by C. E. Hollied of Santa Fé. Here the land, a city block in size, is arranged in four terraces until it reaches halfway to the Ruidoso River. In the days when more cabbage than fruit was grown in the valley, it was a cabbage patch. Later, when the gardens were landscaped, we made sure that Mother's pink and moss roses were included in the plans. To assure that her flowers would get plenty of water, she had set them out in the vegetable garden. After more than fifty years they continue to flourish. This south garden, as we call it, reached by a wide violet-bordered flagstone walk that leads to a rose pergola, is centered by a lily pool surrounded with a boxwood hedge. Descending to another terrace, you come to a lower garden planted with various varieties of shrubs. Reaching above all this are spruce, fir, and long-leaved pine trees, which I dug up in the high elevations of the Mescalero Indian Reservation and transplanted with complete success.

The south patio of the ranch house, accessible through the door of the sun porch, is delightfully warm and bright in the winter sun. Here a gay Mexican-tiled fountain gives a colorful setting even after the roses, peonies, and phlox are gone. For outdoor cooking the same chimney that serves the fireplace of the garden room is used.

For entertaining a large number of guests we use the west terrace, which is reached by the garden walks or through the west entrance of the living room. The brick floor here is constructed around the oldest apple tree in the area, planted by my father when he first took over the ranch. From its trunk, thirty inches in diameter, it spreads its shade over a sixty-foot area in the summer. We still like to sit here and enjoy the surrounding gardens.

The north yard of the ranch house is bounded by an adobe wall and the main irrigation ditch. At each end are colorful red haw trees whose brilliant colors rival those of the roses, lilacs, irises, columbine, lilies, snapdragons, chrysanthemums, and dahlias that grow in profusion in the gardens surrounding the house. From the colorful splashes of three hundred dahlias Louise selected a vaseful that Henriette Wyeth, Peter Hurd's wife, painted for her, and so we see these beautiful flowers the year-round in the dining room.

The forty-by-twenty-foot living room was the original one-room adobe house whose thick walls were assailed by outlaw bullets and Indian arrows. Fifteen heavy beams hand-carved cross the ceiling by Vick Bergman, the Swedish carpenter who had drifted into the village of Ruidoso many years ago and had supervised the remodeling of Coe Ranch in the late 1930's. Also from Vick's skillful hands came the drapery rods and fireplace set which he forged in our own shop. Metal apples dangle from these. Hanging over the fireplace, which is similar to the one

Louise and I had seen in a Taos hotel, is a painting of the ranch by Peter Hurd. Pete also did my own portrait, which hangs on the south wall of the room and reflects in the mirrored wall opposite. With me in the picture are my fiddle and some apples in a silver bowl, which also reflects the artist as he worked. At the foot of a hand-wrought rail along steps leading to the master bedroom, once the Glencoe post office, hangs Henriette Wyeth's portrait of Louise. Eventually it is to be placed in the capitol Senate Chamber in Santa Fé. At this end of the living room is our music area where we roll up the large Navajo rugs and turn the entire room into a dance floor.

The southeast wing of the house contains a bedroom, my office, and a room we use as a museum, which is filled with relics and mementos of the past. Here also are pictures of Mother and Dad and my favorite photograph of Louise. My father's features bear witness to the strength and determination that motivated him. His closely trimmed goatee always made him stand out among the men in this area. His keen, clear eyes have squint-lines at the corners, caused by years of riding under New Mexico's bright skies. Narrow, erect shoulders indicate the litheness and toughness of his body. When I look at the picture I see him again, his restless energy and strong vitality contrasting with his soft voice and gentle manner.

In a smaller frame to the right of the photograph of Dad is one of Mother. Her eyes with their long lashes reflect unfathomed depths. It is no wonder that she won my Dad's heart the first time he looked into them at a country dance in the San Juan valley. Mother's face shows the adaptability and calmness that enabled her to accept gracefully her role as frontier wife and mother. Yet behind her calm acceptance of God's will, she had tremendous courage, a firmness of purpose, and great strength of character. Although she lived to be more than ninety she never lost her zest for life or her compelling personality.

In addition to my office I have a cluttered-up desk at one

end of the sun porch, which has heavy vigas that cross the ceiling and project over the south patio in pueblo style. Scattered over this area are deep couches, Navajo rugs, and comfortable chairs. The mantel has a special built-in niche for Mother's walnut clock, a prized possession. Much of my time is spent here, and whenever fatigue or the problems of the ranch overwhelm me I have but to turn in my chair and look out over the gardens and orchards to Mount Coe in the background. Soon a feeling of rest and calmness comes over me and then I go about my tasks again.

If a warm evening drives us out to the front veranda, which is the same length as the sun porch, we usually find a cool breeze stirring the willow and cottonwoods. The ceiling is made of small willows that have been put close together in sections separated by heavy vigas in herringbone fashion. Across the highway is the mesa where Annie and I used to take our exciting rides as we broke wild broncs to the harness. From the veranda can also be seen the cattle barn and a few other ranch structures. Along the driveway runs a rock wall that surrounds the barn. Inside the enclosure are the loading chutes and corrals.

An itinerant carpenter built the barn in Dad's day. Its first story is of adobe and has a wide center aisle where wagons can be loaded and unloaded. The stalls have chutes that carry hay from the mow to the mangers along the sides. To facilitate the handling of horses that are being harnessed or doctored there are a string of stanchions and some chutes. There is also a tack room in this area. A large window opens at one end of the mow so that hay and grain can be pitched in from the outside.

Across the driveway opposite from the barn stands the hay-barn built on the site of the old one with the cupola playhouse of my childhood. Here a hundred tons of baled hay can be stored at one time. To operate our first baler we drove faithful, reliable old Dimple around in a circle, we kids taking turns riding her. Since tromping down the hay in the baler was dangerous, we had to have a horse that could be depended upon, else the machinery might start moving while someone's leg was down in front of the plunger. The wire was fed by hand, so with the tromping and the riding and the feeding Dad kept most of us busy helping. At times we were in a frenzy to get all of the hay baled before a downpour brought a halt to operations.

Hidden from view by trees and shrubbery on the east side of the house are the shop, corncribs, toolsheds, and blacksmith shop. Although the days of blacksmithing are mostly gone the shop, with its bellows, vises, and drills, is still vital to the repair of farm machinery, windmills, and every kind of farm equipment. The old apple cellar has been converted into a modern cold-storage plant.

The faithful helpers I have had through the years have been the backbone of my farming and ranching operations. One is Alex Gómez, whose family has lived in the valley since the days of the Conquistadores. His home stands near the cattle barn on the main highway. Alex has been a valuable asset because he can do almost anything around the ranch—carpentering, plumbing, cementing, plastering, and masonry work. In addition he is an expert hand with machinery and general farm work.

The first steady hand I hired was Manuel Vigil, the son of Francisco Vigil. Like his father he could handle horses expertly and could never get enough of bronc riding. After he worked all week on the ranch, he would ride down to San Patricio on Sunday and, for a dollar, would ride the meanest outlaw brought out. He was not a hard drinker, but the little whisky that he took at such times made him very daring. All the fiestas and celebrations found Manuel ready to ride a wild bronc, and none was ever too tough or mean for him to handle. As I was also young and "valiente" too in those days, Manuel and I could handle any situation.

Lorenzo Sambrano was a horsebreaker especially skilled in

training ponies for roping and cutting. One of his well-trained horses I sold to the livestock manager of the Wrigley estate; he came to the ranch accompanied by Arthur L. Renton, who is now living at his Rancho Santa Catalina near Atascadero, California. From the first this horse caught Renton's eye, so he later bought him for his own ranch. Because of his roan color he named him Tecolote; with his quick intelligence he soon became a show horse. Several years ago I had a letter from Mr. Renton in which he had this to say of the Coe Ranch horse: "Tecolote surely was a wonderful little cow horse. Two months ago I had to have him put to sleep as his teeth were about gone and he was getting poor even with the special feed mix we had been giving him. It was a sad day around here when he left us. Up until the end he didn't go lame and could still give you a good ride. He never did fall down with me, and I slid off some pretty rough country. He must have been at least thirty years old when he died. The Coe Ranch can certainly be proud of raising that little Steeldust cowpony as he lived up to all standards that a real New Mexico cow horse should." Along with Mr. Renton's letter were two snapshots of Tecolote with the caption, "Thirty years old and still going strong."

Back in the days of Lorenzo and Manuel, our helpers were ready for any kind of job that had to be done. Faithful and tireless, they enjoyed doing their work well without undue regard for hours and wages. They picked cherries, washed dishes, swept the porch, churned the butter, hoed the garden, busted broncs, or cut hay. After feeding and fattening the hogs they butchered them, rendered the lard and stuffed sausages that they had seasoned just right. One winter we killed three hundred hogs and sold the sausage, tenderloins, backbones, and spareribs in El Paso and Roswell. In those days for twenty-five cents you could buy a pound of sausage; spareribs sold for twenty cents.

For the last three years we have employed as manager of Coe Ranch my nephew, David Bonnell, who grew up on

Bonnell Ranch adjacent to my own. He lives on the ranch in a modern two-bedroom house built about fifteen years ago. David is a natural-born, all-around rancher and jack-of-all-trades. He understands machinery, electricity, plumbing, painting, carpentering, and blacksmith work. With cattle he is expert and has continued to upgrade my herd. By converting some orchard land into permanent pasture, we have made the cattle business more profitable. The range land afforded pasture for about one hundred mother cows and their calves, and now with the addition of permanent pasture it will take care of another seventy head.

For work in the orchards, two of my most faithful workers through the years were Leo Chávez and Tránsito Polaco, who have also been neighbors and friends. They helped me plant most of the fruit trees. Both were good pruners and excellent apple pickers.

More recently Damasio Prudencio and his wife, Josefita, have been working for us. Damasio is a good truck and tractor man and a helpful farm hand, and she works in the house. In the summer of 1967 when the state engineers surveyed the center line of an improved stretch of U.S. Highway 70 between Hondo and Coe Ranch, it ran right through the middle of their house. They were paid five thousand dollars for the damage to the house and the right of way. As Josefita and Damasio have great confidence in our judgment and know that we are interested in their welfare, they asked us for advice about a new home. Louise drew up the plans for the house and advised them first of all to drill a well. They had been married ten years and had never had any water except from a bucket. She also insisted they buy bathroom fixtures, a sink for the kitchen, and a hot-water tank. Before the walls of their new place went up these were on hand.

At the peak of our orchard operations we employed as many as fifteen men picking, grading, and packing the fruit. We built a bunkhouse to accommodate these seasonal laborers.

Beginning with the party Mother and Dad gave back in the 1880's to celebrate the new wood floor that replaced the dirt one, Coe Ranch has been an hospitable place. Mother loved to entertain friends, and the girls did not mind if they had to sleep three or four in a bed, nor did I if I was sent off to the barn to sleep with the cowboys.

Louise and I have given many parties, entertaining people from all over the country. As October is irresistibly beautiful in the Ruidoso Valley we often give our larger parties then. Trees have begun to wear their vivid yellows and golden oranges, yet the flowers are still blooming in the gardens. If it is a little nippy the sunny patio provides a warm pleasant place to visit with friends. Also at this time of the year our garden supplies us with fresh corn on the cob, tomatoes, squash, cucumbers, carrots, and green beans, and our orchard trees hang heavy with fruit.

One of our barbecues that I well recall was given on October 4, 1956, in honor of Blanche and Alfred Knopf, the John Herseys, and Grace and Horace Albright. We sent out a hundred and fifty invitations, and our friends came from great distances, among them, my sister Winnie and her husband, Orville Hunt, from Oklahoma City, Clyde and Concie Whittaker from Anderson, Indiana, Dr. and Mrs. Deets Pickett from Kansas City, Missouri, and Dr. and Mrs. Erle Moore from Chicago. These last three couples we have been meeting in Acapulco every winter for years. Other friends came to this party from El Paso, Dallas, Santa Fé, and Roswell. On an open barbecue pit we prepared a fat yearling with the c o e brand, cooked brown, tender, and juicy. (In my early years on the ranch I used my own i n k brand, but later I took over my father's c o e.) The baby beef was served by expert caterers from Roswell, along with frijoles, chile sauce, cabbage slaw, potato salad, Spanish rice, hot biscuits, and plenty of black coffee, with Old Crow to keep the music going.

Louise used lots of colored leaves to decorate the house, but what received the most attention were large hand-woven Mexican baskets of a bushel capacity, each filled with Red and Golden Delicious apples and Bartlett and Anjou pears. On tables throughout the house they made a pretty picture as did the colorful fiesta dresses—so popular in the Southwest at that time—the women wore. I shall never forget the purple one decorated with brilliants worn by Louise Massey. My Louise wore one of this type, of bright blue made for the occasion by Lila Bath in Acapulco and embroidered with sequins. I wore my best red cowboy shirt and purple tie.

By the pool in the south patio filled with floating fresh dahlias, artificially perfumed, and on the terraces, tables and chairs were placed. In addition to the Mexican cancioneros, Peter Hurd serenaded many on his guitar and singing in Spanish. The rugs had been rolled up on the sun porch and living-room floors and when it was time for the dancing I tuned up my fiddle, Louise took over at the piano and, with Ralph Bonnell on the guitar, we started playing. I did several Mexican numbers I had learned from Primitivo Brady, and varied them with Mexican songs. The orchestra was not as large as in the days when my father played the fiddle and we kids joined him with our different instruments, but the dancers seemed to enjoy it just as much as in the old days. With plenty of tequila, apple cider, and other drinks, the guests lingered until late in the evening. As they departed each one was invited to take an apple and a pear from the baskets of fruit.

Because of Dad's interest in promoting projects for the betterment of the community, his own holdings had been enhanced. Our grazing lands include eight sections that are held under permit in the Lincoln National Forest, which he had a part in establishing. In setting up forest preserves the government sought the goodwill and cooperation of the people in the area. Many in our locality were not in favor of having the government take away the range land. Dad believed, however, the only way for one to have a fair share of this land was to have his rights protected by a fence and the law. He knew also that the devastation caused by cutting the timberland for posts and other saw timber for commercial uses would eventually lead to a clearing of the trees from the land. If the forests were to be preserved, the trees would have to be cut in limited quantities and only with the permission of the government. To further this conservation measure, Dad went to Fort Worth in 1910 with a local representative to present arguments for and against the establishment of a forest reserve, and at a later date these recommendations became the foundation of the Forest Reserve Act. After the law went into effect no one could get logs or posts without a permit, and because of this conservation measure much of our timberland still stands today.

Coe Ranch also has under lease some Taylor Grant grazing land and some belonging to the state. In the establishment and protection of water rights, Dad's foresight has caused these leases to be of inestimable value to me today. Since from the 1870's to the present the Coes continually have improved waterings that control the grazing lands, these holdings are considered basic and prior; the law recognizes them as such.

In my time community improvement has been approached in a more organized way, and over the years I have been active in all phases of its development. In my twenties I was an officer in the Ruidoso Cattle and Horse Growers Association, and for forty years I have been secretary-treasurer of the Ruidoso Water Users Association. At the beginning of the Roosevelt administration I was president of the local mediation board which was set up to help farmers with problems of mortgages and land losses. World War II found me serving on the Selective Service Board in our county.

Prior to World War II a county planning board was organized as a part of a nationwide movement to build a better economy. On the local level, plans for improving conditions, especially with regard to farms, roads, highways, and schools were put into action. Recognizing that the tourist business in our state was becoming an important item in the economy, I proposed to the board that the community give an annual pageant based on the history of the county and the career there of Billy the Kid. This would promote the romantic history of Lincoln County and at the same time attract the tourist business. Added interest, I argued, could be gotten from having actual descendants of people connected with the history take part in the pageant. But there was strong opposition. Some wanted no truck with Billy the Kid. Others felt that few people would be interested in the cattlemen's feud of the seventies. George A. Titsworth, however, saw my viewpoint and suggested that the Lincoln County Historical Society take charge of the organization and production of the pageant. Louise, who was then serving in the state senate, worked for the project and secured the full support of the legislators from the other eight counties that originally comprised Lincoln County. A commission was set up and funds were allocated for the restoration and maintenance of the old Lincoln County Courthouse. From its inception the pageant has been a great success, with much of the credit due the local people who gather for rehearsals each summer behind the old courthouse to give of their time and talent to produce the show.

In the fall of 1941 when a devastating flood hit our three valleys I was named chairman of a disaster board on which I served several years. This organization worked to restore dams, ditches, roads, and bridges that had been washed out. To assist in these operations the Upper Hondo Valley Soil Conservation Service, which had been organized only a short time before, went into action. Equipment was brought in and all governmental agencies that could aid were summoned to help us. The Forest Service furnished logs, posts, and other needed timber while the Civilian Conservation Corps cut them and the Soil Conservation Service hauled them. A dredge and a pile driver were sent in by the state to clear the streams and drive the pilings for new dam structures. In addition to all these services the state also furnished seed for the grasslands and spraying equipment for the orchards and cattle. Through hard work and cooperation the land was readied for the spring planting.

Another public activity into which I have put extended work has been rural electrification for the three valleys. Six years after the Rural Electrification Administration was established in 1935 at Washington, the people in the Ruidoso Valley became interested in getting power from it. On their behalf I wrote to President Roosevelt and asked that electric power be made available to our area. Then I called the Ruidoso Water Users Association together to find out whether the members would sponsor a program and submit it to the R.E.A. They agreed and an R.E.A. engineer came to study the situation. His recommendation was that the people in our vicinity tie in with the Cloudcroft Cooperative, which had recently been organized. Subsequently plans were made to go into the Otero County Electric Cooperative to which I was appointed, as trustee to the board, in 1945. But things moved with great slowness. In the meantime the Ruidoso Electric Power Company had constructed a small power unit which was purchased by the Community Public Service of Fort Worth. Only after this small private organization showed interest in extending its lines to the Ruidoso Valley was immediate action forthcoming from Washington; a special engineer was sent at once to survey the situation, the red tape was cut, and delays in contracts were avoided. By Christmas of 1945 R.E.A. lights were shining in the Ruidoso Valley, a forward step that brought light, power, and living comforts to people on outlying ranches at a price they could afford to pay.

During this same period the Peñasco Valley organized another cooperative—this time for telephone service, a plan I long had been thinking about. So in 1949 I worked to organize the White Mountain Telephone Cooperative. A merger formed the Peñasco Valley Telephone Cooperative, which now covers

Otero, Eddy, Lea, Lincoln, and Chávez counties. The loan was approved by the government but with the change of administration it suffered a setback. It was not until 1956 that the money was finally approved, and by the end of that year modern dial telephones connecting us with the entire outside world were ringing in many of the homes of our three valleys.

Another milestone in the progress of our county was made in 1953 when the White Mountain Fruit Growers Association was organized. This, along with other progressive steps, has helped to transform Lincoln County from the raw backwoods to the modern community it is today.

The years spent in making Coe Ranch a place for gracious living and in working for the betterment of our community have been rewarding. But the realization of dreams is not all in the sticks and stones of a dwelling or in the number of cattle counted. Grandfather Coe did not know that he was living out his dream when he rocked wearily in his prairie schooner across the wilderness. Nor did Uncle Lou when he endured the rigors of crossing the Santa Fé Trail. Nor Mother as she lay ill in the back of the carriage on her way to Lincoln County and later when she worked so hard to bring the little Episcopal Church of St. Anne to the old Jap Coe place in Glencoe. Our dreams were fulfilled when we weren't aware they were—the training of a fine horse, the roundup of the cattle, Delicious apples hanging on a limb that bent to the ground, the fragrance of apple blossoms in the spring, Mother as she watched the unfolding of her roses, a star peeping through a hole in the clouds that drifted over the mesa, and, above all, the music that has filled Coe Ranch for almost a century. The echoes of Grandma's organ, of Dad's fiddle, of Mother's sweet voice as she sang "Annie Laurie," and of Agnes calling out the numbers to be played, and of the various instruments of Sydney, Annie, Helena Anne, Winnie, and Edith, and Zubie's songs, latterly with those of Louise's piano and my own violin still sound; these alive in our house today, those in our dreams.

A NOTE ON THE TYPE

The text of this book is set in Caledonia, *a Linotype face designed by W. A. Dwiggins. It belongs to the family of printing types called "modern face" by printers—a term used to mark the change in style of type-letters that occurred about 1800. Caledonia borders on the general design of Scotch Modern, but is more freely drawn than that letter.*

The book was composed, printed, and bound by Kingsport Press, Inc., Kingsport, Tennessee. Typography and binding design by Carl Hertzog.